"I absolutely *love* this book! First, e _____tical component of our evangelical faith ᴀᴺᴅ practice. Second, the authors demonstrate a strong grasp not only of God's Word, but also of the perspective of church history, which is sadly lacking in most contemporary books. Third, these guys write tight, making every sentence count, so even though it's packed with truth, the book is a quick read.

"In 1976, the Regular Baptists of Canada held their annual convention. D. A. Carson was asked to be the morning Bible teacher, and I was asked to be the Bible teacher for the evening sessions. Don was twenty-nine and I was twenty-two! Psalm 145:4 says, 'One generation shall commend your works to another,' so it is fitting that thirty-four years later we team up again to endorse this book by some young friends of ours. I am so proud of these brilliant, godly men, and after you've read their book, you'll understand why Don and I deeply believe in their ministries."

Rick Warren, Pastor, Saddleback Church

"It brings this aging man great joy to see a rising generation address contemporary questions with theologically informed answers. These are the right guys, on the right topics, at the right time."

C. J. Mahaney, Sovereign Grace Ministries

"Sometimes I wonder how I could have spent my entire life in the church, safely ensconced in the evangelical subculture, and yet have such a difficult time articulating the essence of significant biblical concepts and convictions that I claim to have built my life upon. And I don't think I'm alone. *Don't Call It a Comeback* is more than just a primer for the young and uninitiated; it is essential reading for all who want to make sure they are clear and convinced on the things that matter most."

Nancy Guthrie, Bible teacher;
author, *The One Year Book of Discovering Jesus in the Old Testament*

Don't Call It a
COMEBACK

Don't Call It a

COMEBACK

THE OLD FAITH *for a* NEW DAY

EDITED BY KEVIN DEYOUNG

FOREWORD BY D. A. CARSON

:: CROSSWAY

WHEATON, ILLINOIS

Published in association with the literary agency of Wolgemuth & Associates, Inc.

Cover design: Studio Gearbox
Cover illustration: Getty Images
Interior design and typesetting: Lakeside Design Plus
First printing 2011
Printed in the United States of America

Unless otherwise indicated, Scripture quotations are from the ESV® Bible (*The Holy Bible, English Standard Version*®), copyright © 2001 by Crossway. Used by permission. All rights reserved.

Scripture quotations marked KJV are from the *King James Version* of the Bible.

Scripture quotations marked NIV from the HOLY BIBLE, NEW INTERNATIONAL VERSION®. Copyright © 1973, 1978, 1984 Biblica. Used by permission of Zondervan. All rights reserved. The "NIV" and "New International Version" trademarks are registered in the United States Patent and Trademark Office by Biblica. Use of either trademark requires the permission of Biblica.

Scripture references marked NRSV are from *The New Revised Standard Version.* Copyright © 1989 by the Division of Christian Education of the National Council of the Churches of Christ in the U.S.A. Published by Thomas Nelson, Inc. Used by permission of the National Council of the Churches of Christ in the U.S.A.

Scripture quotations marked AT are the author's translation.

All emphases in Scripture quotations have been added by the authors.

Trade paperback ISBN:	978-1-4335-2169-0
PDF ISBN:	978-1-4335-2170-6
Mobipocket ISBN:	978-1-4335-2171-3
ePub ISBN:	978-1-4335-2172-0

Library of Congress Cataloging-in-Publication Data
    Don't call it a comeback: the old faith for a new day / edited by Kevin DeYoung; foreword by D. A. Carson.
        p. cm.
        Includes bibliographical references and index.
        ISBN 978-1-4335-2169-0 (tp)
        1. Evangelicalism. 2. Protestantism. 3. Protestant churches—Doctrines. I. DeYoung, Kevin.
    BR1640.D66 2011
    230'.04624—dc22

                                 2010036244

Crossway is a publishing ministry of Good News Publishers.

DP		22	21	20	19	18	17	16	15	14	13	12	11
14	13	12	11	10	9	8	7	6	5	4	3	2	1

For all the saints who from their labors rest,
who thee by faith before the world confessed,
thy name, O Jesus, be forever blest.
Alleluia! Alleluia!

Contents

Part 3: Evangelical Practice: Learning to Live Life God's Way

Foreword

D. A. CARSON

A year or so ago, in a private conversation, John Piper and I agreed it was a great time to be sixtyish. For—surprise, surprise—the generation below us actually wants to be mentored, wants to hear and read the expositions and theology of quite a number of sixty-year-olds. In the West, it has not always been like that, but it is now. It's a great time to be sixty.

But it would be a huge mistake to imagine for one moment that everything depends on the sixty-year-olds. God is raising up a remarkable generation of twenty-somethings, thirty-somethings, and forty-somethings who are articulate, eager to be faithful to the Lord Jesus and his gospel, hungry to teach the Bible rightly and with unction, eager to use their minds while loving with their whole being, and struggling both to believe and to do the truth. The contributors to this book represent only a small fraction of them.

At one point I met with most of them in a hotel conference room at Chicago's O'Hare Airport. I was happy to try to answer their questions for a couple of hours, on condition that I could then ask *them* questions for a couple of hours. The flow of information and perspective happily traveled in both directions. I went home thanking God for these young Christian servants setting out on a lifetime of gospel focus, the full fruit of which I shall not see this side of eternity.

The twin aims of this book—on the one hand, to unpack what Christians ought to believe and how they ought to act and, on the other, to articulate the essentially theological nature of evangelicalism—are helped along by the writers' ambition to be accessible. In this they have been entirely successful. It would be easy to bemoan topics not treated or criticize treatments not characterized by depth and nuance, but that would be nothing other than telling the contributors to write a different book, a book with quite different aims and intended readers. But any book that sets out "to introduce young Christians, new Christians, and underdiscipled Christians to the most important articles of our faith and what it looks like to live out this faith in real life" (DeYoung) calls forth my gratitude to God for the gifts and graces represented in these pages.

I hope and pray that many Christians will buy multiple copies of this book so as to distribute it with generous abandon.

Introduction

All Grown Up and Nothing to Say

KEVIN DEYOUNG

I didn't just grow up in the church; I practically *lived* there. My family was at church every Sunday morning and every Sunday evening. Weather, band trips, vacation, mild case of whooping cough, Bears in the Super Bowl—it didn't matter. We were in church. We were often there to turn out the lights with the pastor and his family. I attended Sunday school. I was there on Wednesday nights as a kid and on Sunday nights (after church) for youth group. I started doing daily devotions when I was in high school. I read my Bible, had parents who loved God, and generally was surrounded by pretty decent Christian friends. And I *liked* it.

After public high school I went to Hope College in Holland, Michigan. Although it's a Christian liberal arts school, Hope is not a college specifically for Christians. You didn't have to be a Christian, believe like a Christian, or live like a Christian to be at Hope. But like many others, I came to Hope as a committed Christian, having been reared in an ordinary, faithful evangelical church.

I'll never forget during my freshman year having a heated conversation about religion with three other guys from my floor. One was a nominal Christian who grew up in the church but didn't seem to care much about the faith. Another guy was a hedonist. His self-proclaimed goal in life was to have as much sex as possible. This was the good life for him. The third guy was into crystals (seriously). He was a funny New Age dude who liked to watch Rikki Lake and play video games. And then there was me—the little boy Samuel who grew up in the sanctuary.

And yet as we talked on into the night, I felt like I must not have paid enough attention growing up in the house of God all those years.

I don't know whose fault it was, if it was anyone's, but I remember staying awake into the wee hours thinking "I can't articulate what I believe and why I believe it." I felt a bit embarrassed that after all those years I still didn't have a good grasp on some of the most foundational doctrines of the Christian faith. Looking back, I wish I had been challenged more (or had challenged myself more) to really understand Christian doctrine when I was younger. The catechism was being phased out of the curriculum by the time I was going through the later years of Sunday school, and the youth group messages seemed to end with the predictable refrain of asking Jesus into our hearts. I was probably one of the best Bible students in our church, and yet I could barely articulate basic Christian theology past "Jesus died on the cross for our sins." And if I couldn't articulate the basics after seventeen solid, earnest years in the church, what must the predicament be for the seventeen-year-old just converting to Christianity, or for the thirty-four-year-old who's getting serious about her faith for the first time?

What's the Point?

This book has two main aims. The first aim is to introduce young Christians, new Christians, and underdiscipled Christians to the most important articles of our faith and what it looks like to live out this faith in real life. I'll be the first to admit that we are not aiming for originality in these chapters. In fact, we hope that what we are saying has been said by many before us and will be said by many after us. But if we are not claiming any new discoveries, we are eager to communicate Christian faith and practice in a way that resonates with teenagers, college students, young adults, and any others who need to have a better grasp of what they believe and why they believe it. We are all young Christians—in our twenties and thirties when this project began—who want to see the next generation of Christians learn to think, live, and worship in ways that are heartfelt, biblical, and unapologetically theological. We want to see the next generation joyfully embrace and winsomely articulate the truths that matter most.

The second aim of the book is to reassert the theological nature of evangelicalism. In recent years the term *evangelical* has lost almost all its meaning. It has become a political category or a term used by sociologists for Christians affiliated with certain denominations or institutions. *Evangelical* has come to mean everything and nothing. But we think there is still merit to the label, provided it can be infused with theological meaning that manifests itself in some key ethical, social, and ecclesiastical stances and practices.

We realize there are some serious dangers in this second aim. One danger is that we would see ourselves as the be-all and end-all of evangelicalism. We pray this is not our motivation. In fact, the hardest part about editing this book was having to leave out a lot of godly, intelligent, impressive young evangelicals who could have easily written these chapters as well as the rest of us. Evangelicalism certainly does not revolve around us or our ministries. A second danger is that we would be seen as carefully marking out the boundaries for who can and cannot be an evangelical. Understandably, some of this will happen just by virtue of the things we are writing about or not writing about. And frankly we do think the term *evangelical* lacks necessary definition. This book is an attempt to suggest some of the doctrines, ethics, and practices that ought to mark out the evangelical Christian. But we realize for some folks we have not weighed in on enough issues, and for others we have spouted off on too many. Our goal is not to say, "Believe this or else," or "Believe this and nothing else," but to say, "Here are the things that seem most essential and basic to the Christian faith in general and evangelical identity in particular."

Hope for the Future

Our hope is that this book might be of some small use in reforming God's church according to the Word of God and forming Christians in the truth of God's Word. Contrary to the doom-and-gloom reports, the evangelical church is not dead. By God's grace, no matter the financial, military, or political turmoil we may be called upon to endure, the church in North America may have its strongest, healthiest, most vibrant days ahead. Of course, the church will always be "by schisms rent asunder, by heresies distressed," not to mention the problems caused by our own folly and selfishness. But we see signs of renewed interest in the corporate nature of the church, in social engagement, in robust theological commitment, and in a mature, risk-taking, God-saturated faith that has no patience for gimmicks, imitations, or cultural Christianity.

We are sinners, but God is gracious. So the church is bound to be a mixed bag. It is now and will be in the future. For this we can be sorrowful, yet always rejoicing. Sorrowful over suffering, yet always rejoicing in our redemption. Sorrowful for our sins, yet always rejoicing in our Savior. Our prayer is that this book would help a new generation of Christians rejoice in the most important aspects of our faith and walk, instead of sorrowing to discover that we don't know what to think or how to live like Christians.

PART 1

EVANGELICAL HISTORY

Looking Forward and Looking Back

Chapter 1

The Secret to Reaching the Next Generation

KEVIN DEYOUNG

Getting a book published is a funny thing. People you've never met suddenly think you're amazing. Other people you've never met (who may leave a review on Amazon) think you're the scum of the earth (and not the good Pauline kind). And lots of people expect you to be an expert in things you don't know much about.

After my first book came out, *Why We're Not Emergent*, pastors and other Christians started asking me how my church reached out to young people. "We don't want to go emergent," the questioner would explain. "We need sound doctrine. We need good preaching. But what do you do in your church to reach the next generation?" My usual response was, "Nothing." I wanted people to understand that there's nothing fancy or brilliant about our church strategy. We are just trying to be faithful.

But after a while I began to sense that "nothing" was not a terribly helpful answer. So I talked about our campus ministry, and staff structure, and our small groups—all of which matter. Yet this answer seemed like more of the same. "If you want to reach young people, you have to have this program or capture this feel or go for this look." Don't get me wrong; thinking about strategy, structure, and feel is not sinful. I'm thankful for all the people in our church who work hard in these areas. I try to be wise in these areas. But this is not the secret to reaching the next generation.

There have been times as a pastor when I've been discouraged by the slowness of numerical growth in my congregation. I've thought, "Why is that church over there so successful? Why did they go from 150 to 1500 in three years?" I've even been borderline snippy at times: "Lord, if I get to heaven and find out there was some secret musical style or movie clip or new program I was supposed to use in order to be successful, I'm going to feel pretty bummed." But in my saner moments I've come to see two things: (1) It's more my sinful flesh than my sanctified spirit that wants success. And (2) the secret is that there is no secret.

Reaching the next generation—whether they are outside the church or sitting there bored in your church—is easier and harder than you think. It's easier because you don't have to get a degree in postmodern literary theory or go to a bunch of stupid movies. You don't have to say "sweet" or "bling" or know what LOL or IMHO means. You don't have to listen to . . . well, whatever people listen to these days. You don't have to be on Twitter, watch *The Office*, or imbibe fancy coffees. You just have to be like Jesus. That's it. So the easy part is you don't have to be with it. The hard part is you have to be with *him*. If you walk with God and walk with people, you'll reach the next generation.

Let me unpack that a bit. After thinking through the question for over a year, I've come up with five suggestions for pastors, youth workers, campus staff, and anyone else who wants to pass the faith on to the next generation: Grab them with passion. Win them with love. Hold them with holiness. Challenge them with truth. Amaze them with God.

Grab Them with Passion

Increasingly, people do not go to church out of a sense of cultural obligation. This is true especially among the young. Newer generations will not give Christianity a second thought if it seems lifeless, rote, and uninspiring. They will only get serious about the Christian faith if it seems like something seriously worth their time. You can have formal services, so long as you do not have formalism. You can have casual services, so long as you do not approach your faith casually. Your services can have a lot of different looks, but young people want to see passion. They want to see us do church and follow Christ like we mean it.

We would do well to pay attention to Romans 12. "Let love be genuine. Abhor what is evil; hold fast to what is good. Love one another with brotherly affection. Outdo one another in showing honor. Do not be slothful in zeal, be fervent in spirit, serve the Lord" (vv. 9–11). We would be far less likely to lose our young people and far more likely to win some others if the spiritual temperature of our churches was something other than lukewarm. People need to see that God is the all-consuming reality in our lives. Our sincerity and earnestness in worship matter ten times more than the style we use to display our sincerity and earnestness.

I'm tired of talking about authenticity, as if prattling on about how messed up you are or blogging about your goldfish are signs of spiritual maturity. We need passion, a zeal fueled by knowledge (Rom. 10:2). Young people want to see that our faith actually matters to us. They are like Ben Franklin when asked why he was going to hear George Whitefield preach. "You don't even believe what he says," people told Franklin. To which he replied, "I know. But he does." If our evangelical faith is boring to us, it will be boring to others. If the gospel is old news to you, it will be dull news to everyone else.

We cannot pass on what we do not feel. Whitefield blasted the church in his day because "the generality of preachers [in New England] talk of an unknown and unfelt Christ. The reason why congregations have been so dead is because they have had dead men to preach to them."[1] The next generation, every generation really, needs to hear the gospel with personal, passionate pleading. There is a time for dialogue, but there is also a time for declaration. People don't need a lecture or an oration or a discussion from the pulpit on Sunday morning. They need to hear of the mighty deeds of God. And they need to hear the message from someone who not only understands it but has been captured by it.

If we are to grab the next generation with the gospel, we must grab them with passion. And to grab them with passion, we must be gripped with it ourselves. The world needs to see Christians burning, not with self-righteous fury at the sliding morals in our country, but with passion

---

[1] Roger Finke and Rodney Stark, *The Churching of America, 1776–2005* (Piscataway, NJ: Rutgers University Press, 2005), 53.

for God. As W. E. Sangster put it, "I'm not interested to know if you could set the Thames on fire. What I want to know is this: if I picked you up by the scruff of your neck and dropped you into the Thames, would it sizzle?"[2]

Win Them with Love

The evangelical church has spent far too much time trying to figure out cultural engagement and far too little time just trying to love. If we listen to people patiently and give them the gift of our curiosity, we will be plenty engaged. I'm not arguing for purposeful obscurantism. What I'm arguing for is getting people's attention with a force more powerful than the right lingo and the right movie clips.

We spend all this time trying to imitate Gen-X culture or Millennial culture, and to what end? For starters, there is no universal youth culture. Young people do not all think alike, dress alike, or feel comfortable in the same environments. Moreover, even if we could figure out "what the next generation likes," by the time we figured it out they probably wouldn't like it anymore. Count on it: when the church discovers cool, it won't be cool anymore. I've seen well-meaning Christians try to introduce new music into the church in an effort to reach the young people, only to find out that the "new" music included "Shine, Jesus, Shine" and "Shout to the Lord." There's nothing worse than a church trying to be fresh and turning out to be a little dated. Better to stick with the hymns and the organ than do "new" music that hasn't aged terribly well or do the new music in an embarrassing way.

The evangelical church needs to stop preaching the false gospel of cultural identification. Don't spend all your time trying to figure out how to be just like the next generation. Be yourself. Tell them about Jesus. And love them unashamedly. I think a lot of older Christians are desperate to figure out what young people are into because they are too embarrassed to be themselves and too unsure of themselves to simply love the people they are trying to reach.

Jesus said it best: "By this all people will know that you are my disciples, if you have love for one another" (John 13:35). Jesus did not say, "They will know you are my disciples by how attune you are to new

---

[2]Quoted in John R. W. Stott, *Between Two Worlds: The Challenge of Preaching Today* (Grand Rapids: Eerdmans, 1982), 285.

trends in youth culture." Or "They will know you are my disciples by the hip atmosphere you create." Give up on relevance, and try love. If they see love in you, love for each other, love for the world, and love for them, they will listen. No matter who "they" are.

Talk to people. Notice visitors. Invite new people over for lunch. Strike up a friendly conversation at the greasy pizza joint. Let your teenagers' friends hang out at your house. Love won't guarantee the young people will never walk away from the church, but it will make it a lot harder. It won't guarantee that non-Christians will come to Christ, but it will make the invitation a whole lot more attractive.

Hold Them with Holiness

Let me make this clear one more time. I'm not arguing that thinking about music styles or paying attention to the "feel" of our church or trying to exegete the culture is sinful stuff. I'm not saying we shouldn't be asking questions related to cultural engagement. What I'm saying is that being experts in the culture matters nothing, and worse than nothing, if we are not first of all experts in love, truth, and holiness.

Look at what God says in 2 Peter 1:5–8:

> For this very reason, make every effort to supplement your faith with virtue, and virtue with knowledge, and knowledge with self-control, and self-control with steadfastness, and steadfastness with godliness, and godliness with brotherly affection, and brotherly affection with love. For if these qualities are yours and are increasing, they keep you from being ineffective or unfruitful in the knowledge of our Lord Jesus Christ.

Did you pick up on the promise in the last verse? If we are growing in faith, virtue, knowledge, self-control, steadfastness, godliness, brotherly affection, and love, we will not be ineffective ministers for Christ. If ever there was a secret to effective ministry, these verses give it to us. Grow in God and you'll make a difference in people's lives. If nothing of spiritual significance is happening in your church, your Bible study, your small group, or your family, it may be because nothing spiritually significant is happening in your life.

I love the line from Robert Murray M'Cheyne: "My people's greatest need is my personal holiness." I've given that advice to others dozens of times, and I've repeated it to myself a hundred times. Almost my whole philosophy of ministry is summed up in M'Cheyne's words. My congregation needs me to be humble before they need me to be smart. They need me to be honest more than they need me to be a dynamic leader. They need me to be teachable more than they need me to teach at conferences. If your walk matches your talk, if your faith costs you something, if being a Christian is more than a cultural garb, they will listen to you.

Paul told young Timothy to keep a close watch on his life and his doctrine (1 Tim. 4:16). "Persist in this," he said, "for by so doing you will save both yourself and your hearers." Far too much ministry today is undertaken without any concern for holiness. We've found that changing the way we do church is easier than changing the way we are. We've found that we are not sufficiently unlike anyone else to garner notice, so we've attempted to become just like everyone else instead. Today's young people do not want a cultural Christianity that fits in like a Baptist church in Texas. They want a conspicuous Christianity that changes lives and transforms communities. Maybe we would make more progress in reaching the next generation if we were making more progress in holiness (1 Tim. 4:15).

Remember, the next generation is not just out there. They are also in here, sitting in our churches week after week. We often hear about how dangerous college can be for Christian teens, how many of them check out of church once they reach the university. But studies have shown that most of the students who check out do so in high school, not in college. It's not liberal professors that are driving our kids away. It's their hard hearts and our stale, compromised witness that opens the door for them to leave.

One of our problems is that we have not done a good job of modeling Christian faith in the home and connecting our youth with other mature Christian adults in the church. One youth leader has commented that how often our young people "attended youth events (including Sunday school and discipleship groups) was not a good predictor of which teens would and which would not grow toward Christian adulthood." Instead,

> almost without exception, those young people who are growing in their faith as adults were teenagers who fit into one of two categories: either (1) they came from families where Christian growth was

modeled in at least one of their parents, or (2) they had developed such significant connections with adults within the church that it had become an extended family for them.[3]

Likewise, sociologist Christian Smith argues that though most teenagers and parents don't realize it, "a lot of research in the sociology of religion suggests that the most important social influence in shaping young people's religious lives is the religious life modeled and taught to them by their parents."[4]

The take home from all this is pretty straightforward. The one indispensable requirement for producing godly, mature Christians is godly, mature Christians. Granted, good parents still have wayward children and faithful mentors don't always get through to their pupils. Personal holiness is not the key that regenerates the heart. The Spirit blows where he will. But make no mistake, the promise of 2 Peter 1 is as true as ever. If we are holy, we will be fruitful. Personal connections with growing Christians is what the next generation needs more than ever.

Challenge Them with Truth

In the church-growth heyday, scholars and pastors were wrestling with how to reach out without dumbing down. Today I would argue that we reach out precisely by *not* dumbing down. The door is open like never before to challenge people with good Bible teaching. People want to learn doctrine. They really do, even non-Christians. Whether they accept it all or not, they want to know what Christians actually believe. Young people will not put up with feel-good pablum. They want the truth straight up, unvarnished, and unashamed.

Thom Rainer did a study a number of years ago asking formerly unchurched people the open-ended question, "What factors led you to choose this church?" A lot of surveys had been done asking the unchurched what they would like in a church. But this study asked the *formerly* unchurched why they actually were now in a church. The results were surprising: 11 percent said worship style led them to their church, 25 percent said children's/youth ministry, and 37 percent said

---

[3]Mark DeVries, *Family-Based Youth Ministry: Reaching the Been-There, Done-That Generation* (Downers Grove, IL: InterVarsity, 1994), 63.
[4]Christian Smith, with Melissa Lundquist Denton, *Soul Searching: The Religious and Spiritual Lives of American Teenagers* (New York: Oxford University Press, 2005), 56.

they sensed God's presence at their church. For 41 percent, someone from the church had witnessed to them, and 49 percent mentioned friendliness as the reason for choosing their church. Can you guess the top two responses? Doctrine and preaching—88 percent said the doctrine led them to their church, and 90 percent said the preaching led them there, in particular, a pastor who preached with certitude and conviction.[5] One woman remarked,

> We attended a lot of different churches for different reasons before we became Christians. I tell you, so many of the preachers spoke with little authority; they hardly ever dealt with tough issues of Scripture, and they soft-sold the other issues. Frank and I know now that we were hungry for the truth. Why can't preachers learn that shallow and superficial preaching doesn't help anybody, including people like us who weren't Christians.[6]

When it comes to reaching outsiders, bold, deep, biblical preaching is not the problem. It's part of the solution.

The next generation *in* our churches needs to be challenged too. In his book on the religious and spiritual lives of American teenagers, Christian Smith coined the phrase "Moralistic Therapeutic Deism" to describe the spirituality of American youth. They believe in being a good moral person. They believe religion should give you peace, happiness, and security. They believe God exists and made the world but is not particularly involved in the day-to-day stuff of life.[7] We are naïve if we think this is not the faith of some of the best and brightest in our churches, or even those reading this book!

Church people are not stupid. They are not incapable of learning. For the most part, they simply haven't been taught. No one has challenged them to think a deep thought or read a difficult book. No one has asked them to articulate their faith in biblical and theological categories. We have expected almost nothing out of our young people, so that's what we get. A couple generations ago twenty-year-olds were getting married, starting families, working at real jobs, or off somewhere fighting Nazis. Today thirty-five-year olds are hanging out on Facebook, looking for

---

[5]Thom Rainer, *Surprising Insights from the Unchurched* (Grand Rapids: Zondervan, 2001), 74.
[6]Ibid., 62.
[7]Smith and Denton, *Soul Searching*, 162ff.

direction, and trying to find themselves. We have been coddled when we should have been challenged.

Challenging the next generation with truth starts with honest self-examination. We must ask, Do I know the plotline of the Bible? Do I know Christian theology? Do I read any meaty Christian books? Do I know anything about justification, redemption, original sin, propitiation, and progressive sanctification? Do I really understand the gospel? We cannot challenge others until we have first challenged ourselves. That's one of the driving passions behind this book. I want the "average" church-goer to think more deeply about his faith. I want Christians to realize, like I did that night in college, that they have a lot more to learn.

You've heard it said that Christianity in America is a mile wide and an inch deep. Well, it's more like half a mile wide now. Christian influence is not as pervasive as it once was. I'm convinced that if Christianity is to be a mile wide again in America, it will first have to find a way to be a mile deep. Shallow Christianity will not last in the coming generation, and it will not grow. Cultural Christianity is fading. The church in the twenty-first century must go big on truth or go home.

Amaze Them with God

I beg of you, don't go after the next generation with mere moralism, either on the right (don't have sex, do go to church, share your faith, stay off drugs) or on the left (recycle, dig a well, feed the homeless, buy a wristband). The gospel is not a message about what we need to do for God, but about what God has done for us. So get them with the good news about who God is and what he has done for us.

Some of us, it seems, are almost scared to tell people about God. Perhaps because we don't truly know him. Maybe because we prefer living in triviality. Or maybe because we don't consider knowing God to be very helpful in real life. I have to fight against this unbelief in my own life. If only I would trust God that he is enough to win the hearts and minds of the next generation. It's his work much more than it is mine or yours. So make him front and center. Don't preach your doubts as mystery. And don't reduce God to your own level. If ever people were starving for a God the size of God, surely it is now.

Give them a God who is holy, independent, and unlike us, a God who is good, just, full of wrath, and full of mercy. Give them a God who is sovereign, powerful, tender, and true. Give them a God with edges. Give them an undiluted God who makes them feel cherished and safe, and small and uncomfortable too. Give them a God who works all things after the counsel of his will and for the glory of his name. Give them a God whose love is lavish and free. Give them a God worthy of wonder and fear, a God big enough for all our faith, hope, and love.

Do your friends, your church, your family, your children know that God is the center of the universe? Can they see that he is at the center of your life?

Imagine you had a dream of someone sitting on a throne. In your dream a rainbow encircled the throne. Twenty-four men surrounded the throne. Lightning and thunder issued from the throne. Seven lamps stood blazing at the foot of the throne. A sea of glass lay before the throne. Four strange creatures were around the throne, giving thanks to him who sits on the throne. And twenty-four dudes were falling down before the one who sits on the throne. You wouldn't have to get Joseph out of prison to figure out the point of this dream. The throne is the figurative and literal center of the vision. The meaning of the dream is God.

This, of course, is no ordinary dream. It is John's vision from Revelation 4. And it is reality, right now. More substantial and more lasting and more influential than your pain, or fear, or temptation, or opposition, or makeup, or clothes, or boyfriends, or video games, or iPods, or BlackBerrys, or whatever else our culture says should be important to young people is God. What matters now and for eternity is the unceasing worship of him who sits on the throne.

As you try to reach the next generation for Christ, you can amaze them with your cleverness, your humor, or your looks. Or you can amaze them with God. I need a lot of things in my life. There are schedules and details and a long to-do list. I need food and water and shelter. I need sleep. I need more exercise, and I need to eat better. But this is my greatest need and yours: to know God, love God, delight in God, and make much of God.

We have an incredible opportunity before us. Most people live weightless, ephemeral lives. We can give them substance instead of style. We can show them a big God to help make sense of their shrinking lives. We can point them to transcendence instead of triviality. We can reach them with something more lasting and more powerful than gimmicks, gadgets, and games. We can reach them with God.

Imagine that. Reaching the next generation *for* God by showing them *more of* God. That's just crazy enough to work.

FOR FURTHER STUDY

Packer, J. I. *A Quest for Godliness: The Puritan Vision of the Christian Life.* Wheaton, IL: Crossway, 1994.

Piper, John. *God Is the Gospel: Meditations on God's Love as the Gift of Himself.* Wheaton, IL: Crossway, 2005.

Wells, David F. *The Courage to Be Protestant: Truth-lovers, Marketers, and Emergents in the Postmodern World.* Grand Rapids: Eerdmans, 2008.

Chapter 2

The Story of Evangelicalism from the Beginning and Before

COLLIN HANSEN

Virtually impossible to define, even harder to control, evangelicalism is a network of affinity that shares a common history and core theology. While the rest of this book explores that core theology and its implications, this chapter seeks to capture that common history in a sweeping tour through two millennia. Despite the break-neck brevity of this venture, we will pause long enough to learn about those events and personalities that unite a diverse movement with no official membership and no governing body that determines who's in and who's out.

Historian George Marsden has said that an evangelical is "anyone who likes Billy Graham."[1] This description may be somewhat accurate, but it is not sufficient. Surely it is now outdated. Fewer young believers today have even heard of the famed evangelist. They do not know that Graham once divided evangelicals from fundamentalists by working with Protestant liberals and Roman Catholics. They do not remember

---

[1]George M. Marsden, *Understanding Fundamentalism and Evangelicalism* (Grand Rapids: Eerdmans, 1991), 6.

the scorn he incurred from liberals and Catholics due to his funda-
mentalist focus on personal conversion by appealing to the authority
of Scripture.

Today's evangelical movement is more decentralized, more frag-
mented, and more diverse than it was during Graham's heyday. Indeed,
these developments make it increasingly difficult even to describe evangelicalism as a movement, because evangelicals appear to be moving
in several competing directions. Here is where history can guide us.
The future of the evangelical cause has sometimes appeared dire. But
God's faithfulness has never waned. As we become reacquainted with
the evangelical story, perhaps we'll gain more clarity to understand
what it means to bear the good news of Jesus Christ today. Certainly,
we'll see how evangelicals have balanced conviction and cooperation,
continuity and creativity.

Where to Begin?
Despite sharing a common history, evangelicals dispute where exactly
to begin their story. Surely evangelicals trace their roots back to Jesus
Christ himself and the apostles who carried his gospel to the ends of
the known world at the cost of their lives. But we are hardly the only
Christians who claim apostolic warrant. You might also begin the
story with the Reformation, when Martin Luther took his bold stand
for the gospel with a conscience captive to the Word alone. But the
evangelical impulse to reform did not suddenly emerge in 1517 when
Luther posted his ninety-five theses on the door of Wittenberg's Castle
Church. You might, then, begin the story with the trio of John Wesley,
Jonathan Edwards, and George Whitefield. God used these men to lead
spectacular religious awakenings in Great Britain and colonial America
during the mid-1700s. But this beginning might leave the impression
that they invented the concept of revival.

Both of these eras offered something new to the evangelical movement. But to suppose that either of these eras invented evangelicalism
would obscure the substantial continuity throughout varied ages and
places. Evangelicalism was founded on the apostolic convictions of the
early church as taught in the biblical canon. Its theology is consistent
with the Reformation's teaching about God's gift of justification by grace
alone through faith alone. And it was forged through creative coopera-

tion during the transatlantic revivals of the 1700s. Today, it extends around the globe as a vibrant expression of Jesus' commitment to build his church (Matt. 16:18).

Early Church: Christological Consensus

You won't hear evangelicals today arguing over whether Jesus is fully God and fully man or whether God exists in three persons. After much theological wrangling, the early church answered these fundamental questions about the nature and work of Jesus Christ. Countering Arians, who argued that there was a time when the Son did not exist, the Nicene Creed was adopted in its present form at the Council of Constantinople in 381. This statement explains that Jesus was "begotten of the Father before all the ages, Light of Light, true God of true God, begotten not made, of one substance with the Father." The courageous, determined effort of theologians such as Athanasius ensured that official church teaching would recognize Jesus in his rightful place as Lord of all (Acts 10:36).

Yet other influential teachers swung too hard in the opposite direction, exalting Christ's divinity while de-emphasizing his humanity. Once again, church leaders came together to try and strike the appropriate balance that would faithfully represent the apostolic witness. The Council of Chalcedon found that balance in 451. "With one accord," the bishops taught that Jesus is "of one substance with the Father as regards his Godhead, and at the same time of one substance with us as regards his manhood." Like the Nicene Creed, the Chalcedonian definition is recognized by Christians from both the Eastern and Western branches. These foundational statements underscore some substantial unity evangelicals share with the Orthodox and Roman Catholic churches.

During the Reformation in the 1500s, Protestant theologians commonly defended their arguments against charges of novelty by appealing to their forebears. Two in particular stand out for sharing insights still cherished by evangelicals today. Widely regarded as the father of Western theology, Augustine of Hippo abandoned a life of selfish sensuality by the grace of God. The North African bishop, who died in 430, helped Christians anticipate the city of God while the city of Rome crumbled. He also countered the damaging teaching of several contemporaries. Pelagius, a British monk who visited Rome in 400, argued that humans are born with the capability to do good or bad, with the ability to fulfill every command God has given. Augustine responded that original sin renders us unwilling to pursue God (Rom. 3:10–12). God's grace saves us from ourselves. Augustine's compelling theology, built on the foundation of inerrant Scripture, set a course for Western theology that continues today.

Another favorite theologian for the Reformers was Anselm of Canterbury, who died in 1109. He took up the age-old question, Why did God become man? He pursued the biblical trail to teach that a holy, righteous God upholds justice by requiring satisfaction for sin. No sinner can make this sacrifice. "If, then, it be necessary that the kingdom of heaven be completed by man's admission," Anselm wrote, "and if man cannot be admitted unless the aforesaid satisfaction for sin be first made, and if God only can, and man only ought to make this satisfaction, then necessarily One must make it who is both God and man."[2] Indeed, only Jesus Christ could and did offer himself as this atoning sacrifice for sins (Rom. 3:25; Heb. 2:17; 1 John 2:2; 4:10).

Reformation: Gate to Heaven

When Martin Luther spoke out in 1517 to protest the medieval church's practice of selling indulgences, he had no plans to launch a separate church that would rival Rome. In fact, he hadn't even reached many of his most famous convictions, which slowly emerged in his polemics with Catholic critics. But in his study of the apostle Paul's letter to the Romans, he had already crossed the point of no return. For years, his conscience was tormented by fear that the just God would punish his sins. Nothing he could do would please God, so Luther hated him. Then something clicked with Luther's understanding of Romans 1:17.

"Night and day I pondered until I saw the connection between the justice of God and the statement that 'the just shall live by his faith,'" Luther wrote.

> Then I grasped that the justice of God is that righteousness by which through grace and sheer mercy God justifies us through faith. Thereupon I felt myself to be reborn and to have gone through open doors into paradise. The whole of Scripture took on a new meaning, and

---

[2]Henry Bettenson and Chris Maunder, eds., *Documents of the Christian Church*, 3rd ed. (New York: Oxford University Press, 1999), 153.

whereas the "justice of God" had filled me with hate, now it became
to me inexpressibly sweet in greater love. This passage of Paul became
to me a gate to heaven.[3]

After several agonizing fits following promising starts, the time
for sweeping reform had come to Europe. Luther hid from the Holy
Roman Emperor's authorities in the castle at Wartburg during 1521
and 1522. Here, he pored over the Greek text of the New Testament
and began translating the Bible into the vernacular German. With time,
Luther grew more radical in his critiques of Rome, even as he fought to
restrain the radical impulses of some followers. Luther broke the spiritual barrier that separated clergy from laity with his teaching on the
priesthood of all believers. Yet he did not condone the peasant revolts
against established authority. Even though he rejected Rome's teaching
that bread and wine become the actual body and blood of Christ in the
Eucharist, he defended his view of the bodily presence of Christ in the
Lord's Supper against Swiss Reformer Ulrich Zwingli, who maintained
that Christ is present only in the hearts of believers.

Luther and Zwingli were unable to reach a compromise at the Col-
loquy of Marburg in 1529. The Protestant churches did not unite. So
Reformed churches developed on a different trajectory from the Luther-
ans. John Calvin was only eight years old when Luther kicked off the
Reformation. But by the end of the century, the reluctant Genevan
pastor was widely regarded as the Reformation's greatest theologian.
His *Institutes of the Christian Religion* would become a standard for
evangelical theology with its careful attention to Scripture and Christ-
centered focus on salvation.

"This is the wondrous exchange made by his boundless goodness,"
Calvin wrote of his Lord and Savior.

Having become with us the Son of Man, he has made us with himself
sons of God. By his own descent to the earth he has prepared our
ascent to heaven. Having received our mortality, he has bestowed on
us his immortality. Having undertaken our weakness, he has made
us strong in his strength. Having submitted to our poverty, he has
transferred to us his riches. Having taken upon himself the burden

---

[3]Roland H. Bainton, *Here I Stand: A Life of Martin Luther* (New York: Meridian, 1995), 49–50.

of unrighteousness with which we were oppressed, he has clothed us with his righteousness.[4]

Great Awakenings: "Surprising Work of God"

During Calvin's lifetime, which ended in 1564, Genevans lived in nearly constant fear of attack from their Catholic neighbors. Wide tracts of Lutheran territories were reclaimed for Rome during the Catholic Counter-Reformation. The Council of Trent, running through 1563, solidified Catholic teaching against Protestantism, officially condemning anyone who believed in justification by faith alone. Reformation progress in England hinged on who wore the crown. Ruled by Henry VIII's daughter, Queen Elizabeth I, until 1603, England struck a compromise that pleased neither Catholics nor the most ardent reform-minded Protestants.

Many of these so-called Puritans left England with its restrictions on religious practice and settled New England between 1630 and 1640. Here, they planned a great experiment in church life and government. Their community would be a "city on a hill" for all the world to see. Indeed, remarkable events transpired that caught the attention of evangelicals back home in England and Scotland. Jonathan Edwards, a pastor in Northampton, Massachusetts, described a sudden and spontaneous outburst of religious fervor in 1734 and 1735 as a "surprising work of God." According to Edwards, the town "seemed to be full of the presence of God: it never was so full of *love*, nor of *joy*, and yet so full of distress, as it was then. There were remarkable tokens of God's presence in almost every house."[5] Edwards believed only God could send such a remarkable outpouring of his Spirit.

A key figure in what came to be known as the First Great Awakening, Edwards inherited a tradition of seeking these movements of the Spirit, known as revival. Edwards's grandfather, Solomon Stoddard, had presided over several local revivals during his tenure as pastor in Northampton. Echoing the Old Testament pattern of covenant renewal ceremonies, Puritan pastors exhorted their congregations to remember their covenant with God and one another. During a revival, spiritually

---

[4]John Calvin, *Institutes of the Christian Religion*, trans. Henry Beveridge (Grand Rapids: Eerdmans, 1989), 4.17.2.
[5]Jonathan Edwards, "A Narrative of Surprising Conversions," in *Jonathan Edwards on Revival* (Carlisle, PA: Banner of Truth, 1965), 14.

dead or dying church members suddenly could think of little but God in his glory. Every day felt like Sunday with nearly universal longing to worship God in spirit and truth. Sins were confessed, and wrongs were righted. Church leaders proclaimed the Word with renewed zeal.

Presbyterians in Scotland and Ulster were particularly interested in reading Edwards's descriptions of the colonial revival. They not only shared a common Reformed theology with Edwards, but also shared a common longing for spiritual awakening. During "holy fairs," Scots-Irish Presbyterians celebrated days-long communion festivals where they recovered the exuberance and communal spirit of Pentecost. Presbyterian evangelists traveling through colonial America likewise linked communion with revival. Edwards rejoiced in the accounts he heard of revival in the Middle Colonies led by Theodorus Frelinghuysen and the Tennent family.

The English Puritans and Scots-Irish Presbyterians each contributed to the growing evangelical movement during the First Great Awakening. But so did the Pietists, who resisted the nominalism they saw in continental European state churches. During his first journey to America, Anglican priest John Wesley found his faith wanting compared to Moravian believers who calmly weathered a violent storm. These Pietists felt God's presence in a way Wesley did not. But after returning home to London, Wesley experienced a dramatic conversion during a Moravian meeting on Aldersgate Street in 1738. While a Moravian read Luther's preface to the book of Romans, Wesley felt his heart "strangely warmed." Wesley wrote in his journal, "I felt I did trust in Christ, Christ alone, for salvation; and an assurance was given me that He had taken away my sins, even mine, and saved me from the law of sin and death." When Wesley preached the following Sunday, he took up the great themes of the Reformation: salvation by grace alone, through faith alone, in Christ alone.[6]

After three weeks, Wesley traveled to Saxony to visit the Moravian community in Herrnhut, which had experienced revival in 1727. Owing in part to this type of theological cross-pollination, believers in America and the British Isles adopted several continental revival practices. These included field preaching, devotional treatises, and camp

---

[6]Douglas A. Sweeney, *The American Evangelical Story: A History of the Movement* (Grand Rapids: Baker, 2005), 39.

meetings. George Whitefield, an Oxford friend of John and Charles Wesley, became the most famous celebrity in colonial America as he traveled through the colonies urging men and women to be born again by believing in Jesus Christ. But Whitefield and his fellow Methodists did not always agree. The movement split with Whitefield preaching God's sovereignty in salvation, and the Wesleys holding to the Arminian belief that God leaves the choice ultimately to us. Nevertheless, Whitefield recognized the value of cooperation, without compromising the biblical convictions that emboldened his evangelism.

"If the Lord gives us a true catholic spirit, free from a party sectarian zeal, we shall do well . . . for I am persuaded, unless we all are content to preach Christ, and to keep off from disputable things, wherein we differ, God will not bless us long," Whitefield wrote. "If we act otherwise, however we may talk of a catholic spirit, we shall only be bringing people over to our own party, and there fetter them. I pray the Lord to keep . . . me from such a spirit."[7]

Growth and Grief: A Contentious Century

The Methodist movement that emerged in the late 1700s and flourished in the 1800s followed the Wesleys' theology. Methodists also became known as powerful advocates for social change. While many prominent evangelicals in America and Great Britain held slaves, John Wesley opposed the practice with admirable fervency. Methodist circuit riders took the gospel to the rough-and-tumble American frontier where few established churches dared tread. Bishop Francis Asbury blazed the trail. Traveling virtually without break for forty-five years, he logged three hundred thousand miles on horseback. Methodism had been a footnote to religious life in colonial America with only twenty churches in 1770. But that number had grown to nearly twenty thousand by 1860.[8]

Baptists likewise thrived in the new democratic America. Their ranks increased from 150 churches in 1770 to more than twelve thousand in 1860.[9] Lottie Moon embodied the Baptist surge. Converted during an 1858 revival in Charlottesville, Virginia, Moon convened prayer meetings and taught Scripture to fellow female students. John Broadus, chaplain

---

[7]Ibid., 49.
[8]Thomas S. Kidd, *The Great Awakening: The Roots of Evangelical Christianity in Colonial America* (New Haven, CT: Yale University Press, 2007), 322.
[9]Ibid.

at the University of Virginia, challenged students to consider serving as missionaries. Moon heeded the call and headed for China when she was thirty-three years old. She led hundreds to faith in Jesus and inspired Southern Baptist women back home to serve the missions cause. As she expended herself for the Chinese beleaguered by war and disease, Moon withered away, weighing only fifty pounds before she died in 1912.

Even as evangelical denominations grew during the first half of the nineteenth century, trouble loomed over the horizon. While African Americans turned to Christ en masse, Presbyterians, Methodists, and Baptists split over the question of slavery in the years preceding the Civil War. The bloody, prolonged war weakened public confidence in the Bible, which each side claimed supported its cause.[10] Charles Hodge kept busy responding to new theological developments in *The Biblical Repertory and Princeton Review*, the journal he founded in 1825 and edited for forty-six years. Charles Briggs, a student of German higher criticism, taught from his chair in biblical studies at Union Theological Seminary that the Bible errs. The Presbyterian General Assembly suspended his pastoral credentials in 1893, but the tide was turning against evangelicals.

Orthodox Protestants set aside their differences on ecclesiology, eschatology, and several other doctrines to unite around five "fundamentals" that so many of their revisionist colleagues denied: Christ's virgin birth, the Bible's inerrant inspiration, Christ's substitutionary atonement, Christ's bodily resurrection, and the historicity of biblical miracles. These convictions they would not compromise. Though they stood courageously, evangelicals living around the turn of the twentieth century saw many of their cherished institutions slip away. Even Princeton Seminary, once a citadel for Reformed evangelical theology, was reorganized in 1929. Conservatives led by New Testament professor J. Gresham Machen left Princeton and founded their own school, Westminster Theological Seminary in Philadelphia. As far as he was concerned, Machen believed liberalism was no branch of Christianity but another religion altogether.[11]

Postwar Boom: America's Hour Strikes

Though prospects appeared bleak in America, evangelicalism actually expanded around the world in the early twentieth century. The Welsh

---

[10]Mark A. Noll, *The Civil War as a Theological Crisis* (Chapel Hill: The University of North Carolina Press, 2006).

[11]J. Gresham Machen, *Christianity and Liberalism* (Grand Rapids: Eerdmans, 1923).

Revival of 1904—1905 inspired awakenings in Pyongyang, Korea. Working with widows and orphans in India, Pandita Ramabai heard about the revival and saw the Spirit bless her community. Chinese Christianity survived the Boxer uprising of 1900 and enjoyed revivals in Manchuria and Shantung that followed the same pattern of prayer, confession, and evangelism. Anglican missionaries from England encouraged East Africans to seek the higher life by the power of the Holy Spirit.

Perhaps the most significant event for global Christianity in the twentieth century took place in a warehouse on Azusa Street in Los Angeles in 1906. Influenced by Wesley's pursuit of entire sanctification, the holiness movement encouraged Christians to seek a second blessing of the Holy Spirit subsequent to conversion. The Azusa Street meetings, led by African American preacher William Seymour, attracted a racially and economically diverse crowd. For three years, Seymour led three services each day where many sought and received the so-called third blessing, baptism with the Spirit, often manifested by speaking in tongues. Since 1906, Pentecostals have outpaced the growth of all other expressions of evangelicalism. Unfortunately, the Pentecostal impulse is all too often accompanied by an appeal to God to grant health and wealth in return for faith.

When the National Association of Evangelicals organized in 1942, leaders deliberated before agreeing to include Pentecostal denominations. With the motto "cooperation without compromise," the NAE positioned itself between Protestants who pressed for stricter separation and others who embraced seemingly everyone. Carl Henry sought to strike this balance in his landmark 1947 book, *The Uneasy Conscience of Modern Fundamentalism*. He sought to reclaim the evangelical heritage of reforming society on the basis of deep biblical convictions.

"The evangelical task primarily is the preaching of the Gospel, in the interest of individual regeneration by the supernatural grace of God, in such a way that divine redemption can be recognized as the best solution of our problems, individual and social," wrote Henry, who would become the first editor of *Christianity Today* magazine, founded in 1956.

> This produces within history, through the regenerative work of the Holy Spirit, a divine society that transcends national and international lines. The corporate testimony of believers, in their purity of life, should provide for the world an example of the divine dynamic

to overcome evils in every realm. The social problems of our day are much more complex than in apostolic times, but they do not on that account differ in principle. When the twentieth century church begins to "out-live" its environment as the first century church outreached its pagan neighbors, the modern mind, too, will stop casting about for other solutions.[12]

If Henry emerged as the key evangelical thinker, then Billy Graham was the chief spokesman. The dynamic southerner started as the first full-time evangelist for Youth for Christ following World War II. But Graham battled lingering doubts about the authority of Scripture. So he consulted Henrietta Mears, director of religious education at First Presbyterian Church of Hollywood. Mears mentored many ambitious young evangelicals, including Campus Crusade for Christ founder Bill Bright and his wife, Vonette. Graham didn't get answers to every question, but he resolved to trust God at his Word. Graham's 1949 citywide crusade in Los Angeles ran for eight weeks and attracted hundreds of thousands. National media adored the Bible-thumping country boy and made him an overnight celebrity. When crowds in cold New England gave him a similar response, leading evangelicals were convinced that "America's hour has struck." Harold John Ockenga, pastor of Park Street Church in Boston, floated the idea of Graham speaking on the Boston Common in the same location where Whitefield preached to twenty-three thousand without amplification in 1740. On April 23, 1950, about fifty thousand turned out despite dreary, 46-degree weather to hear Graham.

"I believe that 1950 will go down in history as the year of heaven-sent revival," wrote Ockenga, who helped found the NAE, Fuller Theological Seminary, and Gordon-Conwell Theological Seminary.

God is sending the revival for which His remnant all through America—the true Bible-believing Christian who never bowed their knees to the Baal and Ashtoreth of Modernism or Secularism—have been praying. God is moving as He has not moved in America at least for four decades and as He has not moved in New England for two centuries. . . . You do not have to wait till next year. You don't have to

---

[12]Carl F. H. Henry, *The Uneasy Conscience of Modern Fundamentalism* (Grand Rapids: Eerdmans, 1947), 88–89.

wait ten years. You don't have to pray anymore, "Lord, send a revival." The revival is here![13]

The evangelical movement looked to Graham for leadership through the end of the twentieth century. He convened global conferences, raised money for parachurch ministries, corresponded with other leaders, and carved out public space for evangelicals by his friendship with every US president from John F. Kennedy to Barack Obama. He also shaped the terms of evangelical cooperation and debate. By rebuffing invitations from fundamentalists to visit New York City, working instead with the liberal Protestant Council of the City of New York for his 1957 crusade, he ensured that evangelicals and fundamentalists would follow separate paths. When he declined to arbitrate a dispute among faculty at Fuller Theological Seminary, the school moved away from its original commitment to biblical inerrancy.

Today's evangelical movement lacks any comparable central figure. But even the most famous evangelicals, whether Graham or Whitefield or Wesley, never claimed to speak for the entire movement. Personalities come and go, but the Word of the Lord stands forever. And that Word is spreading around the world. Evangelicals believe in the powerful gospel of Jesus Christ that penetrates any culture. On the basis of the divinely inspired Word, evangelicals proclaim the good news that God justifies by faith alone those who believe in Jesus, whose atoning death and triumphant resurrection make it possible for sinners to be born again by the power of the Holy Spirit. Wherever you see cooperation around these core convictions of the gospel handed down through the centuries, you see the evangelical movement.

FOR FURTHER STUDY

Henry, Carl F. H. *The Uneasy Conscience of Fundamentalism.* Grand Rapids: Eerdmans, 1947.

Jenkins, Philip. *The Next Christendom: The Coming of Global Christianity.* New York: Oxford University Press, 2002.

Sweeney, Douglas A. *The American Evangelical Story: A History of the Movement.* Grand Rapids: Baker, 2005.

---

[13]Harold John Ockenga, "Is America's Revival Breaking?" *United Evangelical Action*, July 1, 1950, 3.

PART 2

EVANGELICAL THEOLOGY

Thinking, Feeling, and Believing
the Truths That Matter Most

Chapter 3

God

Not Like You

JONATHAN LEEMAN

Maybe you think God is like Superman. He's basically human but has amazing powers. He likes to help people, at least if he can get there in time. He is a gentleman—well mannered and politically correct. He never imposes himself on people's wills. And he stands for truth, justice, and all that stuff.

Or maybe you think God is like Morgan Freeman. In one movie I saw, Freeman depicts God as a kind older man with a grandfatherly chuckle. He is honest and caring, but he also challenges people. Happily, his harder lessons are for their good.

Or maybe your view of God is not so positive. Honestly, you're a little suspicious of him. Things haven't gone well for you, and the world is too dark to expect much.

We all have slightly different ideas about what God is like. And probably our backgrounds affect our view. But one thing is certain: every one of us, in our natural state, believes that God is pretty much like us. By this, I mean we believe that God is angered at the things that anger us, and treasures the things we treasure. We believe he likes the people we like, and doesn't like the people we don't like. Even when we do wrong, we assume that God basically understands our course of action. He won't make a big deal of it.

We know that God knows more than we do, and that he's morally superior—"better." But we still assume that God, broadly speaking, shares our sense of justice and morality, our views on love and sex, our politics and passions, our ideas of an evening well spent and a life worth living. He's basically like us . . . like me.

It is this assumption that's at the heart of what the Bible calls our sin. The Serpent promised that we could be "like God," which is really just another way of saying, "God is like you, so do as you please." And we have believed this lie ever since. In theological language, we justify ourselves in everything we do or leave undone. Every task we accomplish, every love we pursue, every room we enter, every thought we think—all are done in the grand project of justifying ourselves, our godness, our right to rule, our determination of right and wrong, our assumption that God is like us.

But is God really like you? Like me?

Moses observed that "no one is like the LORD our God" (Ex. 8:10). King David said the same thing: "There is none like you" (2 Sam. 7:22). David's son Solomon said it too: "There is no God like you" (1 Kings 8:23). And, finally, God himself tells us, "I am God, and there is none like me" (Isa. 46:9).

What does the Bible mean when it says that God is not like us? Some theologians, from the early church through today, have used these kinds of phrases to say that we cannot know God "in himself." He's a different kind of thing, and we cannot comprehend him by any analogy of being. (Muslims say something similar.) But look up the context of these Bible passages. They are not saying we cannot comprehend him. They're saying that God is not like us because his purposes cannot be thwarted; he is unimaginably powerful and breathtakingly good; he is shockingly gracious and loving to the undeserving; he has known the end since the beginning.

Over and over the Bible has to say he's not like us because we repeat- edly try to make him like us. We squeeze God into our own mental universes. We domesticate him and fashion him after our image. But what foolishness! This is the God who created the universe with words. This is the God who destroyed the world with a flood. This is the God who struck down two priests for offering unauthorized incense. This is a God who raises up nations and dashes them to pieces. This is the God who put on flesh, died on a cross, and rose again. This is the God who commands us to present ourselves as living sacrifices of worship. Forget Superman, Morgan Freeman, or any other god who looks like us. God is not like us, but far more worthy and far more holy. He is not to be trifled with.

What's more, we *can* comprehend him—not fully, but sufficiently. In the Bible, God opens his throne room doors to a true knowledge of himself. We can enter that throne room with a mere flip of the Bible's cover. Stepping in, what do we see?

Stepping into the Throne Room of the One God

Here is what one person who was there saw:

> And above the expanse . . . was the likeness of a throne, in appearance like sapphire; and seated above the likeness of a throne was a likeness with a human appearance. And upward from what had the appearance of his waist I saw as it were gleaming metal, like the appearance of fire enclosed all around. And downward from what had the appearance of his waist I saw as it were the appearance of fire, and there was brightness around him. . . .
>
> Such was the appearance of the likeness of the glory of the Lord. And when I saw it, I fell on my face, and I heard the voice of one speaking. (Ezek. 1:26–28)

Every description feels one or two degrees removed from the thing itself. The prophet Ezekiel could make out the *likeness* of a throne, the *likeness* of a human appearance, and the *likeness* of the glory of the Lord. He could see the *appearance* of a waist and the *appearance* of fire. But it sounds like Ezekiel doesn't quite see God himself, since "man shall not see me and live," says God elsewhere (Ex. 33:20). God has removed himself from our sight because of sin.

But that does not mean we cannot know God truly. Ezekiel concludes his vision, "I heard the voice of one speaking." God speaks! And consider what God's words give us: God's own thoughts and self-knowledge (1 Cor. 2:11–12). When God tells us that he "is love," for instance, we know that God, in his very essence, knows himself to be love.

Theologians observe that our understanding of "love" will not match God's understanding perfectly—the words are analogical. Yet this doesn't mean our knowledge isn't true. God *acts* in order to help us understand his words rightly. For instance, Psalm 136 points to God's work in creation and redemption to define what God means by "steadfast love." So God acts and speaks in redemptive history, such that his actions give content to his words, while his words interpret his actions.

Stepping into God's throne room, therefore, we become aware, first, that God is personal; he speaks and acts. He is not simply a truth to be discussed or a force to be felt. God is to be encountered through his words and actions. Second, we learn that encountering him means falling flat on our faces, as the prophet Ezekiel did. Why?

The Power and Plentitude of the One God

There are many things a good doctrinal discussion of God should include, such as the fact that God is all-powerful, eternal, everywhere present, unchanging, all-knowing, fully spiritual, and not made up of parts. It should also include his moral attributes: his goodness, justice, truthfulness, righteousness, and more. These are all ways of talking about God's nature, or the attributes of his nature. In the short space here we will meditate particularly on several attributes that should help us quickly see what might be the hardest thing of all to grasp in our day—the fact that God is a King before whom we would fall flat on our faces. He is a King of unrivalled power, holiness, love, and glory.

We live, after all, in a rights-obsessed, entitlement-driven age. We're suspicious of authority. Our sense of reality centers upon ourselves, as if each of us were the sun in the solar system. It's not difficult to see why a Superman God is so appealing. Superman is heroic and inspiring, but he serves us and asks for little in return. Yet what if God really is someone who would destroy the whole world in a flood? What if he is someone who would cause us to fall to the ground in awestruck fear? Wouldn't that change everything, like a new sun showing up in the solar system? Wouldn't it change how we regard sin, or define love, or view our importance?

Let's start then with the first words of the Bible: "In the beginning, God created the heavens and the earth" (Gen. 1:1). Who is the subject? God. The creation account is primarily about God. The story of the entire Bible is about God. The story of our lives is about God. God is the main character and the protagonist.

God is all-powerful. Nothing existed. Then it did. God is eternal. He existed "before" the beginning. And God is utterly self-sufficient. He created everything from the workshop of his own mind. As one writer put it, "If you wish to make an apple pie from scratch, you must first invent the universe."[1] So God did.

Meditating on the self-sufficient power and plentitude of God should shut our mouths whenever we're tempted to think that God owes us, or that we can add to him. The apostle Paul interprets Genesis 1 like this: "The God who made the world and everything in it, being Lord of heaven and earth, does not live in temples made by man, nor is he served by human hands, as though he needed anything, since he himself gives to all mankind life and breath and everything" (Acts 17:24–25; see also Ps. 50:10–12).

God doesn't owe us. He cannot be manipulated by our demands, our claims, or our boasts. He is not beholden to us, and we have no rights independent of him. We cannot instruct him, as if a pot could instruct the potter. The pot is made and unmade as the potter pleases. God is the Creator King, and we do best to close our mouths: "Be not rash with your mouth, nor let your heart be hasty to utter a word before God, for God is in heaven and you are on earth. Therefore let your words be few" (Eccles. 5:2); "let all the earth keep silence before him" (Hab. 2:20).

There is also great relief in discovering the self-sufficient power and plentitude of God. It means we are no longer tasked with filling him up or making the grumpy old man happy. The King of the universe is infinitely happy, and knowing him means bathing in that sunshine. It also means that salvation is free, won by faith. If God is for us, all the resources of his power and plenty are for us.

But is God for us?

---

[1] Carl Sagan, *Cosmos* (New York: Random House, 1980), 218.

The Holiness and Glory of the One God

Standing in the throne room of God, we also encounter his holiness and glory. Listen to another prophet who stood in this place:

> I saw the Lord sitting upon a throne, high and lifted up . . . . Above him stood the seraphim. Each had six wings: with two he covered his face, and with two he covered his feet, and with two he flew. And one called to another and said:
>
> > "Holy, holy, holy is the LORD of hosts;
> > the whole earth is full of his glory!"
>
> . . . And I said: "Woe is me! For I am lost; for I am a man of unclean lips, and I dwell in the midst of a people of unclean lips; for my eyes have seen the King, the LORD of hosts!" (Isa. 6:1–5)

Isaiah hears the angels proclaim that God is all-holy, which they interpret in the next line by saying not that he separates himself from the earth, but that he fills it with his glory. God's holiness is his utter commitment to his own glory. To praise his holiness is to praise his glory:

> Ascribe to the LORD the glory due his name;
> > worship the LORD in the splendor of holiness.
> > (Ps. 29:2; see also Ex. 15:11; Ezek. 28:22)

God is holy in that he is wholly consecrated to his own glory.

But are we? No, we have already said that we center the universe upon ourselves. We devote our entire lives to self-justification and the promotion of our own godness. Movie actor Brad Pitt, explaining why he abandoned Christianity, spoke for many when he said, "I didn't understand this idea of a God who says, 'You have to acknowledge me. You have to say that I'm the best, and then I'll give you eternal happiness. If you won't, then you don't get it!' It seemed to be about ego. I can't see God operating from ego, so it made no sense to me."[2] Pitt's operating assumption, as with every fallen human, is that he is "like God" (Gen. 3:5). After all, he places God and humanity in equivalent moral positions, as if God and humans are entitled to the same things.

---

[2]Brad Pitt, *Parade*, October 7, 2007, http://www.parade.com/articles/editions/2007/edition_10-07-2007 /Brad_Pitt.

But would Pitt or would we be so self-assured if we were all standing in God's throne room with Isaiah? Consider Isaiah's response: "Woe is me!" For the first time in his life, Isaiah's eyes are opened to the utter contradiction that is fallen human existence—the contradiction of a creature posturing as Creator, thereby denying and defaming the Creator. Isaiah, in the presence of God, finally sees his fallen self, and the only proper response is "woe" and "lost."

If God is wholly devoted to his glory (holy), and we are wholly opposed to it (unholy), we cannot survive. He cannot be for us. Indeed, all his power and plentitude will be set against us.

> Fire goes before him
>> and burns up his adversaries all around. (Ps. 97:3)

To enter God's throne room like Isaiah, therefore, is first and foremost to behold a king in his righteous and fiery splendor. It's to be undone. This is not Superman or Morgan Freeman. This is One before whom we would fall on our faces. This is someone altogether more terrifying, beautiful, and mighty.

Seeing a Doorway and God's Three Persons

Yet there is good news from this good God. On one side of the throne room we spy a doorway, a doorway through which the One on the throne stepped from heaven to earth. The One who is "in the form of God" takes on "the form of a servant" or a "human form" (Phil. 2:6–7; also Heb. 1:3). Jesus, the divine Son, became fully man while remaining fully God. Looking through this doorway, then, we see a stable, a hill of judgment, and an empty tomb.

God's plan of salvation, which was promised to Abraham, modeled through Moses, and typified in King David, fully flowers on the pages of the New Testament in the person of Jesus Christ through the power of the Holy Spirit. We discover that the God behind this plan of salvation is in fact triune. The Bible does not use the word *Trinity*. It was devised by the early church fathers to describe what they saw in Scriptures, such as the monotheistic Jewish disciple Thomas worshipping Jesus, "My Lord and my God!" (John 20:28). Sure enough, Scripture affirms that God is one God (Deut. 6:4). There are not three gods. It affirms that the Father is not the Son, the Son is not the Spirit, and the Spirit is not the Father (e.g., Luke 22:42). And it affirms that all three are the one God (e.g., John 1:1). Each shares the essence and attributes of God and is God—without being three gods! The one God subsists in three persons—Father, Son, and Holy Spirit.

As we observe the three persons carry out this plan of salvation, God as he is "in himself" comes into sharper focus.

The Power and Plentitude of the Spirit

God accomplishes his purposes in creation and re-creation through the power of the Spirit (e.g., Gen. 1:2; Ezekiel 37; John 3; 2 Corinthians 3–4). God is everywhere in his Spirit (Ps. 139:7–8). And he knows all things in his Spirit (1 Cor. 2:11). Every member of the Godhead indwells every action of God, yet the Spirit, in some sense, might be said to represent God's power and plentitude.

The Spirit came in partial measure upon Old Testament prophets, kings, and craftsman, but he came in full measure upon the life and ministry of Jesus. He lit upon Jesus as a dove, led Jesus into the wilderness, empowered him to perform miracles, and then raised him from the dead. Jesus promised his disciples that he would send the same Spirit after his departure in order to testify about Christ, convict them of guilt, lead them into all truth, and bring Christ glory (John 15:26; 16:8, 13, 14). After Jesus ascended and sat down at the right hand of God, the Spirit of Christ was given to Christ's people (Acts 2:1–4; 8:14–17; 10:44–48).

The Spirit of God represents the power of God in convicting, regenerating, and sanctifying God's people (John 3:5–8; 1 Thess. 1:5). He seals us now and promises the full inheritance to come (Eph. 1:13–14). He produces the life of the Son within us, and gives us the freedom of Christ's obedience.

The Love and Glory of the Son and the Father

In the life and ministry of Jesus Christ, God provides the clearest picture of his holiness and glory. What's more, he pictures them by pointing to the operations of his love. The holiness of the Father is demonstrated in his perfect love for the Son and in his desire to acquire a loving bride for his Son. The holiness of the Son is demonstrated in his pure love for the Father and in his desire to produce loving worshippers of the Father.

Jesus says that "it is my Father who glorifies me" (John 8:54), and later prays to the Father, "Glorify your Son that the Son may glorify you" (John 17:1). He also remarks, "The Father loves the Son and has given all things into his hand" (John 3:35; 5:20), while simultaneously affirming, "I do as the Father has commanded me, so that the world may know that I love the Father" (John 14:31).

Theologian Jonathan Edwards summed it up this way: "The holiness of God consist[s] in his love, especially in the perfect and intimate union and love there is between the Father and Son."[3] God's holiness is his love of himself and his glory as it is experienced between the different persons of Father and Son.

At the same time, God's goodness, love, and holiness are resplendently demonstrated as he draws once forsaken sinners into the boomerang's arc of this magnificent love—love that comes from God and returns to God, catching us up in its path (Rom. 11:36). We are made recipients of the infinite love with which the Father loves the Son, and we become lovers of the Son and Father in return. Jesus says to his disciples, "As the Father has loved me, so have I loved you" (John 15:9). Then he says to his Father, "The glory that you have given me I have given to them, that they may be one even as we are one . . . so that the world may know that you . . . loved them even as you loved me" (John 17:22–23). Could it be possible? That the Son would love us as the Father loves him? And that the Father would love us as he loves the Son?

Remarkably, we the church are incorporated into the "vast, unmeasured, boundless, free" love of the Father for the Son. The very nature of God, which is revealed most clearly in the Father and Son's love for one another and for God's people, is then to be displayed for the world through the unity and love of the local church (John 17:20–26).

Worshipping the Triune God

Theologians debate whether chapters like this one on the Christian doctrine of God should begin by talking about God's one nature or about his three persons. After all, giving undue weight to his *oneness* can lead to the heresy of viewing God as really just one person who rotates between three different hats. Giving undue weight to his *threeness* can

---

[3]Jonathan Edwards, "Treatise on Grace," in *The Works of Jonathan Edwards*, vol. 21, *Writings on the Trinity, Grace, and Faith*, ed. Sang Hyun Lee (New Haven, CT: Yale University Press, 2002), 78.

lead to the heresy of viewing God's three persons like we would view three human persons. Ultimately, we must not give greater weight to either the oneness or the threeness. As early church father Gregory of Nazianzus put it, "I cannot think on the one without quickly being encircled by the splendor of the three; nor can I discern the three without being straightway carried back to the one."[4]

Yet I began our discussion with the oneness of God because that's where the Bible begins, and I think it does for a clear reason. When we first look upon God, the first thing we see is not the triune Godhead working out the plan of redemption. We see the all-glorious, all-holy, all-powerful God of whose glory we have fallen short (Rom. 3:23). We look upon a mighty and magnificent lion. This is one of the main lessons of the Old Testament.

But as we continue to gaze, and as we consider Jesus' departure and return to heaven, we see something more: a Lamb. The final book of the Bible brings us back once more to God's throne room, where a heavenly elder tells the apostle John, "Behold, the Lion of the tribe of Judah" (Rev. 5:5). Yet John looks and beholds a Lamb, looking as if it had been slain (v. 6). Astounding! The wrathful God is the loving God who is the holy God who is the compassionate God who is the just God who is the good God. God is Lion and Lamb, King and Redeemer.

Why study the doctrine of God? So that we can fall to our faces together with the heavenly assembly, behold the Lion who is the Lamb, and proclaim, "Worthy is the Lamb who was slain, to receive power and wealth and wisdom and might and honor and glory and blessing!" (v. 12). God is not a buddy. We don't saunter up and slap him on the back, as if such casualness were a sign of intimacy. We bow to worship him as the triune God—the Father who has elected us, the Son who has died in our place, and the Spirit who grants repentance and faith and seals us for the Son's return.

The Doctrine of God and the Rest of Theology
God is not like you or me. He's unimaginably better. He's mightier, fiercer, more loving, more majestic. He is holy, holy, holy.

---

[4]Gregory of Nazianzus, *On Holy Baptism* 40.41, quoted in John Calvin, *Institutes of the Christian Religion*, trans. Ford Lewis Battles, ed. John T. McNeill (Philadelphia: Westminster Press, 1960), 1.13.17. Calvin said this passage "vastly delights me."

It's essential, moreover, to get the doctrine of God right before moving on. Either God will be the center of one's doctrinal solar system or something else will. What we believe about God determines what we believe about everything:

- It determines how we view Scripture. Does God talk truthfully? The answer depends in part on what we think of his character.
- It determines how we understand the gospel. Is our problem a lack of knowledge, a broken relationship, or guilt and wrath? The answer depends on how we view God's holiness and glory.
- It determines how we view the church. Is church membership and discipline wrongly exclusive? The answer depends on how we understand the nature of his love.

What we believe about God also determines how we live today. Belief in God is not merely an epistemological matter. It's a matter of lordship and the heart's affections. Either we live in rebellion against God, indifferent to the harm we cause others, or we live in obedience and worship, demonstrating among God's people the loving and holy oneness of the Father and Son through the Spirit (John 17:20–26). A right trust in God ultimately yields holy individuals and a loving church, a community of people who display God's glory before all heaven and earth (Eph. 3:10).

When we belong to Christ, less and less do we believe that God is like us, and more and more do we become like God (2 Cor. 3:18; 1 John 3:2).

FOR FURTHER STUDY

Frame, John M. *The Doctrine of God.* Phillipsburg, NJ: P&R, 2002.
Letham, Robert. *The Holy Trinity: In Scripture, History, Theology, and Worship.* Phillipsburg, NJ: P&R, 2005.
Packer, J. I. *Knowing God.* Downers Grove, IL: InterVarsity, 1973.
Ware, Bruce A. *Father, Son, and Holy Spirit: Relationships, Roles, and Relevance.* Wheaton, IL: Crossway, 2005.

Chapter 4

Scripture

How the Bible Is a Book Like No Other

ANDY NASELLI

I grew up Mormon—sort of. Most of my mom's relatives are faithful members of the Church of Jesus Christ of Latter-day Saints, but my family left Mormonism when I was six years old. I've studied Mormonism a fair bit to try to understand what I might have embraced, and I've found that the most fundamental issue that divides Mormons from evangelicals is what they believe about the Bible.

This dividing line is not unique to Mormons and evangelicals. It's the dividing line between just about all other religious people and evangelicals. That's because evangelicals hold uncommon beliefs about this holy book.

Is the Bible merely a human book with its share of errors? Is it irrelevant and insufficient for life's most pressing problems? Is it too difficult for ordinary people to understand? If the answers to those questions are yes, then evangelicals are fools. If you want to discredit evangelicals, discredit the Bible.

What's the Big Deal?

The Bible is a God-breathed book, completely trustworthy and authoritative. Few things matter more than believing that last sentence.

1. It matters because what you think about the Bible directly affects what you believe and how you live. Is the Bible like an all-you-can-eat buffet where you pick and choose what to believe and obey? Is it merely another moral book, no more historical and inspired than Aesop's Fables?

2. It matters because some people who claim the term *evangelical* have a novel view of the Bible's authority. It is historically recent, for example, for those in the evangelical tradition to claim that the Bible contains historical and scientific errors.

3. It matters because views of the Bible set individuals and institutions on very different trajectories. Institutions that have rejected the Bible's entire trustworthiness have often gone on to embrace beliefs incompatible with the gospel. This controversial issue is a theological line in the sand.[1]

A Book That Is God-Breathed: Inspiration

God has revealed himself to his creatures in two ways. His general revelation includes nature and the human conscience, and his special revelation includes the Bible. Our focus in this chapter is on the Bible. Amazingly, God has chosen to reveal himself using written human language. The process is called inspiration. Inspiration is how God breathed out his words through human authors.[2] "All Scripture is God-breathed" (2 Tim. 3:16, NIV).[3]

But that doesn't mean that the human authors were not actively involved. God didn't dictate the whole Bible the way an executive mechanically dictates letters to his secretary. The human authors' personalities are like musical instruments. If I play the same tune on a

---

[1] For a summary of some recent "battles for the Bible," see Stephen J. Nichols and Eric T. Brandt, *Ancient Word, Changing Worlds: The Doctrine of Scripture in a Modern Age* (Wheaton, IL: Crossway, 2009), 63–85.

[2] B. B. Warfield's classic definition is more precise: "Inspiration is . . . a supernatural influence exerted on the sacred writers by the Spirit of God, by virtue of which their writings are given Divine trustworthiness." *The Works of Benjamin B. Warfield*, vol. 1, *Revelation and Inspiration* (New York: Oxford University Press, 1927), 77–78.

[3] *Spiration* is an archaic word that means "breathing." The *in* prefix on *inspiration* is misleading because 2 Tim. 3:16 refers to a written product that God breathed *out*, not an existing product that God breathed *into* and animated. The prefix *ex* is more accurate, but calling all Scripture expired isn't exactly an improvement. We're stuck with the traditional word *inspired*.

number of wind instruments, each will sound different even if I play the exact melody in the same key and even though it's all coming from the same breath—mine. If I play "Amazing Grace" on a tuba, baritone, trombone, French horn, trumpet, oboe, clarinet, and flute, it is all "Andy-breathed" or "Andy-produced," but it goes through the "personality" of the instrument. In one sense that's how God produced the Bible through human authors. But even further, God worked through their backgrounds—including their skills and training—and research (e.g., Luke 1:1–3).

So who wrote the Bible: God or humans? That's a trick question. The answer is *yes*.

If 2 Timothy 3:16 presents the nature of inspiration, then 2 Peter 1:20–21 presents its method: "No prophecy of Scripture comes from someone's own interpretation. For no prophecy was ever produced by the will of man, but men spoke from God as they were carried along by the Holy Spirit." The Bible is not the product of human invention. The writers did not think up what they wrote on their own. Rather, the human authors "spoke from God as they were carried along by the Holy Spirit." Luke uses the same word for "carried along" in Acts 27:15 and 17 to describe the way a ship was "driven along" by the wind and waves. Like the wind and waves carry along ships in a storm, God carried along the Bible's human authors.

So God breathed out the Scriptures. But how much of it did he breath out? All of it (2 Tim. 3:16). Every single word.

The above summary explains the nature, method, and extent of inspiration, and it lines up exactly with how the Bible refers to itself. The human authors everywhere affirm this view of inspiration. For example, in the Old Testament, the Lord repeatedly speaks to Moses in Exodus, Leviticus, and Numbers; Isaiah quotes the word of the Lord over a dozen times; Jeremiah and Ezekiel say that "the word of the Lord came" to them over one hundred times; Daniel recounts visions from God; Hosea, Joel, Jonah, Micah, Zephaniah, Haggai, and Zechariah each open by announcing that "the word of the Lord came" to them; Malachi writes "says the Lord" twenty-five times.

But the most important example is Jesus.[4] Jesus repeatedly quotes the Old Testament as his final authority. He says, "It is written" (Matt.

---

[4]See John Wenham, *Christ and the Bible*, 3rd ed. (Grand Rapids: Baker, 1994).

21:13); "Have you never read in the Scriptures . . . ?" (Matt. 21:42; cf. 21:16); "You are wrong, because you know neither the Scriptures nor the power of God" (Matt. 22:29); and "Scripture cannot be broken" (John 10:35). He also believes that the miracles recorded in it actually happened. He refers, for example, to Jonah in the belly of a huge fish for three days and nights, Noah's flood, Lot's wife, Moses and the burning bush, and manna in the wilderness (Matt. 12:40–41; Luke 17:26–32; 20:37; John 6:49).

The New Testament authors also refer to the Old Testament as God's word (Rom. 3:2). They regard the writings of other New Testament authors as equally authoritative as the Old Testament and the words of Christ (1 Tim. 5:18; 2 Pet. 3:2, 15–16). They recognize that their writings reveal God's plan more fully than the Old Testament (Eph. 3:2–3; Heb. 1:1–2; 2:2–3).

If the Bible really is this God-breathed book, then two other qualities follow: it's without error and it's authoritative.

A Book That Is Entirely True: Inerrancy
God is entirely truthful—without error (i.e., inerrant) and incapable of error (i.e., infallible) (Num. 23:19; 1 Sam. 15:29; 2 Sam. 7:28; John 3:33; 14:6; Rom. 3:4; Titus 1:2; Heb. 6:18; 1 John 5:6). The Bible is God-breathed (i.e., inspired). Therefore, the Bible is entirely truthful—without error and incapable of error. "Inerrancy means that when all the facts are known, the Scriptures in their original autographs and properly interpreted will be shown to be wholly true in everything that they affirm, whether that has to do with doctrine or morality or with the social, physical, or life sciences."[5]

Since the Bible is God-breathed, God is a liar if it contains errors. The Bible itself asserts that it is true (Ps. 12:6; Prov. 30:5). But it does not merely conform to a higher standard of truth; the Bible itself is the standard of truthfulness, for Jesus said to God the Father, "Your word is truth" (John 17:17). The inerrancy of the Bible is a by-product of the unfailing truthfulness of God.

Some clarifications are in order:

---

[5]Paul Feinberg, "The Meaning of Inerrancy," in *Inerrancy*, ed. Norman L. Geisler (Grand Rapids: Zondervan, 1980), 294.

1. The Bible's inerrancy does not mean that it is truthful only with reference to theology. While it's not a textbook for social, physical, or life science, it is fully trustworthy about whatever it says about any subject. A view that has become common in the last one hundred years says that the Bible is without error when it discusses religion but contains some errors in science and history. But theology and facts are not two separable categories. The gospel itself is irreducibly historical (1 Corinthians 15). A prophet is accredited by the *complete* truthfulness of his words (Deut. 13:1–5; 18:20–22); so is the Bible.

If you can't fully trust the Bible when it discusses science and history (secondary matters that can be verified), how can you trust it when it talks about God and salvation (supremely important matters that we can't verify in the same way)? If you can't trust the Bible, then you can't trust God. If you don't trust God, then you've exalted yourself as the ultimate authority instead of God.

2. The Bible's inerrancy does not mean that it is always precise. The Bible's origin is both fully divine *and fully human.* Though it never affirms what is false, the Bible has the marks of a human book. It is written by human authors with human personalities in human languages in the context of human cultures. For example, you don't question the accuracy of Weather.com when it lists the times of a day's *sunrise* and *sunset* even though the sun technically neither rises nor sets. Nor do you balk if someone tells you that she lives five miles away from your home when in fact she lives 4.857 miles away or that she is twenty-two years old when in fact she was born twenty-two years, 307 days, 4 hours, 37 minutes, and 8.3 seconds ago. Nor is it unusual if two people with very different personalities and backgrounds write about a subject on which they agree—such as their views on politics or sports—and yet sound distinctive in the way they write, the words they use, and the themes they emphasize. We should give the Bible's human authors the same freedom that we routinely give others to use ordinary language.

3. The Bible's inerrancy does not mean that copies of the original writings or translations of those copies are inerrant. Copies and translations are inerrant only to the extent that they accurately reproduce the original writings. God breathed out the original writings, and humans transmitted and translated the copies. This is not sidestepping the issue; this distinction is both accurate and necessary because errors in a copy

or translation are not God's fault but instead reflect the fallible humans who copied or translated them.[6]

So what good is it if only the original writings are God-breathed when we don't possess any of the original writings? A lot of good, actually. It overstates the case to make it sound as if we don't really know what the original writings say because the quality of the Bible's existing manuscripts is so good—far better than any other ancient document. Consequently, existing manuscripts and translations faithfully reproduce over 99 percent of the Bible's original writings. Most of the less than 1 percent that is questionable is about trivial matters like spelling differences, synonyms, and obviously impossible readings. Only about 1 percent of that less than 1 percent that is questionable affects the text's meaning to some degree, and it affects no major doctrines.[7]

4. The Bible's inerrancy does not mean that there are no remaining difficulties or apparent discrepancies. We can't perfectly interpret the Bible for two reasons: we don't have all the data relevant to understanding the Bible (e.g., archeology continually discovers new facts), and we are finite and sinful and thus misinterpret the data we already have. We can't demonstrate inerrancy to everyone's satisfaction until all the facts are available and perfect interpretation is possible. But when that time comes, the Bible's inerrancy will be vindicated. Until then, the only proper response is to trust that what the all-knowing, all-good God has spoken is completely true.

A Book That Is the Boss of Me: Authority

Jesus himself appeals to the Bible as the final authority, affirming that it cannot be shown to be in error: "Scripture cannot be broken" (John 10:35; cf. Matt. 5:17–20). God has supreme authority since he created and controls the universe. If the Bible is God-breathed, then it carries the authority of God himself. It's the final authority. And it's not the final authority merely for "faith and practice" (as doctrinal statements often put it); it is the final authority for every domain of knowledge it addresses. It's supremely authoritative. It's like no other book. So if you

---

[6]See James R. White, *The King James Only Controversy: Can You Trust Modern Translations?*, 2nd ed. (Minneapolis: Bethany House, 2009).
[7]For an accessible introduction to how certain the New Testament text is, see J. Ed Komoszewski, M. James Sawyer, and Daniel B. Wallace, *Reinventing Jesus: How Contemporary Skeptics Miss the Real Jesus and Mislead Popular Culture* (Grand Rapids: Kregel, 2006), 51–117, 272–95.

don't believe or obey the Bible, you are distrusting or disobeying God. It's that serious.

This is what the Protestant Reformers called *sola Scriptura*, that is, Scripture alone. This doesn't mean that Scripture is the only source of any truth in the world, but that it is the only inerrant and infallible authority. It is the final, ultimate, supreme authority.

A Book That Is All You Need: Sufficiency

The Bible is entirely sufficient for its purpose. In the Bible God has given us all we need in order to know, trust, and obey him. "All Scripture is God-breathed and is useful for teaching, rebuking, correcting and training in righteousness, so that the man of God may be thoroughly equipped for every good work" (2 Tim. 3:16–17, NIV). The Bible does not directly answer every question that people can ask. That's not its purpose. Its primary purpose is to reveal the God of the gospel so that we can know and honor him.

The Bible *alone* is sufficient. Its supreme authority is exclusive. No other book is God's word—not the Apocrypha or the Book of Mormon or the Qur'an. Giving such books equal status with the Bible marginalizes and demeans it. It marginalizes the Bible by not adequately emphasizing it, and it demeans the Bible by contradicting it. For example, Roman Catholicism gives the Apocrypha, some church tradition, and some papal pronouncements equal status with the Bible; the Church of Jesus Christ of Latter-day Saints gives the Book of Mormon, the Doctrine and Covenants, the Pearl of Great Price, and statements by its prophets equal status with the Bible; and Islam gives the Qur'an superior status to the Bible. Consequently, they do not adequately emphasize the Bible. They don't think that it's all the special revelation you need to know, trust, and obey him. They think that it needs to be supplemented or supplanted by additional revelation. Their additional revelation is not God-breathed and thus is neither inerrant nor authoritative like the Bible. So it's not surprising that their additional revelation contradicts the Bible in many ways.

Some evangelicals believe that God continues to reveal himself with special words and special guidance. Whether we agree that God still speaks like this or not, we must agree that these special words do not carry the authority of Scripture. We can't be absolutely certain that they actually come from God, so we should never treat these forms of communication the same way we treat God's communication to us in the Bible. Otherwise we would be adding to the Bible, which is already sufficient as it stands.

A Book That Is Actually Understandable: Clarity

It has been said that the Bible is like a deep, broad body of water, shallow enough for a lamb to wade in but deep enough for an elephant to swim in. Not everything in the Bible is equally clear. Peter himself remarked, "There are some things in [Paul's letters] that are hard to understand" (2 Pet. 3:16). But the Bible's central message about God's saving work throughout history is unmistakably clear and easily understood. Its basic storyline—creation, fall, redemption, and consummation—is so simple that a young child can easily grasp it. God's communication in the Bible as a whole is accessible.

This assumes two debated premises. First, the Bible means what God and the human authors intended it to mean. Second, we can understand that meaning. But that doesn't mean that we can understand everything to the fullest possible degree. Case in point: Can a young child understand Genesis 1:1: "In the beginning, God created the heavens and the earth"? Sure, that's not hard for a child to grasp. But that same child's understanding of Genesis 1:1 may continually increase as she learns more and more about the Bible and God's world. We can't know anything absolutely (exhaustively or omnisciently) like God, but we can know some things truly (substantially or for real).

If we can understand the Bible truly, then why don't all humans completely agree with each other on what the Bible teaches? The problem is not with the Bible. The problem is with finite and sinful humans. Were it not for the effects of the fall on our heads and hearts we would interpret the Bible the same way. But the point to stress here is that the Bible's central message is clear.[8]

A Book That Is Essential to Know God: Necessity

The Bible is necessary for us to know, trust, and obey God. You must somehow hear the Bible's message—whether by reading it yourself or

---

[8]Cf. Wayne Grudem's seven sensible qualifications: "Scripture affirms that it is able to be understood but (1) not all at once, (2) not without effort, (3) not without ordinary means, (4) not without the reader's willingness to obey it, (5) not without the help of the Holy Spirit, (6) not without human misunderstanding, and (7) never completely." "The Perspicuity of Scripture," *Themelios* 34, no. 3 (2009): 288–309, accessed at http://theGospelCoalition.org/publications.

hearing someone else read or explain it—in order to become a Christian. "The sacred writings . . . are able to make you wise for salvation through faith in Christ Jesus" (2 Tim. 3:15). "Faith comes from hearing the message, and the message is heard through the word of Christ" (Rom. 10:17, NIV).

And you must keep hearing the Bible's message to grow as a Christian. This means hearing it read and preached, reading it, studying it, memorizing it, meditating on it, and applying it.[9] A Christian needs the Bible like a human needs food and water. The need never goes away. That's why Peter writes, "Like newborn infants, long for the pure spiritual milk, that by it you may grow up into salvation" (1 Pet. 2:2). That "pure spiritual milk" is "the living and abiding word of God," "the good news" (1 Pet. 1:23–25). Can you say with Job, "I have treasured the words of his mouth more than my portion of food" (Job 23:12)?

The Bible is necessary for more than survival. It's our only infallible guide to navigate life wisely because it reveals God's will. "How can a young man keep his way pure?" the psalmist asked.

> By guarding it according to your word.
> With my whole heart I seek you;
>   let me not wander from your commandments!
> I have stored up your word in my heart,
>   that I might not sin against you. (Ps. 119:9–11)

Three Popular Objections

The Bible is God's word—God-breathed, inerrant, authoritative, sufficient, clear, and necessary. This is what evangelicals believe about the Bible because this is what the Bible teaches about itself. But when we talk this way about the Bible, we may have to deal with misguided objections.

1. "Evangelicals are guilty of bibliolatry." No, we don't worship the Bible. We worship God alone. But we esteem the Bible as a unique book because God actively communicates through it: "God has so *identified* himself with his words that whatever someone does to God's words (whether it is to obey or to disobey) they do directly to God himself."[10]

---

[9]See Donald S. Whitney's two chapters on "Bible intake" in *Spiritual Disciplines for the Christian Life* (Colorado Springs, CO: NavPress, 1997), 23–60.
[10]Timothy Ward, *Words of Life: Scripture as the Living and Active Word of God* (Downers Grove, IL: InterVarsity, 2009), 27 (his emphasis).

2. "Evangelicals derive their doctrine of the Bible from the Bible. Isn't that circular reasoning?" Well, yes, but that doesn't necessarily invalidate the reasoning. Our doctrine of the Bible is no more circular than scientific theories. Everyone uses circular reasoning to defend the ultimate authority for beliefs. While the ultimate standard of truth for evangelicals is God and his Word, for most others it is something else—usually themselves. The heated debates about whether the Bible is God-breathed and without error hinge on one issue: whether you accept what the Bible claims about itself. Many useful arguments show that the Bible's claims about itself are reasonable (e.g., its historical reliability and fulfilled prophecies), but ultimately God's Spirit must convince us that its claims are true because sin has distorted how we perceive reality. We can't prove that the Bible is God's word by appealing to any authority besides the Bible itself because such an authority must be superior to God—and there isn't one.

3. "The Word (i.e., Jesus) is what matters, not the word (i.e., the Bible)." As pious as that sounds, it takes a different view of the word than the Word himself. Jesus repeatedly quotes the Bible as completely trustworthy and as his final authority.

How Should We Then Read?
Of course, our high view of Scripture won't matter much if we don't actually read the Bible. But, you may ask, how should we read this holy book? In one sense we should read the Bible like any other book. It consists of different styles of literature that express truth according to the intention of its authors. But we shouldn't read the Bible merely like any other book because it is unique. There's no other book like it.

Because the Bible stands over us, it requires reverence, submission, and obedience. Because it is completely truthful, it requires trust. Because its nature contrasts sharply with our finiteness and sinfulness, it requires humble reading that is always open to correction. And because it reveals God and his ways, it requires careful, prayerful reading that situates passages within its grand story of God's creation, our fall, Christ's redemption, and the universe's consummation.

> Open my eyes, that I may behold
>   wondrous things out of your law. (Ps. 119:18)

Rejoice with John Newton, author of "Amazing Grace," that the Bible is a priceless book—a book like no other:

> Precious Bible! What a treasure
> Does the Word of God afford!
> All I want for life or pleasure,
> Food and med'cine, shield and sword:
>   Let the world account me poor,
>   Having this I need no more.

FOR FURTHER STUDY

Carson, D. A. *Collected Writings on Scripture*. Wheaton, IL: Crossway, 2010.

Feinberg, Paul. "The Meaning of Inerrancy." In *Inerrancy*, edited by Norman L. Geisler, 265–304, 468–72. Grand Rapids: Zondervan, 1980.

Grudem, Wayne A. "Part 1: The Doctrine of the Word of God." In *Systematic Theology: An Introduction to Biblical Doctrine*, 45–138. Grand Rapids: Zondervan, 1994.

Nichols, Stephen J., and Eric T. Brandt. *Ancient Word, Changing Worlds: The Doctrine of Scripture in a Modern Age*. Wheaton, IL: Crossway, 2009.

Piper, John. *Why We Believe the Bible*. Wheaton, IL: Crossway, 2009. DVD and study guide.

Chapter 5

The Gospel

God's Self-Substitution for Sinners

GREG GILBERT

The cross, says Martin Hengel in his classic little book *Crucifixion*, "was not just any kind of death. It was an utterly offensive affair, 'obscene' in the original sense of the word." So obscene was it in fact, that the sophisticated, cultured people in Greek and Roman societies would not even utter the word *cross* in polite company. It was a reviled word, and it conjured disgusting and nauseating images.

Crucifixion was never a private event. It was always raw, and searingly public, because its purpose was to terrify the masses into submission to the authorities. Crosses often lined the main roads into cities, holding the broken writhing bodies of the condemned, or displaying the rotting corpses of the dead. The Romans even scheduled public crucifixions to coincide with religious festivals, insuring the maximum number of people present to witness the horror. Murderers, robbers, traitors, and slaves were crucified, brutally, by the thousands all over the empire and always deliberately in full public view. The horror of the cross was inescapable, and the Romans intended it to be that way.

Given the ubiquity of crosses in Roman society, it's somewhat surprising that ancient accounts of crucifixion are so rare. But then again, nobody wanted to write about such a thing, and why would they? The cross was a government-sanctioned—even government-*encouraged*—opportunity for executioners to carry out on real people their most sadistic, brutal, and viciously inventive fantasies. Thus the accounts we have of it are short, and the authors usually only allude to the horrors rather than describing them in any detail. "You wouldn't want to know," they seem to say.

Shredded flesh against unforgiving wood, iron stakes pounded through bone and wracked nerves, joints wrenched out of socket by the sheer dead weight of the body, public humiliation before the eyes of family, friends, and the world—that was death on the cross, "the infamous stake" as the Romans called it, "the barren wood," the *maxima mala crux*. Or as the Greeks spat it out, the *stauros*. No wonder no one talked about it. No wonder parents hid their children's eyes from it. The *stauros* was a loathsome thing, and the one who died on it was loathsome too, a vile criminal whose only use was to hang there as a putrid, decaying warning to anyone else who might follow his example.

That is how Jesus died.

I think we underestimate just how serious Paul was when he said that the cross was an "offense" to the people around him. We chalk it up to good rhetoric when he says that the message of the cross was a "stumbling block" to some people and "madness" to the rest. But that wasn't just cheap overstatement. It was Paul's matter-of-fact acknowledgment, born of *twenty years* of first-hand experience, that the message he was preaching—that salvation was to be had through a crucified God—was considered by *everyone* to be either deeply obscene or totally, completely, tin-foil-hat ridiculous.

Over and over again, pagan writers pilloried Christians for resting their faith on a crucified criminal. "Seriously?" they asked. "You worship a man who was condemned by the judges and nailed naked to a *stauros*?

And you think this guy was a *god*?" They even drew cartoons in ridicule. One shows a Christian on his knees before a crucified man with a donkey's head. "Alexamenos worships his god," the caption reads. We don't know who Alexamenos was, but it's not hard to imagine him—a child, a teenager?—standing there and having to decide whether following Jesus was really worth being thought a sick fool by his snickering friends.

That was the kind of thing Paul faced every day of his Christian life—disgust, hatred, offense, ridicule. When you think about it, he could have avoided a lot of that pretty simply. He could have just said that Christianity wasn't really about the cross. "Yes, yes," he could have said, "there is that cross thing, but the point isn't the *death* of Jesus, per se. It's his resurrection! Let's talk about *life*, not . . . the *stauros*." Or, "Of course Jesus died on the cross, and that's important. But we should realize that the gospel is bigger than that! It's about God's intention to remake the world!" Surely Paul could have made the gospel more palatable—and less dangerous—by saying it was about something *else*. Something cleaner and less ridiculous than the cross. Something more glorious. Less disgusting.

He didn't do that, though. "I decided," Paul said, "to know nothing among you except Jesus Christ and him crucified" (1 Cor. 2:2). In the face of the worst cultural prejudice imaginable, he fixed the entire gospel squarely and immovably on the fact that Jesus was tacked to a *stauros* and left to die. If he had been *trying* to find a surefire way to turn first-century people off from his "good news," he couldn't have done better than that!

So why did he do it? It's simple. He did it because he knew that leaving the cross out, or running past it with a glance, or making it peripheral to the gospel, or allowing anything else to displace it at the center of the gospel would make it, finally, no gospel at all.

The death of Jesus is—and must be—the heart of the gospel because the good news is precisely that Jesus saves sinners from their sin. Whatever else the gospel promises, at the very beginning of it all is a sinner's sin forgiven.

I'm convinced that part of the reason many evangelicals have begun to lose their grasp on the cross is that we have lost sight of why we need to be saved. We've forgotten, and even in some cases deliberately disregarded, what sin is and how profound is its offense to God.

The Bible tells us plainly that "all have sinned and fall short of the glory of God" (Rom. 3:23), and that at its root, sin is rebellion against God the Creator-King. He made us, Genesis tells us, and therefore he has the right to tell us how to live. When we sin against him, breaking his law, worshipping idols, searching for satisfaction in created things rather than in him, we reject his kingship over us and thereby make ourselves liable to his good and righteous judgment.

It's become popular to soften all that and talk about humanity's problem in very different terms. Sometimes the problem is described in terms of a general sense of meaningless, purposelessness, or disintegration within one's life. Sometimes it's said to be merely a broken relationship with other people, with God, and with oneself. Other times the great problem is said to lie in the corruption of the world's systems and cultures.

The trouble with all those understandings of sin, however, is that none of them does justice to what the Bible says about sin. Throughout Scripture, sin is not simply falling short of one's true meaning or purpose, nor is it merely broken relationship or external systemic corruption. Rather, it is a personal, blameworthy transgression of the law of God, and a rejection of his authority as Creator and King. The point is not that sin *never* results in a sense of purposelessness (it often does), or that it is *not* a breaking of relationship (it is), or that it does *not* have systemic effects (it does). None of those things, however, gets finally at sin's essence. Therefore to lead people to believe that sin is *merely* those things is to misunderstand it, and that will inevitably lead us to undervalue or even misunderstand entirely what Jesus was accomplishing on the cross.

Let me explain in a bit more detail why that is. Take the understanding of sin as a broken relationship, for example. The Bible tells us in no uncertain terms that to sin against God is to break our relationship with him (Isa. 59:2). But we also have to understand what *kind* of relationship has been broken. It wasn't one between equals, or a partnership of some kind. No, the relationship we have broken is that of creature to

Creator, subject to King. If we think of sin as some sort of lovers' quarrel or a spat between friends, we'll lose sight of why it required the death of God's Son to restore. A lovers' quarrel doesn't require all that. You just have to say "I'm sorry" and "That's okay," and it's over. The treason of a rebellious subject against his righteous King, though, is different. That requires something rather more to restore.

If we're going to understand what Jesus accomplished on the cross, we must first understand that sin is a personal offense against God that demands and deserves his judgment. That's why Jesus said that we all "stand condemned already" before God (John 3:18, NIV). It's also why Paul hands down the terrifying verdict that at the end, every mouth will be stopped and all the world will become guilty before God (Rom. 3:19).

It's the guilt that makes the cross necessary. Not the *feeling* of guilt, but the *reality* of it.

The salvation we need is for God's verdict pronounced over us to be something other than "Guilty!" If we are to be saved, and spared the righteous punishment that we have earned by our sin, we need God to declare us innocent, not guilty, even *righteous*.

That's exactly what Jesus accomplished by dying on the cross. He bore the wrath his people deserved because of their sins.

Christians have long called this understanding of the cross "penal substitutionary atonement"—meaning that Jesus paid the *penalty* for his people's sins by dying in their place as their *substitute*. That's not just a philosophical formulation, either. It's the way the Bible talks about atonement, from start to finish.

Think about the Old Testament system of sacrifices. The animal on the altar symbolically represented the people as it died. Through the shedding of its blood, their guilt was atoned for and their punishment deferred for another year. The same imagery operated when the high priest placed his hands on the scapegoat and symbolically transferred the people's sins to the animal before it was sent away to die in the wilderness. Perhaps the clearest example of penal substitution in the Old Testament is the Passover lamb. Each family, God told the enslaved

Israelites, was to take a lamb without any defect, and kill it. Then they
were to put some of the blood around the doorframe of their house. If
they did, God promised that when the angel of death saw the blood, he
would "pass over" that house and spare it the judgment of death. It was
not the people's own innocence that saved them; no, the lamb died so
they wouldn't have to.

It's against this background that Jesus taught the same thing about
his own death. "The Son of Man came not to be served but to serve,"
he said, "and to give his life as a ransom for many" (Mark 10:45). Then
just before his death, at a last supper with his disciples, he took a cup
of wine and said, "This is my blood of the covenant, which is poured
out for many for the forgiveness of sins" (Matt. 26:28).

The apostles, too, said that Jesus had died in the place of sinful
people. Paul described it like this: "Christ redeemed us from the curse
of the law by becoming a curse for us" (Gal. 3:13–14). And in another
place, "God made him who had no sin to be sin for us, so that in him
we might become the righteousness of God" (2 Cor. 5:21, NIV). Peter
wrote, "Christ also suffered once for sins, the righteous for the unrighteous, that he might bring us to God" (1 Pet. 3:18). And, "He himself
bore our sins in his body on the tree, that we might die to sin and live
to righteousness. By his wounds you have been healed" (1 Pet. 2:24).

Do you see what Jesus and the apostles were saying about Jesus'
death? For all the horror that a Roman cross represented, it wasn't finally
the physical pain of it, or even the public humiliation, that marked the
depth of Jesus' suffering. No, the deepest suffering Jesus experienced
was the wrath of his Father poured out on him against sin.

But it wasn't his own sin for which he suffered and died. He didn't
have any! No, it was for his people's sins that Jesus was punished. God
credited all their rebellion, all their disobedience, and all their sin to
him—looked on him as if he had committed it all—and executed the
sentence of death against him. So he became a curse. Became sin. Suffered once for all, the righteous for the unrighteous. Bore our sins on
the tree. So we might live.

And then he rose from the dead. With sin defeated, death conquered,
hell laid prostrate before him, Jesus rose triumphantly from the grave.
Everything he claimed was vindicated, his victory over death and sin

was sealed, and Jesus became the firstfruits of God's promise to redeem and ultimately remake the world.

If that hadn't happened, if Jesus had remained dead, then his death would have meant nothing more than yours or mine. A dead savior can't save. As Paul says in 1 Corinthians 15, if Christ is not risen from the dead, we are above all people most to be pitied. But because he is risen, we join Paul in his exultation: "Where, O death, is your victory? Where, O grave, is your sting?" There is none left, for Jesus the crucified and risen one has absorbed the grave's sting, exhausted sin's penalty, and taken away death's victory!

***

This understanding of Christ's death—that he was dying as a substitute for his condemned-to-die people—is not well received in our world. Because of that, many evangelicals have begun to wonder if there are ways to think about the gospel that don't center so much on a man dying on a bloody cross for sins he didn't commit. I've noticed at least two tendencies in that regard, even among people who would happily call themselves evangelicals.

First is the tendency simply to ignore the cross, to shunt it off to the side and place something else at the center of the good news. Sometimes it's Jesus' lordship, or God's kingdom, or God's purpose to remake the heavens and earth. Other times it's a call for us to join God in his work of cultural transformation. But time after time, in book after book coming off of Christian presses, authors seem to be most excited by something other than the sin-bearing work of Christ on the cross, and their most fervent appeals are for people to join God in doing this or that, rather than to repent and believe in a sin-bearing Savior. In the process, the cross has become (deliberately or not) something of an afterthought in the story of the gospel.

We see this at times, unwittingly perhaps, in the renewed emphasis on the kingdom of God. The kingdom is an important theme in the Bible, and it's a good thing that evangelicals are thinking about it. But very often it seems to me that when evangelicals think about the kingdom, we don't think about the cross, and vice versa. Thus we manage to create in our thought and conversation a rift between the cross and the kingdom.

Some people articulate "the gospel of the cross"—that Jesus died in the place of sinners so they could be forgiven—without reference to the kingdom. And others articulate a "gospel of the kingdom"—that Jesus came to inaugurate a kingdom that will set the world to rights—with little or no mention of the cross (except often as a means of getting Jesus dead so he can rise again). What we're left with then is the "gospel of the cross" over here, the "gospel of the kingdom" over there, and never the twain shall meet. Cross and kingdom are separated by a chasm, and we all crouch on one side or the other of it sneering suspiciously at each other.

I don't think the Bible leaves us with such a division, though. Here's why: *The only way into the kingdom is through the cross.* Yes, Jesus came to inaugurate a kingdom, which will one day be established with perfect justice and righteousness. But that is good news only because he also came to save a people from the wrath of God so that they could be citizens of that kingdom, and the means by which he did that was his penal substitutionary death on the cross. Jesus is not just King; he is suffering King.

Put another way, it is the cross—and the cross alone—that is the gateway to the blessings of the kingdom. You don't *get* the blessings of the kingdom unless you come into them through the blood of the King. Therefore if you preach a sermon or write a chapter on the good news of the kingdom, but neglect to talk about the cross, you've not preached good news at all. You've just shown people a wonderful thing that they have no right to be a part of because they are sinners. That's why we never see Jesus preaching simply, "The kingdom of God has come!" No, it's always, "The kingdom of God has come! *Therefore* repent and believe!" He didn't just preach the coming of the kingdom. He preached the coming of the kingdom *and* the way people could enter it.

So by all means, preach about the kingdom, talk about Jesus' conquest of evil, write about his coming reign. But don't pretend that all those things are glorious good news all by themselves. They're not. The bare fact that Jesus is going to rule the world with perfect righteousness is not good news to me; it's terrifying news, because *I am not righteous!* I'm one of the enemies he's coming to crush! The coming kingdom becomes good news only when I realize that the coming King is also a Savior who forgives sin and makes people righteous—and he does that through his death on the cross. Ignore that, downplay it, shove it out of the center of the gospel, and you make the whole thing not good news at all, but a terrifying message of judgment to rebellious sinners.

A second dangerous tendency is to redefine the cross into something other than the substitutionary, wrath-bearing death of the Savior in the place of sinners. Thus Jesus' death is sometimes said to be the result of human evil or greed or power-lust or culture or any number of other things coming to their lowest, worst, most concentrated point and killing Jesus, who then conquers that worst-of-all-evils through his resurrection.

D. A. Carson hit on this in a blog post some time ago when he wrote:

> In recent years it has become popular to sketch the Bible's story-line something like this: Ever since the fall, God has been active to reverse the effects of sin. He takes action to limit sin's damage; he calls out a new nation, the Israelites, to mediate his teaching and his grace to others; he promises that one day he will come as the promised Davidic king to overthrow sin and death and all their wretched effects. This is what Jesus does: he conquers death, inaugurates the kingdom of righteousness, and calls his followers to live out that righteousness now in prospect of the consummation still to come.

Carson calls this presentation of the Bible's narrative "painfully reductionistic," and he's right. There's no understanding here that sin is an offense against God rather than just an unfortunate circumstance humans have brought on themselves. There's no sense of Jesus standing in the place of sinners to take the punishment that rightly should fall upon them. And for that matter, there's no sense that there's any punishment or divine wrath involved at all—just bad results. Such a presentation of the gospel leaves out exactly what the Bible makes central to it: (1) that on the cross Jesus was dying in the place of his people, and (2) that he endured punishment for their sin (not just the *results* of it, but the *punishment* for it), meted out by God the Father in his righteous wrath.

I wonder if the impulse to decenter the cross or redefine it stems at least in part from the fact that the world just doesn't like the cross. At best, the world around us thinks the gospel of Jesus dying in the place of his people is a ridiculous fairy tale, and at worst a monstrous lie. Add to that the fact that we really want the world to be attracted to Jesus, and there's enormous pressure to find a way not to have to talk about "bloody cross religion" quite so much. So we shade toward a gospel that centers on world renewal or social justice rather than the cross, or at least toward a cross that has nothing to do with Jesus taking God's wrath and punishment for another's sin. If we just do that, we hope, perhaps the world will think us a little less crazy.

One other point demands to be made. Of course it's true that the Bible contains many images of what was happening when Jesus died. Redemption, reconciliation, adoption, healing, conquest—all these are ways the Bible talks about the victory Christ won on the cross.

That does not, however, mean that penal substitution is just one image of the cross among many, and that we may pick and choose which one we want to emphasize. The Bible's images of atonement don't work like that; they are not an all-you-can-preach buffet. Actually, each of the images the Bible uses to describe the atonement finally finds its resolution in the fact that Jesus died in the place of his people. If you trace down the reality that lies behind the images, that is, if you ask enough *how* and *why* questions, what you find at the bottom of every single one of them is penal substitution.

Take reconciliation for example, which is sometimes held up as an alternative to the image of penal substitution. Clearly the Bible talks about the cross in those terms, but if we look carefully at the idea of reconciliation and ask questions of it, what we find is that it *depends* on penal substitution to give it any meaning. Why, for starters, is reconciliation needed? It's because somebody is angry at someone else; a relationship has been broken. So then, is reconciliation needed because we are angry at God, or is it because God is angry at us? And how is reconciliation with an angry God effected at the cross? Is it by something other than Jesus taking the wrath owed to us, becoming a curse for us, the just dying for the unjust? You see? The Bible looks at the cross from many different perspectives, but they all come right back to Jesus taking the punishment his people deserved—that is, to penal substitution.

All this leaves us with an inescapable conclusion: Unless the Son of God died in our place, taking the punishment we deserve for our sins, we will not be saved, and we will not be citizens of his kingdom. Our guilt is too deep. If that is true, then we cannot soften the edges of the gospel message. We cannot move the penal, substitutionary death of Jesus to the side, we cannot replace it with any other truth, and we cannot reimagine it as something less offensive (and ultimately less wonderful!) than it really is. If we do, then we will present the world with something that is not saving, and that is therefore not good news at all.

Let's face it. The apostle Paul knew that the message of the cross sounded, at best, insane to those around him. He knew that by proclaiming the message that "Christ died for our sins" (1 Cor. 15:3), he would incur the world's ridicule. But even in the face of that sure rejection, still he said, "I preach Christ crucified." In fact, he resolved to "know nothing among you except Jesus Christ and him crucified" (1 Cor. 2:2).

That's because, as he put it at the end of the book, the message that "Christ died for our sins" was not just important, and not even just very important.

It was "of first importance" (1 Cor. 15:3).

FOR FURTHER STUDY

Jeffery, Steve, Michael Ovey, and Andrew Sach. *Pierced for Our Transgressions: Rediscovering the Glory of Penal Substitution.* Wheaton, IL: Crossway, 2007.

Letham, Robert. *The Work of Christ.* Downers Grove, IL: InterVarsity, 1993.

Morris, Leon. *The Atonement: Its Meaning and Significance.* Downers Grove, IL: InterVarsity, 1983.

Packer, J. I., and Mark Dever. *In My Place Condemned He Stood: Celebrating the Glory of the Atonement.* Wheaton, IL: Crossway, 2008.

Chapter 6

New Birth

"You Must Be Born Again"

BEN PEAYS

What comes to mind when you hear the term *born-again Christian*?

Generally speaking, the media use *born-again Christian* to describe a particular group of religious people. The media would have you believe that these people are Bible-thumping, hard-line fundamentalists, sadly old-fashioned and out of touch with reality. They are antihomosexual, judgmental, hypocritical, insensitive people who generally feel society is growing continually worse. They are often accused of being too involved in politics and are bent on returning "God's country" back to its Christian roots. Born-again Christians are zealous for "saving the lost," "winning souls," and registering commitments to Christ at evangelistic events. Their biggest enemies are Satan and liberals, and it's often tough for them to tell the difference. They most likely do not drink, dance, or smoke, and especially not on the Lord's Day. They would prefer a closer connection between church and state, as long as it's *their* church. And to accomplish this they often forward mass e-mails in support of the Ten Commandments in courtrooms and prayer in public schools.

Born-again Christians love potlucks, small groups, and cloth-covered Bibles. They can tell you exactly when and where they asked Jesus into their heart. They have a personal relationship with Jesus and readily claim him as their personal Lord and Savior. Above all, they are "people of the Book."

This caricature shows how our sound-bite culture has taken a biblical category—being born again—incorporated some true elements of evangelical faith, but then twisted it to represent something other than what was biblically intended. It is important, however, that we strip away these misconceptions and understand what Jesus means by the term when he says, "You must be born again" (John 3:7). *Born-again Christian* should not be a label we are ashamed to show, but rather a badge that we publicly wear with gratitude and thanksgiving.

Many Name It—Few Can Claim It

Ask Americans, Who has been born again? and around 40 percent would say, "We are!" If you asked Jesus, he would say, "Fewer than you think" (see Matt. 7:22–23; 25:41). The reason for this difference is a distinct shift in the meaning of the term. Jesus used the term *born again* to describe those who had actually experienced the new birth, that is, new spiritual life produced by the Spirit of God. But our culture has distorted it into more of a sociological term—identifying not those who are truly in Christ, but instead a group with certain political or cultural affinities. Rather than letting evidence of the new birth identify those who are born again, we instead ask people to self-identify as born-again believers, to check a box on a survey rather than simply bear the good fruit of a life of faith. The result of this easy-believism is a glut of self-professing born-again Christians whose lives look nothing like those of regenerated people.

In our culture people use the term *born again* in a variety of contexts—often in far less significant ways than intended by Jesus. You may hear a celebrity using the label as a way to announce a career comeback or as a public-relations tool following a moral failure, their way of saying, "I have changed my attitude, I am turning over a new leaf, and I am returning bigger and better." Using *born again* in this context can sometimes be more akin to a second chance, a reinvention of a career or a new lease on life—only this time with the hope of better results. This is not what Jesus meant.

Still others talk about new birth in terms of a spiritual awakening apart from God. A recent study by the University of Chicago showed that an increasing number of people are seeking spirituality, but fewer actually believe in God.[1] This means that they are searching for a quasi-spirituality that is godless versus a genuine spirituality that includes God. Genuine spirituality implies the reception or indwelling of the Holy Spirit while "spirituality" in general implies merely a heightened awareness of or attention to the nonphysical. Jesus says, "That which is born of the flesh is flesh, and that which is born of the Spirit is spirit" (John 3:6). A quest for spiritual birth apart from Christ is doomed to fail. Only the Spirit of God can give true spiritual rebirth. "It is the Spirit who gives life; the flesh is no help at all" (John 6:63).

The Internet is full of retreat centers and programs offering a weekend away from it all to experience a spiritual rebirth. To them, the new birth is about escaping the rough-and-tumble of life, being reflective, tapping into one's spiritual side, or healing from emotional wounds. Spiritual rebirth is reduced to entering the right environment so as to reach a heightened emotional experience. But this is not what Jesus meant when he spoke of the new birth.

There is a big market for this type of spiritual new birth in a busy culture. Spiritual gurus lead seminars to help bored and dissatisfied people experience that spiritual rejuvenation. The *New York Times* recently ran an article about a "spiritual warrior" experience in Arizona where fifty people paid $7,000 each to participate in a spiritual "rebirth" expedition led by a renowned New Age guru.[2] After wandering in the desert during a thirty-six-hour fast, participants meditated in a sweat lodge, leading to three deaths and twenty-one hospitalizations. Unfortunately, many people view Christianity as a similar type of quest for "spiritual enlightenment" with Jesus as the guru leader. They greatly misunderstand spirituality as well as the role of Christ and grace in the process.

These misconceptions about what it means to be born again can easily lead people to mistakenly believe they are born again and, therefore, saved. This means that not only are people living with a false

[1]This report, *Religious Change around the World*, by Tom W. Smith, was published on October 23, 2009, by the National Opinion Research Center at the University of Chicago for the Templeton Foundation.
[2]Accessed at www.nytimes.com/2009/10/22/us/22sweat.html.

assurance of salvation, but they are not experiencing the Christian life at all. No wonder it is sometimes hard to see the difference between non-Christian and Christian lifestyles. Many people believe they are Christians, but they do not actually have the Spirit of God in them.

Understanding Your Salvation

The new birth, or regeneration, is perhaps one of the most misunderstood or neglected dimensions of salvation. Many people could likely tell you *that* they are saved, but it is more difficult to explain *what* actually happened. But it is in the *what* that we truly find the good news of our salvation. When we understand what happened, we more fully grasp how we are changed and what this new life means for our relationship with God and our life on earth and for eternity.

If you ask most evangelicals to share their testimony, you will find some who can tell you *when* and *where* they received Christ. Others may say they cannot remember an exact time or place, but rather slowly began to sense God working in their heart. Sharing a testimony is really an invitation to talk about life before and after becoming a Christian. We tend to focus on the personal aspects of the story—assuming people know the larger, theological truths taking place behind the scenes. The danger of this assumption is that the theology that underpins salvation tends to get overlooked. The result is an impoverished understanding of the gospel.

In our effort to make evangelism simple and accessible, it often becomes oversimplified. Salvation is sometimes presented as something easily obtainable at the end of a series of classic questions and answers. Just "ask Jesus into your heart," "pray the sinner's prayer," "make Jesus your personal Lord and Savior," and "begin a personal relationship with Jesus." If you ask some people to explain what happened to them when they became a Christian, you are more likely to hear these phrases than talk of terms such as *justification*, *sanctification*, *atonement*, *union with Christ*, and *glorification*.

In order to better understand the new birth and what it means to be born again, let's look at what it is, why we need it, what it changes, and why it matters.

The New Birth: What It Is

So what does a *real* new birth look like? *New birth* is a term used to describe the new life the Spirit produces when we trust Jesus Christ.

It's also called regeneration, but perhaps the most popular term is *born again* (from a Greek word *gennaō*, meaning "bear" or "beget"). When we are regenerated, we receive the new birth. We are all born into this world spiritually dead. When God in his grace regenerates our hearts, giving us new life, we become a new creation. God convicts us of our sin and enables us to believe in Christ. This belief unites us to Christ, and in this union we receive the benefits of his work on the cross—justification and forgiveness of sin and eternal life.

The New Birth: Why We Need It

Why do we need a new birth? Because we are dead in our trespasses and sins (Eph. 2:1–2). We need a new life. Apart from this new birth nothing good dwells in us. By nature we are "children of wrath" (Eph. 2:3) and lovers of evil. We need God to cleanse and restore us into a condition that is holy and blameless in his sight. Jesus says that in order to enter the kingdom of God, "You must be born again" (John 3:3, 7). No one can enter heaven apart from experiencing this new life. When we are born again, God gives us new life—eternal life.

Without this new birth, we miss out on everything good associated with the gospel and God's grace (1 Cor. 2:14). Without the new birth, we remain slaves to sin (Rom. 6:17) and Satan (Eph. 2:1–2). Our hearts remain hardened toward God (Eph. 4:18), and we love darkness and hate the light (John 3:19–20). Our condition is corrupt, and we are unwilling to submit to God, to please God (Rom. 8:7–8), or to embrace Christ as Lord (John 6:44, 65; 1 Cor. 12:3).

We need the new birth to save us from God's wrath (John 3:36). Without this second birth, we remain guilty for our sins and at odds with a holy God. All that remains is a fearful expectation of judgment and eternal separation from God in hell (Matt. 25:41; Rev. 2:11; 20:15). We need the new birth in order to experience God to the fullest—his joy, his fellowship, his peace, his promises, and his kingdom (John 10:10).

The New Birth: What It Changes

When we experience the new birth—and we may not always be immediately aware of the experience—our lives are changed forever. We are new creations in Christ, and through faith that follows new birth, God looks at us in a different way.

One of the best-known verses in the Bible is John 3:16. Here it says that if we believe in Christ, then we will have eternal life. But not as well known is *how* this actually works. Jesus Christ is the way and the truth and *the life* (John 14:6). When we receive Christ, we are given the privilege of inheriting that same life (John 6:51). But how do we receive Christ? We receive Christ by believing in him. This belief or "saving faith" is not something that we do of our own will. God gives it to us. When we trust Christ through the miracle of the new birth, we receive him and experience new life (John 20:31).

The new birth transforms our hearts, causing a change in our affections, the things we treasure, and our purpose for life. The Bible describes this as moving from darkness and into light (1 Pet. 2:9). We are brought into fellowship with God and are given the ability to know and love God (John 17:3).

When you are born again, you are adopted into God's family and given the right to become a child of God (John 1:12). You enter his kingdom. All the barriers are removed. You are a legal heir to the benefits of Christ and have been given the right to become a child of God. Our reconciliation is not only to Christ, but also to all other believers. It begins with vertical reconciliation to God through Christ, but then extends horizontally to the other children of God. Similarly, when a mother and father adopt a child into their family, the child is connected vertically to the parents, but also horizontally to the other children in the family.

This new life enables us no longer to treasure the trappings of the world, but to overcome the world and find freedom from the bondage of sin. Our hearts are convicted of sin and turned to Christ. In his grace, God grants us forgiveness and changes the way he views us—from enemies to beloved children. We move from being guilty and condemned because of our sin to being justified and counted righteous because of Christ (Rom. 8:1). In dying the perfect death on the cross, Christ experienced condemnation from God, fulfilled the required sacrifice for our sins, and achieved perfect righteousness. We inherit the benefits of Christ's death, and our lives are changed now and forever.

What Does God Do?

Before we finish by looking at why the new birth matters, we need to explore one crucial question: Who does what in the new birth?

Salvation (i.e., being saved from sin, death, and hell) is a gift from God. So experiencing the new birth, which is an aspect of salvation, is also a gift from God. We are unable to do this on our own. We are not saved by our works. God makes the first move. He stirs, he causes, he reaches out to us in love to make this happen. Just as babies are unable to cause themselves to be born physically, we are unable to cause ourselves to be reborn spiritually.

The Bible makes this clear when Jesus teaches Nicodemus in the third chapter of John. Nicodemus was a prominent Jewish teacher who had respect for Jesus as a result of witnessing his miracles. In a conversation with Nicodemus, Jesus said:

> "Truly, truly, I say to you, unless one is born again he cannot see the kingdom of God." Nicodemus said to him, "How can a man be born when he is old? Can he enter a second time into his mother's womb and be born?" Jesus answered, "Truly, truly, I say to you, unless one is born of water and the Spirit, he cannot enter the kingdom of God. That which is born of the flesh is flesh, and that which is born of the Spirit is spirit." (John 3:3–6)

These words confused Nicodemus. He didn't understand the reality of the new birth or his need for it. Jesus had to explain that salvation came only as a result of being born again and receiving a spiritual new life. He effectively said that Nicodemus was dead and needed new life.

Jesus then offered a second difficult teaching to Nicodemus, saying, "Do not marvel that I said to you, 'You must be born again.' The wind blows where it wishes, and you hear its sound, but you do not know where it comes from or where it goes. So it is with everyone who is born of the Spirit" (John 3:7–8). Here Jesus is saying that the Spirit of God is unpredictable, uncontrollable, and unable to be summoned by humans. Not only do we need to experience this second birth to gain entrance to the kingdom of God, but this second birth is not something we can control. It is God's choice, and we cannot bring it upon ourselves.

Just as this was hard for Nicodemus to accept, it is difficult for us as well. It is disturbing to think that salvation—the most important thing in the world to gain—is out of our control. It is hard to accept that we are dead in our sins and unable to gain this new birth that Jesus says is necessary for salvation.

After Christ died on the cross, the disciples would continue teaching about the new birth and its effects. Peter would say, "According to [God's] great mercy, he has caused us to be born again to a living hope through the resurrection of Jesus Christ from the dead, to an inheritance that is imperishable, undefiled, and unfading, kept in heaven for you" (1 Pet. 1:3–4).

We were able to receive his Spirit based on the work that Christ did on the cross. "No one can come to me unless the Father who sent me draws him" (John 6:44). As sinful humans, apart from God's supernatural work, we are unable to come to him. Apart from God, we do not seek righteousness, we are not able to love God, we continue to sin, we do not truly love others. We must first be reborn, and then we are able to do these things.

In his sovereignty and love, God moves in our lives and calls us to himself. He gives us life. He makes us alive. As a result of these promises, we can have assurance that we are his children, right now.

> [God] saved us, not because of works done by us in righteousness, but according to his own mercy, by the washing of regeneration and renewal of the Holy Spirit, whom he poured out on us richly through Jesus Christ our Savior, so that being justified by his grace we might become heirs according to the hope of eternal life. (Titus 3:5–7)

What Do You Do?

But if God does all that, what is our role in being born again? While it is crucial that we repent, confess, believe, trust, give thanks, and so on, these responses do not bring about the new birth. God causes it to happen, and we live out that transformation.

Here is how it happens. When the Spirit of God works savingly through the Word of God in a person's life, God regenerates the heart (i.e., he gives him new birth), making him a new creation. As a new creation this newborn Christian recognizes his sin and turns to God for forgiveness. God enables him to believe the Word. This is always the case (John 6:37). This belief is what God uses to bind or unite someone to Christ. It is through this union that we then experience the benefits of Christ's work. We are considered righteous because we are now able to inherit Christ's righteousness. It is imputed to us or considered effective in our life. We are not just innocent, but positively righteous.

Moreover, since Christ *is* life (John 14:6), once we are united to Christ, we inherit abundant, eternal life from him (John 6:39–40).

To say it another way, repentance and faith infallibly and inseparably flow from regeneration. True repentance takes place when God enables a heart to turn away from sin. This does not mean believers will not still struggle with sin, but rather they are aware of their sin and they feel sorrow and conviction before God. Faith is more than intellectual assent. It is a God-given, unmistakable holding on to Christ and a total surrender to God's authority (Rom. 3:21–31). This change from rebellion to submission, from unbelief to intelligent trust, is the unambiguous fruit of regeneration.

Practically speaking, regeneration and faith in Christ should be seen as taking place in the same instant. From a human perspective, it may seem like faith precedes regeneration. But from God's perspective, regeneration precedes faith. We cannot believe unless we are born again. The important factor is that God, in his grace, has enabled both regeneration and faith despite your sin. You believe because God has enabled you to do so. Belief is actually an evidence that someone has experienced the new birth. "Everyone who believes that Jesus is the Christ has been born of God" (1 John 5:1).

New Birth: Why It Matters?

Unfortunately, many Christians think of salvation only in terms of getting into heaven and avoiding hell. Christ becomes not a way unto life, but merely a way to avoid death, reduced to a get-out-of-jail-free card or—even worse—fire insurance (you've seen those bumper stickers). This leaves many Christians understanding what they are saved *from*, but not having a good understanding of what they are saved *into*. One danger of evangelism that reduces Christianity to making a decision between heaven and hell is that it overlooks the value of the new birth for our earthly life.

Salvation is most significant for its effects after we die, but we must not neglect its effects on our earthly life. When Jesus says, "You must be born again in order to enter the kingdom of God," he is not only referring to the afterlife. The kingdom of God can, at least in part, be experienced right now. It has already been inaugurated with Christ but will not be fully realized until the coming age. The new birth, however, brings us into the kingdom immediately as children of God.

If evangelism focuses only on what happens *after* we die, it leaves people wondering what Christians should do *until* they die. Salvation is ultimately saving us *from* God's wrath at judgment, but it also saves us *into* a life with Christ today. This reality changes our priorities, our desires, what we treasure, and how we will spend our time and energy on earth.

One of my favorite hymns is "And Can It Be that I Should Gain," by Charles Wesley. There is a verse in that song that always reminds me of the power of conversion for our life on earth:

> Long my imprisoned spirit lay,
> fast bound in sin and nature's night;
> thine eye diffused a quickening ray—
> I woke, the dungeon flamed with light;
> my chains fell off, my heart was free,
> I rose, went forth, and followed thee.

How true are these words! For the redeemed, life really is different. There is freedom, forgiveness, hope, and joy.

If you have been born again, you should live differently. Be who you are. Understand how life is different—what new life in Christ has accomplished—and respond in obedience and love. Seeking to live better is not an attempt to complete or add to salvation, but rather a way to live out our new life in obedience, thankfulness, and love. The born-again Christian's life will show Christ to the world and bring glory to God.

The born-again person is in the habit of practicing righteousness rather than sin, of loving others, of overcoming the trappings of the world, and of placing trust and faith in Christ. Peter says people will know us by the way we love. "Love one another earnestly from a pure heart, since you have been born again" (1 Pet. 1:22–23). This is how the world will know that we have received the Spirit—the new birth. When you experience the new birth, your life should testify to the value of Christ and the power of the Spirit in making someone new.

Just as we heard the gospel through the preaching, reading, study-ing, or hearing of his Word, and we had this Word embedded in our souls through the power of the gospel, we should take this Word and share it with others. God is faithful to bring his power into the gospel message. "You have been born again . . . through the living and abiding word of God . . . . This Word is the good news that was preached to you" (1 Pet. 1:23–25).

The gospel is what God uses to bring us new life. The gospel is the good news that God sent his Son Jesus Christ to die on the cross for our sins and bear the penalty that we deserved. We are no longer seen as being guilty of our sins. We are now able to pursue Christ and righteous living. God now considers us his children, and we enter into the kingdom of God—both now and in the coming age. The realities of the gospel are what enable us to experience the new birth. Our role as born-again Christians is now to share that reality with others—to tell them about it and to model it in how we live.

For Further Study

Carson, D. A. *The Gospel according to John.* Pillar New Testament Commentary. Grand Rapids: Eerdmans, 1991.

Demarest, Bruce. "'Unless a Man Is Born Again': The Doctrine of Regeneration." In *The Cross and Salvation,* 277–309. Wheaton, IL: Crossway, 1997.

Murray, John. "Regeneration." In *Redemption Accomplished and Applied,* 95–105. Grand Rapids: Eerdmans, 1955.

Piper, John. *Finally Alive: What Happens When We Are Born Again.* Ross-shire: Christian Focus, 2009.

Chapter 7

Justification

Why the Lord Our Righteousness Is Better News Than the Lord Our Example

JAY HARVEY

John had blown it. He came into my office more dejected than ever. He could hardly look me in the eye. Once a standout Christian in the community, after six weeks at college he gave way to pressure and temptation and found himself awash in alcohol and sex. He agonized over his sin. He regretted the decisions he made and longed to be back where he used to be. He sat before me feeling condemned and deeply ashamed.

What hope is there for John and millions like him? All of us have experienced the condemnation and shame that accompanies an awareness of our sin. Forget about John, is there hope for us? Much in every way! The good news of the gospel is that we can experience justification instead of condemnation. God offers us the righteousness of Christ in place of our unrighteousness. By faith in Christ we can be holy in God's eyes. This is the doctrine of justification, and there is no Christianity without it.

Thousands and thousands of pages have been written on justification, as much in the past several years as at any time since the Reformation. So the challenge in a chapter like this is how to present this essential doctrine in a way that is substantive, accessible, and brief. I'd like to take a twofold approach. First, I want to talk positively about justification, explaining the doctrine with four "justification is . . ." statements. I'll take the bulk of the chapter to unpack these four statements. Then at the end, I want to approach the doctrine negatively and briefly highlight two different and problematic ways of understanding justification.

First up, however, what is justification?

Statement #1: Justification Is Personal

In justification, God declares us righteous because we have a personal relationship with Jesus. To put it more theologically, we are united to Christ by faith. He knows us, loves us, and shares with us everything that we need for abundant life (John 10:10), including his own life. Christ is our "wisdom . . . righteousness and sanctification and redemption" (1 Cor. 1:30). Our righteousness is an "alien righteousness"; it is outside of us. It belongs to Another, and it is ours only because we belong, personally, to the Other.

Justification changes how we relate to God. We are no longer enemies of God, but friends (Rom. 5:10). Jesus "was delivered up for our trespasses and raised for our justification" (Rom. 4:25). With Christ having satisfied the payment for our sins, God sees us as perfect. Because we have received Christ by faith, we now have "the right to become children of God" (John 1:12). Our Father in heaven sees us as completely righteous children. Consequently, we no longer have to fear being rejected by our Father. In fact, God the Father wants us to grow in our confidence of his love and acceptance. The Holy Spirit himself "bears witness with our spirit that we are children of God" (Rom. 8:16).

We cannot grow in our assurance that God loves us—we cannot truly have a personal relationship with God—without justification and confidence in God's free gift. Justification is personal because it comes through a personal relationship with Jesus, and it allows us to have a personal relationship with our heavenly Father.

Statement #2: Justification Is an Act

Justification is a courtroom word used in reference to a judge's verdict. If a person is innocent, the judge pronounces him justified. This verdict is not a process but an act. Proverbs 17:15 is a good example:

> He who justifies the wicked and he who condemns the
>   righteous
>   are both alike an abomination to the LORD.

If justification were a process, then it would be a good thing to justify the wicked. It would be something we could work at or help them achieve. But justification is not a process; it is a verdict. In Luke 7:29 we read that the people "justified God" (ESV mg.), and in Luke 7:35 we read that wisdom (God's way) is "justified by all her children." Neither God nor the ways of God can be made more righteous than they are. "Justified" is not something we accomplish, but something said about us. That's why it is a gross injustice for a judge to justify—pronounce innocent—the wicked (Prov. 17:15; Deut. 25:1–2).

The Bible repeatedly emphasizes the legal aspects of justification. God does not *make us righteous* in that moment; God *declares us righteous* in that moment, just like a judge passes sentence on the defendant in his courtroom. Through the ministry of the Holy Spirit God will over time make us more and more righteous in the way we live. This process is called sanctification. But we do not grow in sanctification *in order to be* justified. We grow in sanctification *because we are* justified. The declarative act of justification is gracious soil out of which grace-filled lives will grow.

The process of sanctification would be damning drudgery if justification were a process. Rather than joyfully pursuing holiness in view of God's mercies (Rom. 12:1–2), we would constantly be afraid of failure and judgment. By the free grace afforded us in justification, we can joyfully pursue holiness without fear of failure or rejection by God. The guarantee that we are perfectly righteous, accepted, and loved by our Father in heaven is one of our greatest encouragements in the process of sanctification. We are free to love God with all our heart because we know that his love for us is completely secure. We can live as children and not as slaves.

Statement #3: Justification Is by Imputation

If it is an abomination for a judge to justify a wicked person, then how does God get away with it? Is it by sleight of hand or by legal fiction that our just God justifies the unjust? It would be if God overlooked our sin or failed to judge it. But God has not overlooked our sin or failed to judge it. Instead, a great exchange has taken place: our sin is transferred to Christ, and his righteousness is transferred to us. "For our sake he made him to be sin who knew no sin, so that in him we might become the righteousness of God" (2 Cor. 5:21). God really did punish sin. He did not "let us off the hook" by waving a magic wand. He counted Christ as sin and judged him accordingly. Then he looked on us as he looked on Christ and counted us righteous.

Theologians use the term *imputation* to describe this great exchange. There are two aspects to it. First, God the Father reckons to Christ our guilt and punishment. Jesus is crucified for us, bearing the wrath of God that we deserve. It's important to see that Jesus' death on the cross was different from the deaths of the two criminals on either side of him. Jesus bore the full wrath of God for our sins, and this means that his death was even more agonizing than the torture and the physical pain of crucifixion. Jesus bore hell. This spiritual dimension to Jesus' death sets it apart from the death of any other human being. The biblical term used to describe Jesus' death is *propitiation*. On the cross, the Father accepted the sacrifice of the Son, making him (the Father) pro us, or for us. So Paul writes, "God put forward [Jesus] as a propitiation by his blood, to be received by faith" (Rom. 3:25). Similarly Galatians 3:13 says, "Christ redeemed us from the curse of the law by becoming a curse for us." Or as John puts it, "In this is love, not that we have loved God but that he loved us and sent his Son to be the propitiation for our sins" (1 John 4:10). In the cross of Christ we see simultaneously the horror of our sin and the love of God who substituted his Son's life for ours.

So the first aspect of imputation is God reckoning our sin to Christ. The second aspect is the reverse, God reckoning Christ's righteousness to us. When God the Father declares us righteous, he not only declares that we do not deserve to be punished for our sin, but also declares that we have done everything that we should have done. What a strange and wonderful blessing. We obviously have not done all that we should have done. We are sinners. But God the Father credits the righteous life and obedience of Christ to us.

When Adam disobeyed God in the garden of Eden, he became subject to the penalty of death. The apostle Paul draws a contrast between Adam and Christ, emphasizing the disobedience of Adam and the obedience of Christ. "For as by the one man's disobedience the many were made sinners, so by the one man's obedience the many will be made righteous" (Rom. 5:19). The Greek word translated "made" in Romans 5:19 does not mean that over time many will gradually become righteous. The word means "appointed" to a position. It is used by Paul in that sense in Titus 1:5 with regard to appointing elders in the church. Paul is saying that because of the obedience of Christ, those who are in Christ by faith are now considered to be in a new position: we are righteous because of his obedience.

Luke makes the same point by the way he structures Jesus' genealogy between Jesus' baptism and temptation. At the close of Jesus' baptism God the Father says to Christ, "You are my beloved Son; with you I am well pleased." Jesus submits himself to John's baptism to demonstrate that he stands in the place of sinful Israel, to accomplish the mission God intended for Israel. The Father, in declaring that he loves his only begotten Son is also affirming that he loves his son Israel insofar as they belong to Christ.

Likewise, Luke draws a deliberate contrast between Jesus and Adam. Jesus, as a son of Adam (Luke 3:38) will face the same trial Adam faced in the garden. Thus, the Spirit drives Jesus into the wilderness to be tempted by the Devil. But whereas the first Adam sinned and failed the test, plunging the human race into death and condemnation, Jesus, the second Adam, stands fast against the tempter, winning for his people life and righteousness. Jesus succeeds where Adam failed. He demonstrates perfect obedience throughout his entire life, and that obedience is reckoned to us when we are united to him by faith. Praise the Lord we do not depend on our own righteousness, but can rely on a "from God" righteousness that depends on faith (Phil. 3:9).

The importance of imputation cannot be overstated. It is our confidence, our hope, and our joy. As the great British preacher Dr. Martyn Lloyd-Jones put it, "Out of my ledger goes my sin, put to His account; then His goodness, His righteousness, His purity are put into my account under my name! . . . God sees me in Him clothed with His righteousness."[1]

Being clothed in the righteousness of Christ is not just the heart of justification; it is the heart of the Christian faith. Adam receives garments of skin in place of the fig leaves he sewed himself that proved inadequate to cover his nakedness and shame (Gen. 3:7, 21). Joshua the high priest receives pure vestments in place of filthy garments to signify that the Lord has taken away his sin and Satan can no longer accuse him (Zech. 3:2–5). The dirty prodigal son receives the best robe of the house, his father's robe, to cover the garments he made filthy while indulging in his sin (Luke 15:22). Believers in heaven are clothed in white robes, because "they have washed their robes and made them white in the blood of the Lamb" (Rev. 7:14). No more dirty clothes, nothing but clean clothes— that's the good news of justification through imputation. Clothed in the righteousness of Christ we find relief from the burden of guilt and shame. Though we still sin, we are nevertheless considered righteous, perfectly loved and accepted by our Father in heaven.

Statement #4: Justification Is by Faith Alone

Because we are justified solely because of the righteousness of Christ, our role in justification is not to obey but to have faith in Christ. Our obedience cannot justify us: "We know that a person is not justified by works of the law but through faith in Jesus Christ" (Gal. 2:16a). Paul says that the whole purpose for believing in Christ is "in order to be justified by faith in Christ and not by works of the law" (Gal. 2:16b). Even if "works of the law" refers specifically to Jewish badges like circumcision and kosher food, the reference is still to things we do. And if we are saved by obedience, Paul argues, then "Christ died for no purpose" (Gal. 2:21). When we seek to justify ourselves by human effort of any kind, we undermine the sufficiency of Christ's atoning work. Only justification by faith alone preserves the honor and glory of what Jesus did on the cross.

Faith in Christ for our righteousness requires a radical change in the way we view ourselves. The apostle Paul said that he came to see not only his sins but also his very best accomplishments as "rubbish, in order that I may gain Christ" (Phil. 3:8). The word *rubbish* translates a

---

[1]Martyn Lloyd-Jones, *The Kingdom of God* (Wheaton, IL: Crossway, 1992), 80.

Greek word that was used for animal excrement, garbage, or any worthless thing. Paul knows that because he is a sinner, even his righteous deeds are worthless before God. The prophet Isaiah makes the same point: "All our righteous deeds are like a polluted garment" (64:6). This polluted garment is a menstrual cloth, fit only to be discarded after use. This strong language about our righteousness before God is intended to counter one of our strongest sinful tendencies: pride.

We constantly want to justify ourselves before God, to be good enough without Christ. But God does not want us to trust in our goodness. He does not want us to make up for our past sins through present obedience. He does not want us to think that we are good enough to go to heaven by comparing ourselves to the Hitlers and Stalins of the world. Comparisons are useless when it comes to establishing righteousness before God. God crucified his one and only Son for our justification, and he wants us to trust in him alone. When it comes to being justified, faith plus anything else is quicksand. The only ground for right standing before God is Christ Jesus grabbed ahold of by faith.

Two Problematic Ways to Look at Justification

The doctrine of justification affects every aspect of the Christian life. But before concluding this chapter with an examination of why the doctrine matters, we need to look briefly at two different and problematic ways of understanding justification.

The Roman Catholic Church understands justification to be a process. They believe that through our faith in Christ and participation in the sacraments of the church, God supplies grace so that we can live an obedient life. When we die, God will declare us righteous in part because of what we have done to obey him. The answer to the question "What must I do to be saved?" is, in Catholic theology, "Repent, believe, and live in charity."[2] Because nearly everybody who dies is not completely righteous, most people will spend time in purgatory to be cleansed of their remaining sin.

Besides the whole notion of purgatory itself, the Catholic understanding of justification cannot be squared with the biblical evidence. Nowhere in Scripture do we find that baptism wipes away original sin. Just as crucially, it's hard to see how the Catholic idea of "charity," even

---

[2]Peter Kreeft, *Catholic Christianity* (San Francisco: Ignatius Press, 2001), 130.

the acts empowered by grace, does not repeat the same mistake the Galatians made concerning works of the law. The Bible simply will not allow obedience—whether in deeds of love or in fulfillment of the law—to serve as a ground of our justification.

Certainly, Roman Catholics, those who know their official theology anyway, are quick to assert that it is only by grace that a Christian can do the righteous acts to be justified. But in the end it is the inherent personal righteousness of the believer and not the alien righteousness of Christ that is the basis for justification. For Catholics, justification is not just a legal declaration but an actual change wrought in us. Once changed in our moral state, then we get a fresh start with God and embark on a journey that requires penance and confession along the way. In the end, the Catholic view leaves the believer without assurance of final acceptance by God. Something is required of us for salvation other than faith alone.

A more recent challenge to the historic doctrine of justification is loosely termed the "New Perspective on Paul." What is "new" about this perspective is its thesis that Paul's teaching on justification in Galatians, Romans, and Philippians was not intended to challenge legalism (the view that salvation is by faith in Christ plus works of obedience). Instead, Paul's primary concern was with Jewish Christians' attitude toward Gentiles. Because the Jews felt themselves to be superior as the chosen people of God, they expected Gentile converts to observe key Jewish ceremonial laws like circumcision, the Sabbath, and dietary restrictions. "Works of the law," according to the New Perspective, does not mean acts of obedience to law in general, but refers narrowly to these Jewish boundary markers. Therefore, when Paul says that we are justified by faith and not by works of the law, he is saying that Jewish Christians should not force Gentiles to become Jewish in their way of life by obeying these laws.

The New Perspective wants to make sure we do not read Luther's struggles with the Catholic Church back into the New Testament. This is a good warning. The Jews of the first century did not think of themselves as legalists pulling their souls up to heaven by their moral bootstraps. But there's no reason to think "works of the law" did not have a legalistic component to it. As I've already argued, no matter what kind of laws they were, they were still works that the Jews depended on and insisted on for their good standing before God. Jesus himself saw the legalistic tendencies in Judaism when he "told the parable to some who trusted in themselves that they were righteous, and treated others with contempt" (Luke 18:9). In this parable, a Pharisee thanks God that he is not like other sinners. The tax collector (typically regarded as "sinful" in Jesus' day) simply pleads for God to have mercy on him as a sinner. Jesus says that the tax collector "went down to his house justified, rather than the other" (v. 14). Jesus is making the same point that Paul makes: don't be confident in your own righteousness, even if you imagine your righteous deeds are owing to God (v. 11).

First century or twenty-first century, it is human nature to struggle with legalism and self-reliance. In our pride we want to assert our own righteousness before God rather than cast ourselves completely upon the righteousness of Christ. This tendency is universal; it is not limited to Jew or Gentile, ancient or modern, young or old. Legalism was a first-century Jewish problem whether they saw it or not. It is our problem today as well.

Conclusion: Why Justification Matters

Justification matters because there is nothing more essential in life or in death than what God thinks of us. Ultimately there are two options: God looks upon us either as justified or as condemned. Likewise, we look upon God as either our loving Father or a fearful judge.

The good news is that God offers us justification by faith alone in Jesus Christ alone. For the justified in Christ, there is no condemnation. "There is therefore now no condemnation for those who are in Christ Jesus" (Rom. 8:1). No doubt, many of us still struggle with feelings of condemnation, haunted by past sins and loaded down with present shame. Some Christians are crippled with guilt. But learning to "forgive ourselves" or making resolutions or paying for our sins with our own misery won't work. We cannot bury the baggage of past sins underneath supposed achievements and accomplishments. The stain remains. Only justification by faith alone can give our consciences rest and free us to live the life Christians are meant to live.

If you are a Christian but believe that God will never use you or could never forgive you because you have already lost your virginity, had an abortion, experimented with homosexuality, been into drugs, or done anything else that is on today's "A" list of sins, you need to personalize Psalm 32. "Blessed is Jay Harvey, whose transgression is forgiven." Put your name in Romans 8 and Psalm 51. In Christ, God is completely and permanently for you, not against you.

Patterns of recurring condemnation will persist in any person who does not have a hearty grasp of the doctrine of justification. As a pastor, I've seen this time and again, especially in persons involved in sexual sins and the occult. These sins come loaded with images, emotions, and memories that are powerful. In our increasingly non-Christian culture, more people in our churches will come to Christ with deep struggles in their past or present. Young people are more likely to engage in sexual sins of all kinds at younger ages than before. Pornography threatens to strangle a whole generation of young men. Of course, these sins must be fought against. But they cannot be battled until we know they are forgiven. Satan is the great accuser, always pointing a cruel finger at our transgressions. But God has put these spiritual forces "to open shame, by triumphing over them" in Christ's crucifixion (Col. 2:15). The debt has been paid. The law has been fulfilled. Our justification is real. The pattern for the church remains unchanged. God wants us to be changed by the Spirit, filled with hope, delighting in Christ, loved by the fellowship, and free from shame. And it is all possible because we are justified by faith alone.

FOR FURTHER STUDY

Ferguson, Sinclair. *The Christian Life: A Doctrinal Introduction*. Carlisle, PA: Banner of Truth, 1981.

Mahaney, C. J. *Living the Cross Centered Life*. Sisters, OR: Multnomah, 2006.

Oliphint, K. Scott, ed. *Justified in Christ: God's Plan for Us in Justification*. Ross-shire: Christian Focus, 2007.

Packer, J. I., and Mark Dever. *In My Place Condemned He Stood: Celebrating the Glory of the Atonement*. Wheaton, IL: Crossway, 2008.

Waters, Guy Prentiss. *Justification and the New Perspectives on Paul: A Review and Response*. Phillipsburg, NJ: P&R, 2004.

Chapter 8

Sanctification

Being Authentically Messed Up Is Not Enough

OWEN STRACHAN

What does it mean to be sanctified? Does it refer to

1. being broken?
2. not dancing?
3. being relevant?
4. not smoking (and not hanging out with those who do)?
5. living righteously?

Clearly I've stacked the deck here. My target answer is obviously 5, living righteously. That's what sanctification is, after all. It's about living in a righteous way that pleases the Lord.

Even though this seems rather plain, we Christians can easily become confused about what sanctification is. Instead of emphasizing its connection to the Lord and his Word, we can make it merely about certain external behaviors and mind-sets, select methods and practices. For past generations of Christians, it was of paramount importance to appear holy and composed, to avoid certain practices (among them dancing, smoking, and even playing cards), and to embrace certain behaviors (rigorously attending church, reading the Bible, and praying). While there is wisdom in this mind-set, it easily falls prey to legalism, the joyless following of codes and practices that one mistakenly thinks leads to good standing with God.

You may have noticed a little different mind-set with many Christians today. Where our parents' and grandparents' tendency toward legalism may have led them to focus more on avoiding the culture, today many Christians go the opposite direction toward a vague antinomianism, an anti-law kind of spirit. Following the postmodern mood of society, they do away with pretense and formality and prize such things as "authenticity" and "brokenness." Though these concepts relate to certain aspects of Christian doctrine, they are merely parts of biblical sanctification.

We need not fall prey to legalism on the one hand or antinomianism on the other. The Bible offers us a vibrant and exciting portrait of sanctification, which we will explore in this chapter. First, we'll dig into the core theological realities of biblical sanctification. Second, we'll look briefly at several biblical passages on the topic. We'll conclude with some comments about key matters to keep in mind regarding sanctification.

What Is Sanctification? A Theological Look

Sanctification may sound like a daunting concept, but it's really not. Here's how theologian Wayne Grudem defines it: "Sanctification is a progressive work of God and man that makes us more and more free from sin and like Christ in our actual lives."[1] We see here that sanctification is "progressive," meaning that it unfolds over the course of one's life. It is completed only when the believer goes to heaven. In addition, God and man participate together in the work of sanctification. Unlike justification, which is achieved only by the initiative and power of God, sanctification involves effort on our part. We cannot experience increasing conformity to the will of God without our effort and investment, even though all of the effort we expend is ultimately and

---

[1]Wayne Grudem, *Systematic Theology: An Introduction to Biblical Doctrine* (Grand Rapids: Zondervan, 1995), 746.

graciously from God (Phil. 2:12–13). As John Murray put it, *"Because God works we work."*[2]

Sanctification is fundamentally a battle against sin. It is a fight for holiness. Nineteenth-century Anglican bishop J. C. Ryle explains:

> Sanctification is that inward spiritual work which the Lord Jesus Christ works in a man by the Holy Ghost, when He calls him to be a true believer. He not only washes him from his sins in His own blood, but He also *separates* him from his natural love of sin and the world, puts a new principle in his heart, and makes him practically godly in life. The instrument by which the Spirit effects this work is generally the Word of God . . . . The subject of this work of Christ by His Spirit is called in Scripture a "sanctified" man.[3]

Fundamentally, to be sanctified is to become holy. It is a conflict. God and his children team up to fight Satan and sin. The believer is "washed" of sin by faith in the work of justification. In sanctification, the Lord "separates" the believer from the "natural love of sin." The struggle against our inherent unrighteousness is not a one-time cataclysm, but a lifelong war. Satan will attempt repeatedly to discourage us as we falter, but we must persevere in our war against him, daily taking up our cross as we journey to the rest that awaits us (Luke 9:23).

In this sense, we recognize that we are very much broken by sin, unable to help ourselves outside of the intervening grace of God. We must experience the humiliation of confession before we can taste the goodness of grace. This means acknowledging our utter wickedness and dependence on the Lord. All of our efforts to make ourselves pure and holy before the Lord fail without his help. Though we know this as Christians, we repeatedly forget it and must continually pursue a repentant brokenness before the Lord in order that we might be restored.

We must also remember that this fight is not a fair one. Though Satan's temptations are strong, and though our flesh is weak, God has conquered both of these foes through the death of his Son. In the crucifixion and resurrection of Jesus Christ, sin has lost and Satan has been crushed. All who experience the new birth in believing in Jesus

---

[2] John Murray, *Redemption Accomplished and Applied* (Grand Rapids: Eerdmans, 1955), 149.
[3] J. C. Ryle, *Holiness: Its Nature, Hindrances, Difficulties, and Roots* (1877; repr., Moscow, ID: Charles Nolan, 2001), 19.

Christ and repenting of their sins are unified with Christ through the Holy Spirit.

Sanctification proceeds from the realities of the gospel. It does not happen without the gospel. It's like a computer sitting in a room. Without power, the computer can do nothing. But once the computer is plugged in, it can work wonders. The same is true with us. Without the power of the Holy Spirit, received by faith in the person and work of Jesus Christ, we can do nothing to please God and will only taste his just wrath and eternal judgment. But when we believe the gospel, and the Holy Spirit resides in us, we are free to experience the explosive current of holiness that flows from the Godhead into the soul of a believer. Sanctification is no meek and mild affair, no mere rearranging of spiritual furniture. It is an electric process, an exhilarating experience of the power of God within us. It births a hunger and thirst for the things of God that is satisfied only in him. As we daily believe the gospel and apply it to our lives, we taste the essence of biblical sanctification.

So to summarize: sanctification is progressive; it involves our partnership with God; it is rooted in the gospel; it is carried out by faith. Sanctification is the experience of the power of God in the heart of the believer. All this work is driven toward the end that we might glorify God. Sanctification is doxological, motivated by an overarching purpose transcendent above all others: the glorification of the God whose perfect holiness requires nothing else. Sanctification is *of* God, and sanctification is *for* God.

What Is Sanctification? A Biblical Look

Having established a theological foundation for understanding sanctification, let's look more closely at the biblical text itself. Sanctification is a many-sided reality, and the Bible considers it from many angles. Each of these angles informs our conception of holiness.

When Jesus Christ came as the fulfillment of the Old Testament and its teachings and prophecies (Luke 24:44–45), he came as the Messiah, the one whose personal sacrifice would cleanse the guilty and render them pure in the eyes of the Lord (see Isaiah 53). Jesus began a new age in which all people who trusted the Lord would grow holy by following Christ by faith, not the law that pointed to him. Jesus repeated the call to holiness, but he executed a new work: he gave the Holy Spirit to people who believed in him as Messiah. The Spirit empowered Christ's followers to leave their sinful ways behind and adopt a new way of life, a life of holiness and conformity to Christ (see Rom. 8:1–4).

Elsewhere, Paul presents sanctification as a full-fledged war against "the schemes of the devil" that requires putting on "the whole armor of God" (Eph. 6:11, 13). Our battlefield attire includes "the belt of truth," "the breastplate of righteousness," "shoes" of the "gospel of peace," "the shield of faith," "the helmet of salvation," and "the sword of the Spirit" (Eph. 6:14–17). Fueling all of our conflict against Satan is prayer: we are to pray "at all times in the Spirit" for the promotion and success of the gospel (Eph. 6:18). We need to pray, as 1 Thessalonians 5:17 also teaches, "without ceasing."

Colossians 3:1–17 offers a memorable image of the pursuit of holiness. There Paul says that we are to "seek the things that are above," not earthly things, which we are to "put to death" (Col. 3:1–2, 5). This is a visceral picture. Sanctification is not an antiseptic affair. It is raw, rough, and not for the faint of heart. To please the Lord, we do not "let go and let God"—we reach out and kill the sin that threatens to kill us. This sacred responsibility is not offered to us as an option. The Scripture, after all, does not suggest to us that we change our lives by the power of the Spirit for the glory of God. The authors of Scripture—and the Author of Scripture—*command* us to do so. This fits with the general character of the Bible. Breathed by God (2 Tim. 3:16), it does not meekly submit itself to mankind for consideration. It confronts us, to borrow an Old Testament description of the Lord, as "a consuming fire" (Deut. 4:24), a transcendent reality that swallows us whole.

In 1 Timothy, Paul exhorts his young disciple Timothy to "flee" earthly temptations and to "take hold of the eternal life to which you were called" (1 Tim. 6:11–12). The mentor seeks to put steel in his charge's backbone, exclaiming, "I charge you in the presence of God . . . to keep the commandment unstained and free from reproach until the appearing of our Lord Jesus Christ" (1 Tim. 6:13–14). This call is sobering. Holiness is not often the sudden, Damascus Road kind of experience. It is Israel walking for forty years in the wilderness. It is the apostles following the leading of God's Spirit to a martyr's cross. It is modern Christians in Dubai and China and Sudan fighting for their very survival and doing it day after day after day. Sanctification is at base a tenacious grip on the robe of Christ, a wrestling with the Lord to bless us, a sojourn in the valley of death in pursuit of a city we cannot see.

How to Fight for Personal Sanctification Today

In this last main section, I offer some plainspoken advice to readers who want to live for the Lord in an unholy modern world. Here are three exhortations to keep in mind as you develop your understanding of the doctrine of personal holiness.

Be aware of some of the major sins of this age and fight them specifically.

Following the first point, it is important that we fight sin not merely in a general sense. In our walk with the Lord, we face a definite foe, not an abstract one. We're not simply killing Sin; we are killing sin in its specific manifestations personal to us.

Let's make this concrete. Here are some major problem areas for many of us in the present day. Keep in mind that these are just a fraction of the problems we could cover.

Love of self. In the Bible, being holy before the Lord fundamentally means that the sinner acknowledges before the Lord that he is nothing and the Lord is everything. Consider the words of Isaiah when he realizes just how unholy he and his people are before the Lord: "Then said I, Woe is me! for I am undone; because I am a man of unclean lips, and I dwell in the midst of a people of unclean lips: for mine eyes have seen the King, the LORD of hosts" (Isa. 6:5, KJV). This is a powerful statement of God's magnificence and our insignificance. As those who have recognized that God is great and we are not, and who have been left "undone" by this realization, we are called to exalt the Lord and not ourselves.

Yet exalting ourselves is just what our modern culture encourages us to do. For example, though it has many positive uses and features (which I myself enjoy), the Internet seems to encourage us to assume the role of self-appointed celebrity. Many of us spend a great deal on various social media outlets calling attention to ourselves. We "tweet" our latest brilliant insight, blog our daily events, post on Facebook the latest silly picture of ourselves and our friends. This kind of behavior crops up in the real world as well. Few of us listen well; many of us talk a great deal, and often about our own lives; most of us worry far more about our own happiness than that of others. We try to advance our careers, to selfishly grab blessings that we believe God owes us. We are a generation afflicted with ourselves. Whether we're aware of it or not, we spend a great deal of time exalting ourselves, and little time exalting the Lord. This way of life is shot through with sin. The scary thing is that these patterns are almost too big to see. Many of us need to repent of narcissism and to take definite steps to counter it by the power of the Holy Spirit.

Love of sports and trivial things. This follows from the last point. When we are not updating our Facebook page and focusing with tenacious determination on our own small existences, many of us busy ourselves with trivial things. This conflicts with what Paul tells us to focus on in Romans 12:1–2:

> I appeal to you therefore, brothers, by the mercies of God, to present your bodies as a living sacrifice, holy and acceptable to God, which is your spiritual worship. Do not be conformed to this world, but be transformed by the renewal of your mind, that by testing you may discern what is the will of God, what is good and acceptable and perfect.

The apostle instructs us to seek the "renewal" of our minds, a process that happens when we focus on God and his grandeur. As John Piper, following Jonathan Edwards, has pointed out in books like *Desiring God*, we have been created to adore and exult in God, to gaze on his beauty, to delight in his mercy, to cherish his goodness. These are weighty ideas. These are transforming realities.

Much of what many of us focus on is anything but weighty and transforming. It is trivial and shallow. For example, how many guys spend hours on sports? Watching them, playing them in person, playing them on Xbox or Wii, talking about them in person, chatting about them online, reading about them in books, reading about them online, playing fantasy football, daydreaming about them in class or at work—we could go on for paragraphs. Many of us are obsessed with sports. The culture aids this obsession. The drama and spectacle of a routine sporting event often outdoes any other earthly pastime. No wonder so many guys have so much trouble staying interested in church.

To be frank, this is ridiculous. Think about it: many of us guys ignore our children, disdain our churches, and harm our work and studies for the sake of games. Sports are games. They are not life-and-death. They are superfluous. Is there something wrong with a game? No, not at all. I enjoy few things more than a good pickup basketball game. But I try to remember—and I have to do this intentionally as a modern man—that sports are, in themselves, relatively unimportant. My wife, my daughter, my church, my job, my studies, my friends—these things matter. Most of all, God matters. The cause of the gospel matters. Unsaved people dying all around me matter. Christians not knowing the basics of the faith matter. A broken world matters. If my life does not reflect these truths, and if yours does not, then we are in sin. Big-time. We need to repent. We need to seek the grace of God to rebel against modern culture, which insists that our diversions consume our devotion, and to live according to scriptural wisdom.

The same goes for other activities. Do we spend hours shopping? Are we enchanted by celebrity fashion? Do we care more about pop culture than we do the work of the gospel? Do we worry a great deal about our appearance? These are struggles that many of us face today and that claim way too much of our attention and concern. A large number of young women are tempted by such distractions. They are challenged to care far more about their weight than their soul. They are tempted to fritter away time in gossip and silly conversation that could be spent in edifying others. They are called to embrace an unscriptural pattern of life, a selfish pursuit of career and one's own indulgences rather than to lay their lives down for others in the name of Christ. Many young women spend less time at sports than young men do, but equally significant temptations entice them to live trivial lives.

Love of sex. The apostle Paul knew that life in a sinful world involves considerable sexual temptation. At one point in Romans he speaks to this issue, declaring, "Let not sin therefore reign in your mortal body, to make you obey its passions. Do not present your members to sin as instruments for unrighteousness, but present yourselves to God as those who have been brought from death to life, and your members to God as instruments for righteousness" (Rom. 6:12–13).

Little has changed in roughly two thousand years. The body still attempts to make us "obey its passions." The world in which we live is intensely sexual. Sex, one could say, is for many the dominant narrative of life. Stages of life are increasingly measured not by certain virtuous behaviors, but by sexual involvement. We are a sex-oriented society.

Though Christians are called to honor the Lord with their bodies, many struggle greatly in this age to do so. Countless Christian young people are sexually compromised today. I have heard several theologians observe that pornography usage is now the norm among young men. Many young women struggle as well, whether in the mind or physically. Because it is considered normal for almost anyone above the age of twelve to be in some kind of relationship—an insane proposition— many young people have lost their virginity. This is true of many professing Christian youth. Those who have not physically compromised themselves often struggle mightily to trust the Lord and his timing for relationships. For many young women, relationships are a kind of holy grail (a mind-set celebrated in popular culture). Many young men have the opposite viewpoint and are delaying the responsibilities of manhood, incurring the kind of struggles mentioned above. This is a disastrous situation.

There is a great deal that needs to be said in proposing a solution for this situation. For now, we can only suggest that Christians caught in these struggles need to own up to their sin, to repent before the Lord, and to seek the help of their church and their friends in the fight for holiness. Sex is a good gift of God, but our age tempts us to make it a god. In whatever situation we find ourselves, we need to keep God and his good gifts in proper perspective.

Recognize that the church is the outpost of sanctification.
In the eyes of the New Testament writers, the local church—ordinary as it may be—is the fundamental work of God on the earth. It is the center of his kingdom. It is the outpost of his gospel. It is the foremost display of his glory. It is the laboratory of sanctification, the entity that, as the dwelling place of God, we are to love, serve, edify, pray for, and devote ourselves to. It keeps us accountable through church discipline (Matt.

18:15–20; 1 Cor. 5:1–5, 9–13), it hosts the Lord's Supper and baptisms (1 Corinthians 10; Matt. 28:16–20; Acts 2:38), and it calls for our regular attendance and service (Heb. 10:25).

This is especially important in light of the previous section. Many of us have been well served by parachurch groups and by Christian friends. We all need the local church, however. It is where we find all the resources we need to love God in a sin-stricken world—exhortation, encouragement, rebuke, opportunities for service, enjoyment, edification, and so much more. It is specially set up and calibrated to mature us, to lift our eyes from ourselves to see the needs of those around us and the glory of the church's Lord. The local church is not designed to bore us and cause us to live small lives, but to grow us, to bring us into close contact with other believers for mutual accountability and help, and to give us a transformative vision of a mighty Lord who is carrying out a cosmic mission of deliverance and salvation.

The church may not seem exciting on the outside—the chairs may not be comfortable, the main hall may smell a bit, and some of the people may know little about cultural awareness. Just as we should not judge a book by its cover, though, we should not judge a church by its chairs. Every local church that preaches the true gospel is a part of the most dynamic movement the world will ever know. By the power of God working in the hearts of men, the lowly are great, the weak are mighty, and the mustard seed of faith topples a mountain (Matt. 17:20). The local church is not the B team—it is ground zero for God's kingdom work. Join it, serve it, love it, and experience the satisfaction that comes with involvement in the gospel cause that transcends all others.

Keep in mind the hard work of sanctification involves deliberate action while resisting easy categorization.

Many of us have bought into the postmodern "mood" of our culture, which is anti-authority, anti-discipline, anti-effort. Today we pat ourselves on the back if we are "true to ourselves." This is a very tricky theme for a Christian to handle, because while our "true selves" bear the image of God and the mark of his conversion, they are also shot through with sin (Rom. 3:10–18). Furthermore, while it's fine to reject an appearance-driven Christianity, being authentically messed up is not what the biblical authors call for. While they knew the depth of their sin—the apostle Paul called himself "the chief of sinners" in 1 Timothy 1:15 (see KJV)—they also knew the power of God inside them. They recognized that the power of the indwelling Spirit was far greater than that of indwelling sin. Like David after the death of his son, they could know the cleansing power of God and rise from out of the ashes to live once more for the Lord. So it must be with us on a regular basis—humbled by our wickedness, restored by God's righteousness.

With the need for discipline firmly in view, we also need to make clear that holiness is not reducible *merely* to certain behaviors. Holiness stems from the gospel, and holy living drives the gospel. The embodiment of true Christianity requires wise thinking and careful discernment rooted in the *evangel*. We need to saturate our minds and hearts with the riches of biblical theology, such that we think and act from a profoundly scriptural base. We need to be in the Word constantly. We need also to pray hard and regularly, asking God to give us wisdom for our daily lives and power to kill our nagging sins. We need to continually reapply the gospel to our specific sins and weaknesses.

Conclusion: So Much More Than a List or Mood

As we seek to live righteously before the Lord, we must cling to the gospel and recognize the power of the Holy Spirit inside us. God lives inside us. He is making all things new, as Paul says in 2 Corinthians 5:17: "Therefore, if anyone is in Christ, he is a new creation. The old has passed away; behold, the new has come." This accords beautifully with Hebrews 12:1–2:

> Therefore, since we are surrounded by so great a cloud of witnesses, let us also lay aside every weight, and sin which clings so closely, and let us run with endurance the race that is set before us, looking to Jesus, the founder and perfecter of our faith, who for the joy that was set before him endured the cross, despising the shame, and is seated at the right hand of the throne of God.

In the face of our indwelling sin, we need to look to Christ and to remember the work of God in us as the central reality of our lives. Sanctification, after all, is not a mood. Neither is it a code. Sanctification is a dynamic outworking of the gospel in the life of every believer. This process of conformity to God thrives not when we tweak our attitude here, and modify our behavior there, but when we grow entranced with God, and Christ the "founder and perfecter of our faith" looms large before us, magnificent in holiness, awesome in splendor, tenacious in love.

FOR FURTHER STUDY

Anyabwile, Thabiti. *What Is a Healthy Church Member?* Wheaton, IL: Crossway, 2008.

Bridges, Jerry. *The Discipline of Grace: God's Role and Our Role in the Pursuit of Holiness.* Colorado Springs: NavPress, 2006.

Ryle, J. C. *Holiness: Its Nature, Hindrances, Difficulties, and Roots.* Darlington, UK: Evangelical Press, 1979.

Strachan, Owen, and Douglas Sweeney. *Jonathan Edwards on the Good Life.* Chicago: Moody, 2010.

Chapter 9

Kingdom

Heaven after Earth, Heaven on Earth, or Something Else Entirely?

RUSSELL MOORE

Can there be anything more haunting than the sound of a child screaming from a grave?

Marcus Garvey is remembered by Americans as one of the precursors of the civil rights movement in the United States. He led millions of his fellow African Americans to protest against the image of black inferiority projected by the Jim Crow era. And yet Garvey's cause never became the kind of age-transforming movement led later by figures such as Rosa Parks or Martin Luther King Jr. That's partly because, unlike the "beloved community" envisioned by the mid-twentieth-century civil rights movement, Garvey's message was of a kind of separatism and self-sufficiency that grew more and more extreme as his crusade for justice carried on. Garvey learned the self-sufficiency that would drive his life's philosophy, historians tell us, at the bottom of a newly dug grave.

Garvey's father was a professional mason, whose responsibilities included making cemetery plots. Once, the story goes, Garvey's father took the child with him as he was digging a grave and threw him into the pit below. Marcus's father pulled up the ladder and left him alone. No matter how Marcus would scream, his father wouldn't answer.

Garvey's father's action was abusive, to be sure, but he thought he was teaching his child a life lesson. The older man was a former slave, and he wanted his son to learn a hard lesson about making his way in the cruelty of this world: you can only rely on yourself. The young child learned the lesson and carried it with him throughout his life, preaching a virtual gospel of individual responsibility and self-sufficiency.[1]

Most of us can feel, when we read this story, the psychic trauma of being a child left alone in an empty grave, crying out to a silent father as we claw at the clay around us, feeling about for a ladder that isn't there. Yet most of us have never actually been in that situation. Or have we?

The gospel of Jesus Christ tells us that all of us have been, at some point in our lives, in a state of slavery "through fear of death" (Heb. 2:15). We are born into a world cut off from communion with its Father, an executed world waiting for the dirt to be shoveled onto its face. The Scripture also tells us that, left to ourselves, we'll learn the wrong lesson from all this horror. We'll stop screaming and start clamoring with more ferocity, or we'll just sit in our dirt and call it home.

Against all of this, the gospel calls us from self-sufficiency—indeed from "self" itself—and toward an entirely new reality: the kingdom of Christ. Sometimes even those who've followed Jesus for a long time find the kingdom message a difficult one to grasp. We sometimes assume *kingdom* is just a metaphor for "getting saved" or for another denominational program or political crusade.

Part of that is our context. Most of us in the Western world have seen parodies of kings and crowns and kingdoms, but we've never seen anything approaching the real thing. So the language void is filled with all the chatter around us about the Prince of Wales or the local high school homecoming queen or the advertising slogans of the "King of Beers" or the "Dairy Queen."

---

[1] This anecdote was part of an oral history documentary on Garvey on the PBS *American Experience* series. The transcript can be found online at http://www.pbs.org/wgbh/amex/garvey/filmmore/pt.html.

And yet, the Bible we believe—and the gospel we preach—is constantly slapping us back to the message of kingdom, kingdom, kingdom, repeated throughout Old and New Testaments and in every generation of the church ever since. The mission of Christ starts and ends not just in the announcement of forgiveness of sins or in the removal of condemnation—although both of those things are true and essential. The mission of Christ starts and ends with an announcement that God has made Jesus emperor of the cosmos—and he plans to bend the cosmos to fit Jesus' agenda, not the other way around.

The Collapse of the Kingdom

The world around us looks like pretty good proof that the gospel isn't true. If we're really honest with ourselves, don't we have to admit the universe does seem to be just what the Darwinists and the nihilists tell us it is—a bloody machine in which power, not goodness or beauty, is ultimate? The gospel, though, doesn't shy away from such questions.

The book of Hebrews quotes a passage from the Psalms that reflects on the biblical truth that God created humans to have the rule over everything that exists:

> You have crowned him with glory and honor,
>   putting everything in subjection under his feet. (Heb. 2:7–8)

This song reiterates what the Genesis account tells us from the very onset of creation itself. God gave the man and the woman dominion "over the fish of the sea and over the birds of the heavens and over the livestock and over all the earth and over every creeping thing that creeps on the earth" (Gen. 1:26). God did this because the man and the woman would represent him, bearing his image, governing the cosmos he created for them (Gen. 1:27). But the book of Hebrews brings up a difficult point about this Bible passage.

It isn't true.

The writer of Hebrews points out what ought to be obvious— whether one believes the biblical creation accounts or not: we don't have "dominion" over the universe around us. The Spirit tells us, "At present, we do not yet see everything in subjection to him" (Heb. 2:8). We can see that in everything from the natural forces that sap the color from our hair to the bacteria that grind our bodies to pulp as we lie in our caskets. The universe rolls around about us frenetically and, in every single case, eventually kills us. We are not the kings and queens of the world.

Now our problem is that we think this "kinglessness" that we experience is normal. We are like historians looking at the ruins of a Nazi-era synagogue in Vienna and concluding that these Jewish Europeans must have been self-loathing Hitler sympathizers because of all the swastikas painted on the walls. Before one can learn much about the synagogue, one must distinguish between the original structure and the hate-speech graffiti left on it by its enemies. This is also true of the universe.

Early humanity lost the rule over the universe, the Scripture tells us, to an invading power: Satan. Even those who've never seen a scrap of biblical revelation know of this Presence, and they tremble. This being, through his cunning speech, persuaded our first ancestors to join his insurrection against the Creator, in an attempt to become "as gods" with him (Gen. 3:5, KJV).

The man and the woman surrendered their kingdom to the very "creeping thing" over which they were to rule. The king and queen of the universe now pictured the chaotic and murderous reign of Satan, rather than the orderly, love-driven rule of God. Their communion with God, with one another, with their future offspring, and with the creation itself was disrupted (Gen. 3:14–19). Instead of joining God in his rule, they joined Satan in his guilt, bearing the sin that calls out for the judgment of God and is incapable of conformity to the love of God. They now were those for whom a just inheritance could only be "the eternal fire prepared for the devil and his angels" (Matt. 25:41; see also Rev. 20:10).

The satanic powers—the power of accusation and the power of death—now gained power over humanity. God then exiled the man and the woman from the life-giving tree that was to fuel their kingdom expansion (Gen. 3:24), an exile that meant they were destined to wither away into the judgment of death.

The creation then, designed as it was to recognize God's image in its king and queen, revolted against humanity. As Paul put it, the cosmos is in "bondage to corruption" (Rom. 8:21), and so the universe is "groaning together in the pains of childbirth until now" (v. 22), waiting "for the revealing of the sons of God" (v. 19).

And so, throughout the generations since this catastrophe, human beings have been governed by "the prince of the power of the air" (Eph. 2:2), who drives humanity along by our cravings and by the sway he has over us through deception (2 Cor. 4:4) and accusation (Rev. 12:10).

The Creator God, though, threatened the snake, at the outset, that his aggression would not long stand. And so God called together a new people, a kingdom of priests who were being trained in righteousness by his Word. He promised that through this people he would establish a glorious reign in which the symphony and peace between humanity, nature, and God would be restored.

God set over his people Israel a line of kings, promising them that it would be through the Spirit-anointed wisdom and power and righteousness of their king that the kingdom would stand or fall (Deut. 17:14–20). It fell. And fell. And fell. And fell. The Israelite outpost of God's kingdom was itself ripped to shreds. And the collapse of the kingdom left wreckage throughout history.

Now, this is not just the story of the ancient people of Israel. It's your story, and mine. The Scripture tells us what the end result of a loss of kingship is: moral rebellion. The old book of Judges puts it this way repeatedly: "In those days there was no king in Israel. Everyone did what was right in his own eyes" (Judg. 21:25).

The kingdom of God in Adam collapsed in the rebellion at Eden. It is collapsing around us even now as Satan's reign is being charged back. If we're in Christ, it must collapse in our own lives, as we evacuate our fiefdoms before the coming kingdom of Jesus.

With this the case, evangelical Christianity speaks to contemporary culture by pointing out what everyone instinctively intuits—something is wrong. Even then the most hardened and vocal atheist reflects something profoundly right—twisted and misdirected as his argument is—when he points out how suffering and evil seem inconsistent with the goodness of God. That's why a truly evangelical (that is, gospel-centered) Christianity will teach our people to *groan* at the world of divorce courts and abortion clinics and torture chambers and cancer wards around us.

And that's why a central focus of evangelical Christianity's emphasis on the kingdom is to show us what's wrong with the present regime. As we grow in Christ, we grow in discontentment with the "kingdoms of the world" offered to us by their ruler even while we perceive the glory of the new kingdom breaking in through Jesus.

The Reinvasion of the Kingdom

Earthly revolutions almost never turn out to be as revolutionary as one hopes. But the kingdom of Jesus fulfills and perfects the hopes behind every utopian or countercultural vision one could imagine. The gospel is good news, and the good news is the announcement of a kingdom and how we can enter that kingdom through faith in the King. This starts with the glad declaration that the old order—whether it's imperial Rome or imperial Me—has been overthrown.

When Jesus stands up to preach to the people in his hometown synagogue, he declares that the kingdom of God has shown up; now the day of the Lord is here (Luke 4:16–30). His sermon caused a violent riot, prompting his fellow villagers to create a Via Dolorosa three years ahead of the cross, as they dragged him up a mountain to throw him from the cliff. Why? Jesus' hearers understood how insane and megalomaniacal it sounded for Jesus to identify the coming of God's new order with his own voice.

But Jesus didn't back down at this point. Everywhere he went he announced the kingdom was on its way, and he demonstrated it by turning back the curse in all its forms. Jesus seemed completely unperturbed by the evil spirits, by the natural order, by biological decay—they all turned back at the sound of his voice. Why? Because, as he put it, "If it is by the Spirit of God that I cast out demons, then the kingdom of God has come upon you" (Matt. 12:28). Jesus overcomes the power of the evil principalities precisely because, as one who is without sin, he is free from the accusation of Satan (John 14:30).

Jesus as King, then, reestablished human rule over the angelic and natural orders. He lived out everything that it means to be human, establishing himself as a wise ruler with dominion over his own appetites, with a will, affections, and conscience guided by the direction of his Father—and not by that of Satan. He walked through human suffering, temptation, and, ultimately, the curse of death itself—standing in the place of wrath itself—to wrest humanity from the Accuser's fingers.

Imagine hearing the voice of a Middle Eastern criminal, screaming through his bloody mouth as he's being executed, in a language you don't know, to the soon-to-be corpse on the stake next to him. His voice would seem desperate, I'm sure, even haunted, but that voice sums up the gospel: "Remember me when you come into your kingdom" (Luke 23:42). The robber understood that "the unrighteous will not inherit the kingdom of God" (1 Cor. 6:9), and that this condemnation fell rightly on him (Luke 23:41). As he looked to Jesus, he saw a rightful world ruler suffering in the place of humanity, and he pinned all hopes for mercy and redemption on this King of the Jews.

This is precisely how Jesus explained the kingdom to Nicodemus of the Pharisees. The old order of flesh and blood will stand condemned, Jesus said, and "unless one is born again, he cannot see the kingdom of God" (John 3:3). The kingdom is made up, not of the old order of flesh and blood, but of those who have been re-created by the Spirit (John 3:5–8), who have looked to Jesus as sacrifice for sin (John 3:14–15), and who have entrusted their future judgment to the mercy found in Christ Jesus (John 3:16–21).

Jesus' kingdom fulfills all the kingdom promises God made to the people of Israel. He and his apostles applied the language of Israel—including the imagery of temple, vine, shepherd, light of the nations, and so forth—to himself first and then to all those who are found in him. God's promise of a kingdom for Israel—with all enemies put under the people's feet—is found when God does just what he promised to the people: he raises Israel from the dead and marks him out with the Spirit (Ezek. 37:13–14). Jesus in his teaching prepared his people, through stories and pictures and rebuke and encouragement, for life in this new kingdom. And then he ushered it in as the "firstborn from the dead," the "firstfruits" of God's new creation project.

Jesus' own closest followers didn't quite get what the kingdom would be like. When he told them the kingdom would be global, they still didn't anticipate Pentecost. Above all, they couldn't comprehend one of the most troublesome mysteries of the kingdom: it doesn't arrive all at once.

It's the same basic concept the second-century Christian preacher Justin argued with a Jewish friend named Trypho: Jesus' kingdom has come in two stages. The key to what's "already" about the kingdom and what's "not yet" isn't some secret code to the Bible; it's the Christ/church mystery. In Hebrews we see Jesus "crowned . . . with glory and honor" (Heb. 2:7), but that's not the kind of thing we perceive in the starry sky or in the fossil record. We see it through the proclamation of the gospel, and through the invisible rustling of the Spirit (John 3:8). God exalts Jesus, grants him the kingship, but Jesus doesn't yet rule over the whole universe.

This means we find the kingdom, then, not where we most expect to find it: in the whirl and pomp of political campaigns or in the splendor and glory of great movements. We find the kingdom, often, in the place where we, like our ancestor apostles, would be least likely to even think about something as majestic as a messianic reign: in a local church.

Just like the *kingdom* language, evangelical Christians often try to make *church* language abstract and idealistic. We sometimes talk as though *church* were simply a synonym for "everybody with Jesus in his or her heart, all together." But that's not it. The Scriptures do speak of the church as that great, majestic gathering of all of God's people in Christ—those in the heavenly places and those scattered across the earth, one body with one Spirit. But this church is manifested in particular local gatherings.

The church at Ephesus (or any other congregation you see mentioned in the Bible) wasn't a super-spiritual place. The people there would have been a lot like the people seated around you on Sunday morning. Not everyone would have had his subjects and verbs in agreement all the time. People would have squabbled from time to time over whose turn it was to set the table for the Lord's Supper or who forgot to announce the offering to help pay Sister Eunice's back taxes.

But the kingdom was there, and King Jesus was there—and in every congregation gathered in his name (Matt. 18:15–20; 1 Cor. 5:4). The church is an outpost of the coming kingdom. Part of this is the very existence of the church itself as a sign of the kingdom. These gatherings of sinners reconciled to God and to one another are, Paul says, so "the manifold wisdom of God might be made known to the rulers and authorities in the heavenly places" (Eph. 3:10). Your church might be struggling to make budget, and you might not be able to agree on whether to sing Bill Gaither or Chris Tomlin songs in worship, but the very fact you're here says to the demons, "Your skulls are about to be crushed" (cf. Rom. 16:20).

The Future of the Kingdom

I suspect that many evangelical Christians, perhaps even you, if strapped to a gurney and given truth serum would have to admit that heaven seems a bit, well, boring. That's because our vision of heaven—so much of our preaching and singing and funeral eulogizing—is, well, boring. We think of our future glory as a church's midweek choir practice that goes on and on and on and on—and when we've been there ten thousand years, we still have infinity ahead of us to sing and gaze into the light.

But that's not what we have in Christ Jesus.

Yes, the Bible teaches that immediately at death, those in Christ are spiritually in heaven—where Jesus is (2 Cor. 5:8; Phil. 1:23). But our purpose is not to live as spirits, but to live as whole God-imaging persons, body and soul together. This is why we bury our dead in hope, as though planting seeds, waiting for the day when this dead tissue will be called to life again, patterned after Jesus' own resurrected body (1 Thess. 4:13–5:11; 1 Cor. 15:35–49).

The kingdom, then, is described as everything it means to live: feasting together as a family around the table (Isa. 25:6; Matt. 8:11; Luke 22:18), personal relationships filled with love (1 Cor. 13:8–13), and meaningful labor, as we join with Jesus in governing the universe (Matt. 19:28–29; Rev. 2:26–27). As a matter of fact, much of what life will be like in the kingdom is veiled to us yet because there's just no adequate way of comprehending, based on what we know now, "the glory that is to be revealed to us" (Rom. 8:18). We shouldn't think of our resurrection lives as being a capstone of what went before. The kingdom of God is life, not an afterlife.

If the kingdom is what Jesus says it is, then that means what matters isn't just what we neatly classify as spiritual. The natural world around us isn't just a temporary environment. It's part of our future inheritance in Christ. The underemployed hotel maids we walk past silently in the hallway aren't just potential objects of our charity; they are potential queens of the cosmos (James 2:5). Our jobs—whatever they might be—aren't accidental. The things we do to serve in our local churches aren't random. God is designing our lives—individually and congregationally—as internships for the eschaton. We're learning in little things how to be put in charge of great things (Matt. 25:14–23).

That's because the kingdom is, after all, the kingdom of Christ—and it's all about God's purpose to make him preeminent in all things (Col. 1:18). To be part of the kingdom, we must be "born again" (John 3:3). We must, as Jesus first told us on the shores of Lake Galilee, follow him.

But Jesus made it clear, "Where I am going you cannot follow me now, but you will follow me afterward" (John 13:36). This isn't just straight to glory. It's, first, right behind Jesus. He isn't ushered straight from the Bethlehem feeding trough to the New Jerusalem throne. He "learned obedience through what he suffered" (Heb. 5:8). As he relied on the Spirit, not on his own eyes or appetites, he was matured as the rightful human heir of the kingdom, made "perfect through suffering" (Heb. 2:10).

We too must learn to increase "in wisdom and in stature and in favor with God and man" (Luke 2:52). We must through life in the church be brought, ever so slowly, "to mature manhood, to the measure of the stature of the fullness of Christ" (Eph. 4:13). We too must walk through the wilderness of temptation and into the agony of the crucifixion, before we join Jesus at the feast table of the firstborn (Rom. 8:17). We must learn, by patiently enduring evil in a world that seems demon haunted, not God governed, to be the kind of king (or queen) who judges "not . . . by what his eyes see" (Isa. 11:3), to "walk by faith, not by sight" (2 Cor. 5:7).

The future of the kingdom gives evangelical Christianity a telescopic, global perspective. There's no aspect of life we don't care about because there's no aspect of life—except for death and sin and curse—that isn't headed somewhere in our future. At the same time, the fact that the kingdom is future keeps us from the hubris (and eventual despair) of thinking we can rule over the world or right every wrong now (1 Cor. 4:8). Every time we speak out for justice, every time we make peace, every time we strike out the ravages of the curse, we're announcing that this wreck around us isn't yet the kingdom—it gets better than this. At the same time, we recognize that the kingdom is fully here only when we see—by sight, not just by faith—the unveiling of Christ. Until then, there is no lasting "peace and justice," and we can't find a "moral majority," not even among us.

Conclusion

If evangelical Christianity is about anything, it ought to be about the gospel—that's the meaning of the term *evangelical* itself. If so, we must recognize that our mission is to be found in what makes the good news good. We don't have to be left to our own striving and clawing. And we don't have to try to be emperor of our own lives, or of those around us. We point instead to a kingdom that overshadows—and knocks down— every rival rule, including our own.

This means our proclamation agrees with our non-Christian friends that something's deeply wrong with the way things are, even as we show them how they're not nearly outraged enough by the world the way it is. We tell them—and remind ourselves—of the good news of an invisible kingdom now in heaven, showing the pockets of the kingdom in our struggling little churches, and singing out for the glorious kingdom that will one day explode through the eastern skies.

But, most importantly, we announce who is King in that kingdom: the One who joined us in our grave holes, even as we alternated between a hardened self-sufficiency and a screaming for the snake father we'd chosen for ourselves. Our Brother/Lord brought the kingdom in a way we'd never have thought of. He stopped looking for the ladder, and cried out to his Father.

And he was heard.

For Further Study

Goldsworthy, Graeme. *Gospel and Kingdom: A Christian Interpretation of the Old Testament*. Carlisle: Paternoster, 1981.

Hoekema, Anthony A. *The Bible and the Future*. Grand Rapids: Eerdmans, 1979.

Ladd, George Eldon. *The Gospel of the Kingdom: Scriptural Studies in the Kingdom of God*. Grand Rapids: Eerdmans, 1959.

Chapter 10

Jesus Christ

The Only Way and Our Only Hope

TIM CHALLIES

We live within a pluralistic culture of many faiths. Most often, the faiths coexist peacefully. This is good. Living in multicultural Toronto, a city in which over 50 percent of the population was born in another country, I have seen this religious diversity firsthand. As people immigrate to Toronto, they bring with them their religion. My son's best friend at school is Muslim, the neighbor across the road from us is Buddhist, and just down the way is a Hindu from South Africa. Atheists, Roman Catholics, universalists, Mormons—all of them are within a stone's throw of my front door. Look closely and you can even find the occasional evangelical. Within just our small neighborhood is a virtual pantheon.

While we regret the necessity of this pluralism, wishing that all men would be saved and come to a knowledge of Jesus Christ, we are grateful for laws that allow us freedom to worship our Savior. We may not agree with the tenets of other faiths, but if every religion has freedom, we will too. This religious pluralism allows us to worship Jesus Christ in freedom and peace, without fear of interference or persecution. It is a profound blessing.

Another Pluralism

This is one use of the word *pluralism.* But there is another kind of pluralism that is of equal concern to Christians. This brand of pluralism asserts that all religions in some way lead to God and to salvation. In affirming this, it necessarily denies that Jesus Christ is the only Savior the world will ever know. In the end, it says, all faiths, whether Christianity or Islam or Buddhism, lead to God and have the same ultimate benefit for their adherents.

This kind of prescriptive pluralism, standing as it does in direct opposition to what Scripture makes so clear—that Christ is the only way to the Father—must be rejected unapologetically and out of hand. If any (or almost any) approach to God is as good as another, how do we make sense of the Bible's insistence on monotheism, its consistent rejection of all forms of idolatry, and the missionary impulse—that the nations would turn to the true God—running from Genesis to Revelation? Most crucially, pluralism cannot do justice to the privileged place the Bible gives to Jesus Christ. *Every* knee must bow before him. He will judge *all* peoples. The God of the Bible, revealed as Yahweh in the Old Testament and incarnated at Jesus Christ in the New, is nothing if not a universal God who accepts no rivals. To reject the unique person and work of Jesus Christ is to make an utter mockery of the Bible. To reject his claims is to reject God himself and to steal from him the glory that is rightly his. Ultimately it is to turn one's back on the Bible and on the God of the Bible.

A More Tantalizing Option

While pluralism falls far outside the bounds of Christian orthodoxy, there are many evangelicals who believe that God's saving grace is not limited to those who explicitly profess Christ. Some "believers" may receive salvation because of their faith in God or their sincerity or because of their response to the light they had, even though they have not turned to Christ or even heard of him. These "anonymous Christians" are still saved by grace through Christ's work, but there is no expression of faith in the person and work of Christ.

Here we need to distinguish between two important terms that set the stage for this chapter. *Exclusivism* states that Jesus Christ is the only Savior the world will ever know and that in order to be saved, a person must hear and respond to the gospel message, placing his faith in Christ. Though there may be elements of truth in other religions, only those can be saved who turn to Christ in repentance and faith. All others, bearing the stain of original sin and the weight of their own sins, will be justly punished.

Inclusivism, on the other hand, says that though Christ is the world's only Savior, a person does not need to hear and believe in the gospel in order to be saved. While inclusivism and exclusivism agree that Christ is the Savior of the world, they disagree on the necessity of responding to God's special revelation in order to receive salvation. Inclusivists argue that, while putting one's faith in Christ is the *best* way to honor God and receive the benefit of what Christ has accomplished, it is not the *only* way.

Prescriptive pluralism is easy to dismiss, but inclusivism merits a closer look. The appeal of inclusivism is not so much in its apparent consistency with Scripture but in its ability to deal with some of the uncomfortable realities faced by exclusivists. It offers emotionally satisfying answers to difficult questions. Can those who have never heard the gospel still be saved? Yes, they can, it says. Can good people in bad religions be saved? Yes! Would God condemn a person for not trusting in Christ even though he never had a chance even to hear his name? No, not necessarily. It even offers an explanation for some of the apparent exceptions in the Bible—people who, for one reason or another, did not fit the mold of a typical believer: Rahab, Cornelius, and others. In these ways it has greater immediate appeal than the supposed harshness of exclusivism. But while it may succeed on this emotional level, it does not fare as well under the light of Scripture.

The Case for Exclusivism

We cannot simply assert that exclusivism is correct (and I believe it is); it must be shown to be true from Scripture. To do this we will visit three New Testament passages, each of which proclaims that faith in Christ is a prerequisite for those who would be saved. Yet they are controversial passages that remain at the heart of the dispute between inclusivism and exclusivism. We will turn to those objections at the end.

The Gospel of John

A fine place to begin is with the well-known and much-loved words of John 14:6. There Jesus proclaims, "I am the way, and the truth, and the life. No one comes to the Father except through me." The question before us is whether "through me" refers only to the work of Christ or to the work of Christ *and* faith in him. To resolve that dilemma it is important that we view this verse within the context of the entire book of John. John wrote his gospel specifically to prove that faith in Christ is the God-given remedy for those who dwell in sin. It was not written to address concerns with the unevangelized or those who may never have heard of Jesus, but to show that all men are under God's curse and that Christ is the unique solution for those who will be saved. John himself states the purpose of the book in 20:30–31, where he writes, "Now Jesus did many other signs in the presence of the disciples, which are not written in this book, but these are written so that you may believe that Jesus is the Christ, the Son of God, and that by believing you may have life in his name." So the entire purpose of the book is to introduce Jesus so that people may believe in him and find life.

While the word *faith* is not present in John 14:6, it is implied throughout the passage (see vv. 1, 10). Just as important, the theme of believing in Christ, placing faith in him, is present throughout all of John. Think of the beautiful words of John 3:16: "For God so loved the world, that he gave his only Son, that whoever believes in him should not perish but have eternal life." What warrant is there to suggest that the qualification ("whoever believes in him") applies only to those who have heard his name? What reason is there to think that the statement in verse 18—"whoever does not believe is condemned already"—refers to anything *less* or anything *other* than an explicit faith in him?

We may turn also to John 5:22–24 where we read:

> The Father judges no one, but has given all judgment to the Son, that all may honor the Son, just as they honor the Father. Whoever does not honor the Son does not honor the Father who sent him. Truly, truly, I say to you, whoever hears my word and believes him who sent me has eternal life. He does not come into judgment, but has passed from death to life.

Here Jesus draws a link between faith in Christ, faith in the Father *through* Christ, and salvation. The necessary conclusion is that to be saved a person must believe in the Son, and through the Son the Father who sent him. Only these people will pass from death to life.

Thus we appeal to John 14:6 as an apt summary of the entire teaching of John's gospel. John makes it clear from the first verse to the last that Jesus Christ is the world's only Savior and that those who would be saved must believe in him. "Whoever believes in the Son has eternal life; whoever does not obey the Son shall not see life, but the wrath of God remains on him" (John 3:36).

Acts 4:12
Acts 4:12, speaking of Christ, says, "There is salvation in no one else, for there is no other name under heaven given among men by which we must be saved." True, this passage does not explicitly state that faith in Christ is absolutely necessary for salvation. However, to deny that faith in Christ is necessary we would have to prove that "no other name" means something more (or less) than knowing the name of Jesus and declaring allegiance to him. Can we do this without doing damage to the text and without ignoring the wider context of both the passage and the book? We might also wonder why Luke did not simply state, "There is no other *person* by whom we may be saved." What would he gain by speaking of a name that his readers did not need to know?

What is the significance of the phrase "no other name"? The context points us in a clear direction: Jesus Christ must be known and embraced by anyone who would be saved. After all, here John and Peter have been arrested by the religious council and are declaring why they must preach the good news of the gospel. They preach the good news of Jesus so that men might hear of Christ and believe in him. Though in this passage they speak to a devoutly religious Jewish audience, there's no reason to suppose that pagans have less need to hear and respond to the name of Jesus. After all, throughout the entire book of Acts, the apostles travel far and wide, face pain and persecution, even give up their lives to take the name of Jesus to those who have never heard it. The clear testimony of this passage and this book is that anyone who will be saved, will be saved by Christ; anyone who will be saved by Christ will be saved by grace through faith in him. In its context Acts 4:12 admits no thought of salvation apart from a profession of faith in the Savior.

Romans 10

Space won't allow us to examine Romans 10 thoroughly, but we may point to several key verses. Verse 9 proclaims, "If you confess with your mouth that Jesus is Lord and believe in your heart that God raised him from the dead, you will be saved." Could we ask for more clarity than this?

Consider also verses 14–17 in which Paul expounds on the great need for the name of Jesus to go to all corners of the globe:

> How then will they call on him in whom they have not believed? And how are they to believe in him of whom they have never heard? And how are they to hear without someone preaching? And how are they to preach unless they are sent? . . . So faith comes from hearing, and hearing through the word of Christ.

This passage is as clear as any in the Bible. Those who are to be reconciled to Christ must know of Christ so that they may put their faith in him. This fact provides the impetus for Christian mission; preaching and evangelism are motivated by a desire to take the message to all men, so they may be saved to the glory of God. "There is no distinction between Jew and Greek; the same Lord is Lord of all, bestowing his riches on all who call on him" (v. 12). There is no distinction between those who may be saved because there is no distinction in how men are to be saved.

Even from these three passages, only three of many we could turn to, we see little reason to believe that Scripture allows for the possibility of "anonymous Christians," people who will be saved though they have not put their trust in Jesus Christ. The whole burden of the New Testament is that we are saved only through Christ and only through faith in him.

Answering the Questions

It may be useful here to anticipate a handful of the most common objections to exclusivism.

Is it fair for God to punish those who have never heard of Jesus Christ?

Lying behind this common question is an implicit but erroneous assumption—that people are condemned only (or primarily) for rejecting Christ. Therefore, those who explicitly reject Christ have knowingly turned their backs on him and invited God's wrath, but those who have neither known nor rejected Christ are in a state of innocence toward God.

Here we do well to turn to the first several chapters of Romans. There Paul tells us, beyond any doubt, that all men are under the just wrath of God. It is not their rejection of God's special revelation of Jesus Christ that is at the heart of their condemnation, but their rejection of God himself, even despite his natural revelation. General revelation communicates truth to everyone—truth that ought to lead each of us to turn to God. And yet nowhere in the Bible is there record of anyone turning to God on the basis of general revelation alone. This shows a problem with neither the revelation nor the Revealer, but rather, with the human being. All men reject this revelation of God. A good person who obeyed all of God's commandments—were that possible—would have the right to plead his case before God, but there are none who can do this. Therefore all people are under God's condemnation for their hatred of him, their rejection of him. Those who explicitly reject Christ further their punishment but do not in that act instigate it. Anyone who wishes to be saved without placing his faith in Christ ought to have lived a sinless life.

We can argue from a slightly different angle and say that no one is in a state of innocence before God. God owes salvation to no one. This is not a question of fairness, but a question of justice. All men have accrued a sin debt, and all thus stand guilty before God. We argue here from human depravity. There is only one kind of man—the man trapped in the total depravity of his sinful nature, inherited from his father Adam (Rom. 5:18). And since there is only one kind of man, there is only one kind of salvation—faith through the second Adam, Jesus Christ.

So is it fair for God to punish those who have never heard of Jesus Christ? Yes, it is, for all men are sinful to the core. All people have a sin nature, and all continually defile themselves with sinful acts. Though we hope and pray that everyone would hear the good news of Jesus

Christ and respond to it in faith, we know that all men need to hear that news only because they are already dead in sin, condemned to an eternity of justice.

The Old Testament saints did not know of Jesus Christ and yet they were saved. Couldn't this happen today?

Many Christians believe that those in the Old Testament who were accepted by God were accepted on the basis of their works. Because Christ had not yet been born, the argument goes, these people could not trust in him. Therefore, it must have been on the basis of their love for God that they were acceptable to him.

But Abraham stands as a firm example of one who was saved on the basis of his faith in a Messiah who was yet to come. Genesis 15:6 reads, "And he believed the LORD, and he counted it to him as righteousness." To grasp this, we have to understand exactly who or what was the object of Abraham's faith. What or who did Abraham believe? We find an extended discussion of the faith of Abraham in the third chapter of Galatians. It should not go unnoticed that this discussion utterly rejects works or law keeping as the basis of anyone's salvation either before or since Christ. "Is the law then contrary to the promises of God? Certainly not! For if a law had been given that could give life, then righteousness would indeed be by the law" (Gal. 3:21).

Looking to the biblical account of humanity's fall into sin, we find the object of Abraham's faith, for in Genesis 3:15 God promises a Messiah.

> I will put enmity between you and the woman,
>   and between your offspring and her offspring;
> he shall bruise your head,
>   and you shall bruise his heel.

This offspring, this seed (as it is often translated) is none other than the promised Messiah. We find that Abraham had faith in the Seed who had been promised by God. Knowing of his own sin and unworthiness before God, Abraham trusted in a Savior who was to come. Where today our faith looks *back* to the cross, Abraham's faith looked *forward* to it. We see with the benefit of hindsight and with greater (though still less-than-perfect) clarity; Abraham saw only vaguely. But still he believed, and it was counted to him as righteousness. Abraham had faith in Christ just as we must today.

Weren't there "holy pagans" in the Old Testament who believed even though they were outside of God's covenant community?

Having already established that faith in the promised Savior was the key to Abraham's salvation, we are now in position to ask whether there are exceptions—whether anyone in Scripture who was outside of God's covenant community was saved apart from faith in the coming Messiah. We might think of Rahab or Melchizedek in the Old Testament or even Cornelius in the New.

Let's look briefly to Cornelius as a representative example. Appealing to Acts 10:2 (". . . a devout man who feared God . . ."), Acts 10:15 ("What God has made clean, do not call common"), and Acts 10:34–35 (". . . in every nation anyone who fears him and does what is right is acceptable to him"), inclusivists argue that Cornelius stands as an example of someone who was a believer even though he had not turned to Christ in faith. In reality, though, the passage teaches just the opposite; it teaches that it was necessary for Cornelius to hear the good news and to place his faith in Christ in order to be saved.

In Acts 11:13–14 we read Peter's words as he describes the angel's appearance to Cornelius. "He told us how he had seen the angel stand in his house and say, 'Send to Joppa and bring Simon who is called Peter; he will declare to you a message by which you will be saved.'" Two of the pieces of information the angel told Cornelius are extremely important to this discussion. First, the angel said that it would be by means of a message that Cornelius would be saved, and, second, he made it clear that this salvation was a future event, dependent on the message. When Cornelius heard the message, he would then believe it, turn to Christ in faith, and be saved. Here it is clear as day. Cornelius may have been a decent God-fearing man, but he could not yet be counted as a justified child of God. He was not already saved but was in desperate need of salvation through the message of Jesus Christ. And God graciously granted him the privilege of hearing this message and responding to it.

What about infants and the mentally disabled?

I often wonder why God did not speak explicitly about the eternal state of infants or the mentally disabled—those who, though they may die, do not have the ability to respond to Christ in faith. In fact, they do not have the capacity to reject God's general revelation, not to mention his special revelation. Not only has the infant who died at two days never had an opportunity to turn to Christ, but she has not had the ability to respond positively or negatively to God's revelation of himself in creation. What can we say about the eternal state of such a child? This is not the place to provide a discourse on the eternal security of the mentally handicapped or of children who die in infancy. But we can make one helpful clarification.

We must be careful not to assume a one-to-one relationship between infants or the mentally disabled and adults who have never heard the gospel. Which is to say that this is not strictly an issue that ought to fall under the banner of inclusivism or exclusivism. For when we talk about inclusivism, we are discussing those who have been exposed to general revelation but not to special revelation—they have seen God's revelation of himself in creation but have never encountered the name of Jesus. It is an issue of whether a person can be saved on the basis of general revelation even without special revelation. Yet when it comes to the question of children and the mentally disabled, we are discussing people who are able to respond to *neither* category of revelation. They are still children of Adam and, in that way, inheritors of a sin nature. And yet they are in a state that precludes them from understanding or responding to any manner of God's revelation. They do not reject God because, by God's design, they have no knowledge to reject.

We believe what the early chapters of Romans teach us—that all men leave themselves without excuse because of their rejection of God's revelation of himself in creation. We see, then, that at least to some degree we are judged on the basis of what we know, on the basis of knowledge we have access to. Those who have no knowledge must be distinguished from those who have knowledge and yet choose to reject it. Therefore, children and the mentally handicapped simply cannot be pressed into the same category as the man or woman who has never heard the gospel. Whether infants and the severely mentally handicapped are all converted (à la John the Baptist or David in the womb) and have some latent faith that can't be expressed, or whether they simply fall into a different category altogether is beyond the scope of this chapter, but we can conclude they are not analogous to those who have never heard.

Conclusion

Jesus Christ is the only Savior the world will ever know. Those who are to be saved by God will be saved only through faith in this Savior, this Messiah. Knowing as we do that countless millions on this earth have never heard the name of Jesus, we may be tempted to fall into despair, hopeless before this harsh and terrifying reality. And yet in the midst of this despair, God gives hope. The church is the hope for the world. You and I and all of our brothers and sisters in Christ are the hope for the world. It is the church that God has called and commissioned to take the name of Jesus to all lands. Knowing that God saves only those who trust in Christ, we feel the urgency and the burden to take this good news to all the world so that all may hear and believe.

Living as we do in a pluralistic culture and situated as we are in an increasingly inclusivistic church, it can be difficult to stand firm on the truth of God's Word. But stand we must, for this is no small matter, no fine point of lesser doctrine. To deny that Jesus Christ is the only Savior is to deny the utter seriousness of the human condition and the gravity of the offense against God. To deny that faith is the only way by which we may apprehend Christ's riches is to deny the uniqueness of the person and work of the Savior and to deny the clarity of his Word. At stake when we consider Jesus' claims to exclusivity is the gospel itself. The stakes could not possibly be any higher.

FOR FURTHER STUDY

Macleod, Donald. *The Person of Christ.* Downers Grove, IL: InterVarsity, 1998.

Morgan, Christopher W., and Robert A. Peterson, eds. *Faith Comes by Hearing: A Response to Inclusivism.* Downers Grove, IL: InterVarsity, 2008.

Piper, John. *Jesus: The Only Way to God: Must You Hear the Gospel to Be Saved?* Grand Rapids: Baker, 2010.

PART 3

EVANGELICAL PRACTICE

Learning to Live Life God's Way

Chapter 11

It's Sometimes a Wonderful Life

Evangelicals and Vocation

TED KLUCK

The trouble with my generation is that we all think we're . . . geniuses. Making something isn't good enough for us, and neither is selling something, or teaching something, or even just doing something; we have to be *something. It's our inalienable right, as citizens of the twenty-first century. If Christina Aguilera or Britney or some* American Idol *jerk can be something, then why can't I?* —Nick Hornby, *A Long Way Down*[1]

I've always kind of hated the movie *It's a Wonderful Life*. The protagonist, George Bailey, resents the fact that he never has a chance to live his dreams. He mopes around, convinced that his life is meaningless, only to be patted on the proverbial back by various people who assure him that he actually is a great guy and his life isn't nearly as meaningless as he feels. This is, of course, an extremely sellable thesis—essentially telling

---

[1](New York: Riverhead, 2005), 30.

your audience (because most of us are completely unremarkable) that it's okay to be average. This used to really chafe me when I was young and thought I was going to live all of my dreams and do something amazing. That is also the expectation lots of Christians carry with them as they think about their work.

My vocation, today, is "writer." It says so on my tax returns. This made me feel really good in an ego-boosting, living-other-people's-dreams sort of way for a few minutes until I looked at the section on "income." As a writer I write books and magazine articles, as well as the occasional screenplay on spec. I also do lots of other things to pay the bills, including coaching high school football and teaching community college writing courses. I live in a perpetual cycle of coming up with book ideas, writing proposals for those book ideas, doing radio interviews about previously acted-upon book ideas, gathering blurbs from more famous evangelicals about those book ideas, and then hoping/praying that important evangelical bloggers will like my book, which I liken (from a sales perspective) to just less than being kissed on the forehead by God Almighty himself. I also spend a little time writing.

I've learned a few things about my current vocation. I've learned the difference between actual sales figures and sales figures post-returns. I've learned not to trust my calculations on royalties, because the actual royalties are always much less. I've learned that when I coauthor a book, I make about fifty cents on each copy sold, and that going into a bookstore and looking at the thousands of books there (most of which are selling better than mine) is among the most humbling experiences possible.

But I've also learned what it feels like to teach a fifty-year-old laid-off factory worker how to write a really good thesis statement (it feels amazing). I've been able to coach a 160-pound nose tackle who showed up for the first day of practice in a *Miami Vice* T-shirt into a starting defensive lineman. I've not known how we were going to pay the bills on multiple occasions, curled up on the floor in the fetal position and prayed, and then eventually (though not immediately) seen God meet our needs in unique ways. I've felt what it actually means to pay more than lip service to the idea of "trusting God to meet our needs."

I've learned to be thankful for my vocation—this after spending most of the first decade of postcollege married life in several jobs and hating almost all of them uniformly. I was the guy who grumbled his way into the cubicle, grumbled through a long, boring day at work,[2] and then grumbled home, always feeling like God must have bigger things in store for me. Which ended up being both true and untrue. The bigger thing, as it turned out, was finding my happiness and identity in him, and growing in holiness in both good and bad work times. And the bad times didn't end immediately when I became a writer (as I think I had mistakenly dreamed they would). In some ways they became worse as the failure became more personal and there was nobody to blame but myself.

My goal for this chapter is to write something other than young Reformed pontification. You know, the "God is sovereign, which means he's with you even as you stamp out insurance claims or empty the garbage, so just be happy," or a "Go engage the culture by quitting your job at the factory to write piano sonatas" message.[3] Most of these types of vocational books/chapters/articles are written—no disrespect intended—by the sorts of guys who sound like they haven't worked a day in their lives (grad school/seminary doesn't count, even though it is a particular kind of hard work).

Milkmaids Matter

> Only let each person lead the life that the Lord has assigned him, and to which God has called him. (1 Cor. 7:17)

> God is milking the cows through the vocation of the milkmaid. (Martin Luther)

God may be milking the cow through the vocation of the milkmaid, but that doesn't always mean it's easy to be the milkmaid. Being the milkmaid means sore hands, a sore back, a drafty barn, and a cow that won't hold still. It means people in your family not so subtly insinuating that you should be more than a milkmaid, or people in your church intimating that women shouldn't be milkmaids (outside the home) in the first place. It means feeling like you'd rather do anything but go into

---

[2]Caveat: There were some truly great people, and great times, at these jobs even though I wasn't entirely (or even sort of) content. It wasn't all drudgery.

[3]That said, this perspective may very well be right. I just didn't want to write it again.

the barn. Working, by its very nature, is complicated. You can both be thankful for something (your job) and at the same time hate almost everything about it. To deny that this happens occasionally, even to Christians, would be silly.

But we need milkmaids (and everything else) because, as Gene Veith writes:

> God protects us through the vocations of earthly government, as detailed in Romans 13. He gives his gifts of healing usually not through out-and-out miracles (though he can) but by means of the medical vocations. He proclaims his word by means of human pastors. He teaches by means of teachers. He creates works of beauty and meaning by means of human artists, whom he has given particular talents.[4]

That said, there is a greater reason for the things we do, provided those things aren't in opposition to the truths we find in Scripture. I thank God for doctors (even non-Christian ones) who can heal my separated shoulder, prescribe medication, or stitch up my son's face after he falls off a log. I'm thankful for the first-grade teacher who willingly goes into work to spend time with twenty-five six- and seven-year-olds each morning (though I think she's insane). And I'm thankful for pastors and missionaries who bring the Word of God to their congregations and unreached cultures. Their work matters.

Before we hear from a few people on why work matters, we need to dispel a few myths about work.

A Few Myths Regarding Christians and Work

Going to work in a standard job makes you a "missionary." Some of the people I love most on earth are missionaries, which makes it uncomfortable when pastors (with the best of intentions) occasionally say things like, "Hey, if you leave your house in the morning to go do a job, you're a missionary." Not exactly. I get what they're trying to say, which is, "Make sure you're looking for opportunities to share the gospel in your everyday life." But shouldn't we make an important distinction between slapping a Jesus fish on your Honda Odyssey and actually, say,

---

[4]Gene Edward Veith, "Our Calling and God's Glory," *Modern Reformation* 16, no. 6 (2007), accessed online.

going to the mission field? Bruce Wilson, missions pastor at College Church in Wheaton, Illinois, sums this up well:

> The church's activity to proclaim the gospel and make disciples within our culture is termed "near-culture ministry." The church's activity to proclaim the gospel and make disciples across language and/or ethnic boundaries is termed "missions." Missions is advancing Christ's kingdom cross-culturally.[5]

Being a vocational Christian means you're in "the center of God's will" (which also means that nothing bad will ever happen to you). One of the things we were sometimes told by well-meaning folks during our year on the mission field in Lithuania was that "the center of God's will is the safest place to be." Loosely translated, this meant: God will take care of you, and you probably won't get sick/injured/killed/broken financially in this cold, scary, sometimes-dangerous post-Soviet country, because you're in ministry.

Don't get me wrong, I think God takes care of people. We also know that he is sovereign, and he gives and takes away, regardless of our vocation. Just to be safe though, in Lithuania, I still triple-bolted the door to our drafty Soviet-style apartment and balled up my fists every time we walked downstairs past the thugs who used to congregate outside the front door of our building to drink beers in the morning. I should have been concerned with sharing the gospel with them, but I spent more time thinking about how I would take out all three of them if they tried to mug my wife.[6]

I also know that for much of that year in Lithuania, I was doing a, quote, "professional ministry job," but as is the case for many early-twenties evangelicals on their now-almost-obligatory self- (or spouse-) finding years abroad disguised as short-term missions trips, my head was often somewhere else. For much of that year I wasn't growing in holiness or sanctification—I was just a guy doing a job; it's just that I happened to be doing it halfway around the world for a school that had "Christian" in its name, while living in a much crummier apartment than the one I had in the States.

---

[5] Accessed at http://www.college-church.org/missions/YouandMissions.htm.
[6] Which actually meant a lot of time reflecting on fight scenes from movies like *Roadhouse*.

Engaging the culture means opening a fair-trade coffee shop in your city (usually called "Ekklesia"), doing something in the inner city, painting pictures, making a short film, or starting a band. One of the by-products of making my living in the popular-today-lame-tomorrow Christian book industry is that I've been able to observe the life cycle of cultural engagement literature. It's very exciting to think about doing all of the things mentioned above, and for certain there are Christians who are called specifically to do each of those things. More than likely they're Christians who have some talent in those areas to begin with. Unfortunately, there are a lot of Christians who don't have gifts in those areas, who end up doing those things and doing them badly in the name of cultural engagement. I would argue (and in fact, do, below) that there are lots of Christians engaging their cultures in lots of pretty effective, under-the-radar ways.

Christians always like their jobs and always feel "called" to their careers. A great deal of our church-lobby rhetoric can make you feel like if you don't love your job and/or feel completely thankful for it at all times, you are somehow less than spiritual. And most of the Christian men I know (and admire) happened onto their careers in ways that felt less than intentional, and less than an act of God "calling" them to become factory workers, lobbyists, salesmen, or engineers. The fact of the matter is that there are things we like doing, there are things we have some degree of aptitude and talent at doing, and there is the not-small consideration that we need, as men, to provide for our families. And somewhere in the middle of all of that we end up finding our jobs and (hopefully) making a living.

A Few Lessons from Christians Who Do Something

There are few things I feel more apathetic about than "Christians in culture" discussions. But I am particularly inspired by men and women in nonministry vocations who seem to be especially blessed in their work while also being a blessing to those around them. That, to me, is engaging the culture in a more real (or, at the very least, as real) way than making short films on your Mac, painting in the inner city, or enjoying the perfect cup of organic, fair-trade coffee. Call me a Philistine, but that's just me.

Below are snippets of conversation with some of these Christians: a factory worker, a financial planner, a teacher, and an executive. They discuss their choice of vocation, their particular vocational challenges, and the ways God has been glorified in their work.

God Wants Us to Do Something

> Make it your ambition to lead a quiet life, to mind your own business and to work with your hands, just as we told you, so that your daily life may win the respect of outsiders and so that you will not be dependent on anybody. (1 Thess. 4:11–12, NIV)

My friend Peeter is a factory worker in his early fifties. He describes himself as "an employee of Government, er, _General_ Motors." More specifically, he shoots rivets into pieces of metal that are flying by him at high speeds. He does this all day, every day, and barring injury will do so for the rest of his life.

"I did indeed have a 'calling' to this job, a very distinct audible voice, that I can remember to this day," he writes, explaining his call to General Motors. "The voice said, 'Mr. Lukas, this is Ms. Smith from G.M. Could you come to the personnel office next Thursday for a second interview?' In reality, I didn't have any idea what to do after college. I wanted to live near a good church, G.M. was hiring in a town with a good church, and so, I enlisted."

Enlist, as in the military? This sounds especially challenging, spiritually.

"The entire atmosphere of a factory is challenging. Do you conform to your peers in ways that go far beyond cursin' and drinkin'—their laziness, abject indifference, utter cynicism, bitterness, hopelessness, idle gossiping, and a countless number of other forms of self-destruction and squeezing into a world's mold that 'takes no prisoners'? The work is largely mindless, and I'm sure that I've lost a goodly number of the original brain cells that God gave me, but the challenge is to still believe that God is with me each day, even as the machines whirr and the people shout. The work defines the word _repetitious_. Can I each day (mostly) thank God for it and show that thanks by repetitive, conscientious diligence? The work can be discouraging, joyless, numbing—but will I live life in a bigger context, with an ultimate meaning that isn't defined by what I do but Who I know?"

That may be, in fact, one of the most poignant things I've ever heard on vocation, made more poignant by the fact that it was written by someone who, at least on paper, shouldn't be thankful for what he does for a living. For me, it's easier to hear this "Who I know" message from a factory worker than it is from a pastor or (worse) a full-time academic.

He adds, "I ultimately find myself as one who has gained more than he has given. There realistically are days that are like treks through a parched desert, but God has used the factory to make me more of his. . . . When I first came to the Lansing plant, I literally had to pray every bolt into every car that I built for the first month. Approximately 12 bolts a car, 350 cars a day, for 30 days. I have a depth perception problem and age is making it worse. Quarter-inch holes flying by at 200 mph (well, that's what it feels like!) make for much prayer.

"How have I had to trust God in my work? When I first began at G.M., I noticed many people in their forties and fifties who were burned out, cynical, depressed, etc., and I prayed a simple prayer: 'God, please protect me from becoming like that when I'm their age.' Thank you, Lord, thank you, Lord, for answering my prayer."

God Sometimes Uses Our Vocations to Humble Us

> Cursed is the ground because of you;
>   in pain you shall eat of it all the days of your life;
> thorns and thistles it shall bring forth for you;
>   and you shall eat the plants of the field. (Gen. 3:17–18)

Seth owns an investment business that deals primarily with retirees and those close to retiring. The company focuses on investing through the stock market, commodities, and world markets. He chose the field "when I was young, to get rich" but now sees it as a fertile ground for ministry "behind the gated communities of rich people." He writes honestly about the challenges that are inherent in working with money.

"My income is directly related to the stock markets worldwide," he explains. "When the accounts go down, my income goes down. My trust can come in the form of the Baal of Wall Street instead of the God of Abraham and Isaac. I sometimes pray to the Bull of New York when the Bear of Main Street is showing too much of its head. This is a struggle. My idol becomes what most of my clients' idols are: money. I find it hard to not let their attitudes and love of the dollar impact me, instead of my trust in the Lord impacting them."

It's no secret that many Americans are losing more than they're gaining financially in these tough economic times, and Seth faces tough questions from his clients on a regular basis. The Lord uses these questions, and these challenges, to steer us away from self-reliance.

"I tell them I am trying to trust in Christ, knowing he gives and takes away for his glory. I know that he is in control, but I also struggle spiritually to actually believe this in practice. This answer always makes people think, and they really don't know what to do with an honest Christian."

God Wants Us to Use the Talent He Gave Us

> From the fruit of his mouth a man is satisfied with good,
>   and the work of a man's hand comes back to him. (Prov. 12:14)

Ruth, a young teacher in Manhattan, teaches tenth-grade geometry in a public school where many of her students are first- or second-generation immigrants. There are very few Christians on staff or in the student body. She is honest about her "call" to teaching.

"Several things lined up for me that made teaching make sense," she writes. "(1) I loved math and was good at it. I enjoyed explaining my knowledge to others. (2) I had a phenomenal female math teacher in high school who was very passionate about math. She inspired me. (3) I wanted to impact people's lives and be a positive influence. I guess I was able to see that this was a passion that God had placed inside of me. I mean, how many people can say they are passionate and excited not only about math but about teaching math?"

Ruth sees firsthand the needs of students (and faculty) in her school, and works hard to incorporate gospel truth into her daily interactions in the workplace. She's thankful that God has given her people to pray for, and a chance to use her talents to be salt and light.

"When you work with people so closely (students and teachers but especially students), it's hard sometimes feeling like I'm building into them half-truths or only addressing their intellectual needs," she writes. "When students share with me their struggles, I want to tell them about Jesus and how he is the answer! However, I have to say things like, 'Get more rest,' or 'Forgive this person or they will have power over you.' While none of these things are untrue, they aren't addressing the root of the issue—you are sinful and need Jesus. There is so much need, so much pain, and so much hurt that you see so clearly in these young lives and in my coworker's lives.

"I should stick out as I exude Christ," she continues. "I am to be a 'little Christ,' as C. S. Lewis puts it, so my life and worldview should be different than what the world has to offer."

God Wants Us to Be Excellent at What We Do

> Do you see a man skilled in his work?
>   He will stand before kings;
>   he will not stand before obscure men. (Prov. 22:29)

Jeff, a mechanical engineer by training, a father of four young children, and an elder at his church, runs a technical assistance center for a large cell-phone insurance company.

"When I was in college, I expected that God would call me to the mission field, maybe in a tent-making role where I could use my skills and training for the kingdom," he writes. "I inquired with various missions organizations and prayed for God to open a door for me in foreign missions during my senior year in college. When nothing ever developed, I took the one job offer I had received and headed off to the secular marketplace as a manufacturing engineer at General Electric.

"There was nothing inherently spiritual about my job (improving weld quality on steam turbine parts!), but I found that I was constantly around nonbelievers and that I had many opportunities to share my faith. Also, just by doing my work 'as unto the Lord,' I enjoyed success in the projects assigned to me. Soon, I found myself being promoted into positions of increasing responsibility, and ultimately into management roles. I discovered that I enjoyed these management roles and that leadership came naturally to me. Since then, I've had a number of different roles in quality, engineering, purchasing, and operations.

I've found that my calling is not to a particular job or industry, but to use my gifts in whatever job God provides for me, in a way that honors him."

Fugitives, Wanderers, and Hope: Who I Know

> When you work the ground, it shall no longer yield to you its strength. You shall be a fugitive and a wanderer on the earth. (Gen. 4:12)

> So I saw that there is nothing better than that a man should rejoice in his work, for that is his lot. Who can bring him to see what will be after him? (Eccles. 3:22)

To be a working writer is to be a fugitive and a wanderer. This is what I think at 1:08 a.m., mentally calculating what I'll make in the coming months, and realizing it will probably leave me short of what I need. This should probably fill me with despair,[7] because like Nick Hornby's character, I long not only to "do" something, but to "be" something. And some nights, like tonight, I'd like to get on with the "being something."

In six and a half hours I'll be standing in front of a group of college students, trying to teach them something about communication. After that I'll sit in my car on a cell phone, doing a radio interview about a book I pretty much stopped thinking about a few days after I hit "send." Still, I'm thankful and grateful to God for my work, especially after realizing, partly via the interviews above, that there are Christians for whom vocation is more than just a set of circumstances that can swing one way ("I'm successful—so God is blessing me") or another ("I'm failing—so God must be punishing me"). And writing is nothing if not swinging circumstances.

But work, especially in this economy, is an occasion to trust God (Lord, please provide for my family's needs), thank God (Lord, thank you for the work you've given me), and love God (Lord, help me to work in such a way as to bring glory and honor to your name). Am I seeking my identity not in what I do, but in Who I know?

---

[7]It does, to a certain extent. I trust that God will provide (he always has), but I still have trouble sleeping. Being a Christian author, for me, hasn't meant the cessation of all of my worry.

For Further Study

Keller, Timothy J. *Counterfeit Gods: The Empty Promises of Money, Sex, and Power, and the Only Hope That Matters.* New York: Dutton, 2009.

Terkel, Studs. *Working: People Talk about What They Do All Day and How They Feel about What They Do.* New York: New Press, 1997.

Veith, Gene Edward. *God at Work: Your Christian Vocation in All of Life.* Wheaton, IL, Crossway, 2002.

Chapter 12

Social Justice

What's God Got to Do, Got to Do with It

DARRIN PATRICK

When I parachuted into the city of St. Louis to plant The Journey Church, I had tension on two fronts. First, I did not know anyone who was interested in our new church, though I had talked to strangers about how our new church could make a difference in our broken city. But thankfully, you can fool some of the people some of the time, which is apparently good enough to get you a core group. Our small church, which consisted of my wife and one-year-old daughter, began to gather people in my basement with a vision to preach and live the gospel in a city of more than 2.5 million people. Our next-door neighbors were Ukrainian and Filipino, while we were a cornbread, lily-white, early-twenties church. How could we possibly build a church for this kind of city?

We were also in tension because our city was racially divided, poverty-stricken, and abandoned by most churches in the urban core; many churches followed all the white folks into the suburbs. The questions ringing in our ears and hearts were these: How do we preach the gospel here? How do we offer living water and give a cup of cold water in the name of Jesus? How do we do both word and deed ministry? How can we be faithful in our proclamation of the gospel and in our demonstration of gospel living?

Feel the tension! Biblically speaking, it is simply unacceptable for us to jettison gospel proclamation in favor of alleviating temporary sufferings in this life. Likewise, we cannot ignore biblical commands to do justice and mercy in our broken cities under the guise of "holding true to gospel proclamation." Our cities desperately need word and deed ministry, which means the church must live in this tension.

What Is Social Justice?

The term *social justice* means many things to many people. For some it is a political term. For others it encompasses nearly every good deed imaginable. And others question whether the term is helpful at all. When I use the term, I am simply referring to the efforts we make to demonstrate care and concern for the needs of those around us, especially those least able to help themselves.

Working off this loose definition, we can take a closer look at what it looks like for Christians to do social justice. Dr. Tim Keller, pastor of Redeemer Presbyterian Church in New York City, suggests four main themes for social-justice ministry: neighbors, justice, service, and mercy.[1]

Neighbors. First, we must understand who our neighbors are. Neighbors are not just those who look, spend, and think like we do. Drawing from Jesus' words in Luke 10:25–37, Keller writes, "Your neighbor is anyone you come into contact with who lacks resources, even someone of a hated race or of another religious faith."[2] Thus the call in Leviticus 19:18 to "love your neighbor as yourself" extends well beyond your social or financial class.

Justice. Second, we must strive against injustice. If there is social justice, there is certainly social injustice. Social injustice is taking advantage of those who have little or no economic or social power (Isa. 58:6–10). According to Scripture this includes the physically disabled, widows,

---

[1]Timothy J. Keller, "The Gospel and the Poor" (unpublished outline, New York: Redeemer Presbyterian Church, 2009), 5–7.
[2]Ibid., 5.

orphans, the poor, and a whole host of others who may be abused by socio-economic power structures. Biblical justice includes dealing fairly with the disadvantaged and fighting systemic oppression where it exists.

Service. Third, we must be willing to humbly serve those with basic needs.[3] Radical service, Jesus said, means throwing a party for "the poor, the crippled, the lame, [and] the blind" (Luke 14:13, see vv. 12–14). The protodiaconate in Acts 6 was given the task of serving meals to widows. Such service was well beneath respectable citizens of the Greek culture of the time. Keller contrasts Plato and Jesus to delineate Greek norms and Christian ethics. Plato said, "How can a man be happy when he has to serve someone," while Jesus said, "I am among you as the one who serves" (Luke 22:27).

Mercy. Finally, to do social justice we must engage in acts of mercy. Keller differentiates between justice, service, and mercy by looking at the three offices of Jesus: Prophet, Priest, and King. Justice, Keller suggests, is the prophetic action of speaking against acts and systems of injustice while advocating for those who are neglected. Service is having a kingly perspective on most practically, concretely, and effectively meeting the needs of the poor. Mercy, then, means moving toward the poor with a priestly, Christlike compassion and concern.

Both-and Tension: Gospel Proclamation and Social Justice

As soon as we talk about social justice, however, we are immediately enmeshed in more tension. In our pursuit to serve the "least of these" we must be careful not to overlook the church's primary ministry, which is gospel proclamation. Before we go further, I need to explain briefly what I mean by the term *gospel*, so that my intent is clearer when I speak of gospel proclamation.

Fundamentally, the gospel is the good news that the eternal Son of God entered our sinful world and lived a life of perfect obedience to the Father, died as a sacrifice in the place of sinners, and rose triumphantly from death as a sign of sin's defeat and the Father's acceptance. In all this, the Son established a righteousness for those who had no righteousness of their own. Therefore, there is "now no condemnation"

---

[3]My forthcoming book with Matt Carter, *A Church for the City*, will deal in greater detail with practical principles and examples of how churches can serve those with the greatest needs in our cities.

(Rom. 8:1) for those who trust in Christ alone. Jesus' death and resurrection are the permanent placeholders for the sinner's right standing before the holy God.

At times, evangelicals passionate about the gospel have thought only about conversions. As D. A. Carson notes, "For some Christians, 'the gospel' is a narrow set of teachings about Jesus and his death and resurrection which, rightly believed, tip people into the kingdom."[4] While belief in the gospel does indeed bring the Christian into the kingdom, this is not the only implication of the good news. The gospel is the "embracing category that holds much of the Bible together, and takes Christians from lostness and alienation from God all the way through conversion and discipleship to the consummation, to resurrection bodies, and to the new heaven and the new earth."[5] The gospel informs everything. And as Christians grow in the grace of the gospel, they will find themselves eager to respond with compassion to the myriad needs in their midst (1 John 3:18).

But here's the tension again: we may not substitute social justice for spiritual transformation. While our heart for social justice grows out from the gospel, social justice by itself will not communicate the gospel. We need gospel proclamation, for as much as people may see our good deeds, they cannot hear the good news unless we tell them. Social justice, though valuable as an expression of Christian love, should, especially as a churchwide endeavor, serve the goal of gospel proclamation. We care for people because we love them as creatures made in God's image and lament their suffering. But believing in the reality of eternal suffering, we also hope that giving a cup of cold water in Jesus' name will win us a hearing for the gospel. We long to tell the story of Christ's ultimate act of service, of his satisfying of divine justice, of his mercy toward the spiritually bankrupt sinner through his incarnation, crucifixion, and resurrection.

Tension in the Church
Though we tend to believe we are all unique snowflakes and the most intellectually advanced and progressive generation in history, thankfully we are not. And we are not the first Christians to wrestle with this

---

[4]D. A. Carson, "The Gospel of Jesus Christ (1 Corinthians 15:1–19)," *The Spurgeon Fellowship Journal* (Spring 2008): 6.
[5]Ibid.

tension. After receiving the gospel, the early church responded in two primary ways.

First, they preached—anywhere and everywhere. While the apostles often invoked different arguments for different contexts,[6] the essence of the gospel remained the same. Second, the first Christians took a comprehensive strategy to engaging their culture, from initiating spiritual conversations, to "gossiping the gospel" in their homes, to planting new churches.[7]

As it grew, the church struggled to deal consistently with the non-believing world. Take the medieval monastery for example. They fluctuated between being havens for the poor and the marginalized and being hideaways for hermits pulling away from society in order to seek God apart from any "worldly" tentacles. A similar dynamic was at play in the evangelical awakening of the eighteenth century. Despite the attempts of John Wesley and Jonathan Edwards to live within the gospel tension by championing gospel proclamation and social justice, many Christian leaders still ignored the practical needs of those around them.

More recently, Walter Rauschenbusch, who lived prior to World War I, appropriately critiqued the church for not acknowledging Jesus' reign as King over social structures, but the social gospel movement he started was marred by human-centered optimism and the other-worldly dimensions of the historic Christian faith.

Social Justice in the Bible

Having dealt with definitions, history, and general themes, we now come more explicitly to the Bible and what it says about our responsibility to care for the needy.

The people of Israel were warned continually by the prophets to have a godly sensitivity to the poor. In Job 31:16–22, we see God's heart for the downtrodden. A godly person, this text says, cannot and will not stand idly by when aware of destitution and abject poverty. Job says he will withhold nothing from the poor, that orphans will eat before he does, and that if anyone dies from lack or want on his watch, "Let my shoulder blade fall from my shoulder, and let my arm be broken from

---

[6]In Acts 13, Paul preached Christ to the Jews through the timeline of Jewish history. In Acts 14, Paul and Barnabas convert many pagan "blue-collar" Gentiles who thought the missionaries were gods, and in Acts 17, Paul preaches the gospel to Greek intellectuals at the Areopagus in Athens. In other words, the same gospel was preached, but adapted to most effectively reach the people group being addressed.

[7]See Michael Green, *Evangelism and the Early Church* (Grand Rapids: Eerdmans, 2003), 23–26.

its socket" (Job 31:22). Elsewhere, the prophets roundly rebuke Israel for their idolatrous materialism. Isaiah 3:16–26 shows the harshness with which self-centered hoarders of wealth will be treated.

> The Lord will take away the finery of the anklets, the headbands, and the crescents; the pendants, the bracelets, and the scarves; the head-dresses, the armlets, the sashes, the perfume boxes, and the amulets; the signet rings and nose rings. . . .
>
> > Instead of perfume there will be rottenness. . . .
> > Your men shall fall by the sword
> >   and your mighty men in battle.
> > And her gates shall lament and mourn;
> >   empty, she shall sit on the ground.

But the sin of God's people was not limited to their desire for wealth. By focusing on personal accrual of riches, God's people were not only failing to share with the poor; they were also failing to empower them to live productive lives on their own. Deuteronomy 15:12–15, along with other passages, makes clear that the poorest of the poor are not to be left empty-handed, but are to be set up to succeed, furnished "liberally," for "as the LORD your God has blessed you, you shall give to [the poor]."

The same concern for the poor is found in the New Testament as well. In Matthew 25:44–46, after establishing a ministry of extraordinary and often miraculous care for the poor (Matt. 11:1–6), Jesus instructs his hearers that those who truly trust in him will necessarily serve the hungry, the thirsty, the strangers, the naked, the sick, and the prison-ers. True faith in Christ results in true care for those with the greatest needs. Most of all, this means caring for our Christian brothers and sisters (Matt. 25:40), but it also means doing good to the world around us when we can (Gal. 6:10).

Changed at a heart level by the gospel, the apostles modeled care for the poor in their speech and in their actions. Leaving none of the Old Testament's commands behind, the Epistles actually expand on them. In 1 John 3:16–17, John recalls the heart behind the Deuteronomy passage above. He reminds the church that because Christ laid down his life for us, we ought also to lay down our lives for our brothers and sisters in need. Like Isaiah, James reminds his Jerusalem congregation that ill-gotten wealth is an out-and-out sin, highly offensive to God, and will reap terrible results for the guilty. The brother of the Lord, angered by the hoarders in his church, wrote, "Your gold and silver have corroded, and their corrosion will be evidence against you" (James 5:3). The implication for James's sheep is that it is better for them to serve their brothers and sisters in need than to have the possessions they've garnered "eat [their] flesh like fire" (James 5:3).

What of the example of Jesus himself? As someone who has read the Gospels faithfully for more than twenty years, I have grown increasingly cautious trying to systematically deduce a predictable method for how Jesus went about enacting his divine mission on earth. He declared that his main ministry was preaching (Luke 4:43), yet how he went about this preaching priority was not uniform. Many times he entered a town, wandered over to a place where a group of sick people gathered, healed one or two of them, and continued on his way. On a couple of occasions he fed the hungry crowds so that they could hear him teach about the kingdom of God and experience a miracle that authenticated his message. He physically healed everyone who came to him,[8] and was unashamed and unafraid to touch those deemed most sinful and unclean (Matt. 11:19; 24:49; Luke 7:34). Other times, he told his disciples to find a boat, so he could get some space and teach. Still other times, Jesus antagonized the religious leaders regarding their hypocrisy, which was often revealed by their lack of concern for the poor and marginalized (Matt. 23:23). In the end, it's hard to make definite conclusions from the example of Jesus. But this much we can say with certainty: while Jesus did not want his teaching to be sidetracked by the needs of the crowd, neither did he ignore the suffering all around him. He was committed to staying on mission. He was also full of mercy.

We cannot faithfully follow Christ and avoid acts of mercy. The practical question the church must address, then, is this: To what extent is the church to participate in social justice in the form of individual deeds, intentional systems of mercy, and community development? My contention, which I'll unpack below, is that the church as church should focus on the Great Commission (making disciples), while it lives out the Great Commandments (love God and love your neighbor) along the way. The church's priority must be Christian discipleship. No other

---

[8]John Wimber, *Healing Seminar* (London: Vineyard Ministries International, nd), 11.

institution on earth will carry out this mission. This does not mean our churches are wrong to adopt a school or support a homeless shelter. Certainly not. But for the most part the work of social justice will fall to the church scattered, to individual Christians banding together or even working with nonbelievers to show mercy and offer help to a broken and hurting world.

As this chapter draws to a close, I draw the following conclusions based on biblical understanding, the lessons of church history, and my own experience as a pastor in a racially divided, once-thriving-and-now-impoverished rustbelt city.

Conclusions

I've talked a lot about tension. Maybe you even felt that in the back-and-forth, give-and-take in this chapter. Understanding social justice is not for the faint of heart. But there must be some take-home lessons in all this both-and. Let me offer five practical points of application.

1. *Admitting the tension is the first step to living in it fruitfully.* The Bible is no stranger to tension. The kingdom, for example, is already here, but not yet fully arrived. This tension helps us understand the tension we feel with a commitment to social justice.

On the one hand, we know that true social justice awaits the new heaven and the new earth, but on the other hand we are compelled to extend mercy according to the word and examples of Jesus, the apostles, and the Old Testament. On the one hand, we are called by Scripture to engage the culture, to show how the gospel challenges unjust social and political systems and to fight for the good of those oppressed by such systems. On the other hand, we must expect sin and poverty in this life and not utopia. The already and not-yet of the kingdom means that we are right to feel a tension between doing good works as an expression of the kingdom come, all the while understanding that the kingdom will not come by our good works.

2. *The church is called, first and foremost, to proclaim the gospel.* As The Gospel Coalition states in its ministry vision statement, "We are neither overly optimistic nor pessimistic about our cultural influence, for we know that, as we walk in the steps of the One who laid down his life for his opponents, we will receive persecution even while having

social impact (1 Pet. 2:12)."[9] Timmis and Chester say it well: "If we do not keep people's eternal plight in mind, then immediate needs will force their way to the top of our agenda, and we will betray the gospel and the people we profess to love. The most loving thing we can do for the poor is to proclaim the good news of eternal salvation through Christ."[10]

3. *You must not use social justice to avoid the offense of the cross.* As Paul notes in 1 Corinthians 1:23, the gospel is "a stumbling block" and "folly" to those who do not believe. No matter how well Christians articulate the gospel, no matter how effectively and compassionately we serve, the gospel will always be offensive to those whose hearts are opposed to God. To think otherwise is as foolish as the gospel sounds to nonbelievers.

This should not be a surprise to us for two primary reasons. First, Jesus himself was an offensive person to those who did not receive him (Matt. 11:6; 15:12; Luke 7:23). He preached unadulterated truth, which ultimately led to his death (Matt. 12:14). Second, the horror of sin in us and its ravages in our world are very real, and this will be the case until Jesus returns to ultimately establish the fullness of his kingdom. Promoting social justice as a remedy for our sin not only is theologically incorrect; it leads to utter disappointment for those who place their ultimate hope in cultural renewal.

Lest we remain unconvinced, the Apostle of Love, John, makes no bones about it in 1 John 3:12–14. Drawing on the biblical account of the world's very first murder, John notes that Abel, the righteous servant of God, was murdered by his own brother because of his obedience to God. Therefore, John says, "Do not be surprised, brothers, that the world hates you" (v. 13). The gospel is offensive to those who oppose God, and leads to suffering to those who love him. No amount of righteous service will change that reality.

4. *The "institutional" church must equip individuals who will become the "organic" church.*[11] The language of the institutional church and the organic church comes from the Dutch neo-Calvinist Abraham

---

[9]See http://thegospelcoalition.org/about/foundation-documents/vision/.

[10]Tim Chester and Steve Timmis, *Total Church: A Radical Reshaping around Gospel and Community*, (Wheaton, IL: Crossway, 2008), 78.

[11]Abraham Kuyper, "Common Grace," in *Abraham Kuyper: A Centennial Reader*, ed. James D. Bratt (Grand Rapids: Eerdmans, 1998), 165–201.

Kuyper.[12] Do not let the term *institutional* take you mentally to a dusty old 1950s-style library that needs to have the windows opened to let in fresh air. Institutional churches, in Kuyper's view, can be brand-spanking new churches. The institutional church, said Kuyper, is the church as most of us know it: elders preaching and leading, deacons serving, and members observing the sacraments. In other words, the institutional church should do what we said in point 2 above: use all of its influence and creativity to promote and proclaim the biblical gospel of Jesus. The goal is not just to convert non-Christians with the gospel, but to preach the gospel to Christians, enabling them to see the all-encompassing scope of the gospel and its authoritative power in every sphere of life.

The organic church, then, as I alluded to above, consists of the individuals who have been equipped with the gospel proclaimed by the institutional church. They then tease out the implications of the gospel in real life. This means that while the institutional church is equipping through gospel proclamation, the organic church is living it out as scores of Christians perform individual acts of service to the poor and marginalized. Further, the organic church produces individuals who organize themselves to form nonprofits, guilds, community development agencies—the list goes on and on. As individuals are equipped with the gospel, they mobilize in order to partner with and even start nonprofits and other social and political reform advocacies.[13]

I believe this distinction between institutional and organic churches does much to alleviate the fears of many evangelicals who are afraid that programmatic approaches to social justice will dilute the message of the gospel in a lost world.

5. *Gospel-centered churches should plant other gospel-centered churches.* Churches that not only understand but implement points 1 and 2 above will make a significant gospel impact in the neighborhoods in which they are established. But these churches will not make significant impact in neighborhoods outside their immediate geographical area. This is why institutional churches that develop organic churches should plant other institutional churches that develop and equip organic churches in other

---

[12]David F. Wells, ed., *Reformed Theology in America: A History of Its Modern Development* (Grand Rapids: Eerdmans, 1985), 140–43.
[13]See http://www.missionstl.org and http://www.hfny.org for examples of how church-spawned nonprofits are addressing the felt needs of both minor and major US cities.

neighborhoods. New churches reach non-Christians at a much higher rate than older churches.[14] This is not to say that established churches cannot make a gospel impact in their neighborhoods and win lost souls for Christ. It is simply stating a reality that statistics bear out. Studies show that churches under three years of age lead three times more people to Christ than churches fifteen years of age or older.[15] The good news for existing churches is that when they take the bold step of investing in young church planters, it revitalizes the "mother" church as well.[16] Church planting gives life to new churches and established churches alike.

And how does social justice fit into the call for church planting? The way for the church to prevail is to focus on the preaching of the gospel, which will challenge people to carry the gospel into the brokenness of the city. Gospel-centered churches will challenge people to be good neighbors, to be embedded in their city/neighborhood, not just to use the city for play or to flip houses for profit, but to meet people's felt needs as an entry point for meeting people's eternal spiritual needs. Just as Christ's miracles were not a suspension of the natural order, but a "putting back together" of what was supposed to be before sin, so also will followers of Christ seek to make things right within their sphere of influence, which includes places where they live, work, and play. Is social justice the main program of the church? No! Is social justice an important intentional and organic part of discipleship for the individual Christians mobilized and equipped by their local church? Yes!

For Further Study

Blomberg, Craig. *Neither Poverty nor Riches: A Biblical Theology of Possessions*. Downers Grove, IL: InterVarsity, 2001.

Fikkert, Brian, and Steve Corbett. *When Helping Hurts: Alleviating Poverty without Hurting the Poor . . . and Ourselves*. Chicago: Moody, 2009.

Keller, Timothy J. *Ministries of Mercy: The Call of the Jericho Road*. 2nd ed. Phillipsburg, NJ: P&R, 1997.

Kuyper, Abraham. "Common Grace." In *Abraham Kuyper: A Centennial Reader*, edited by James D. Bratt, 165–201. Grand Rapids: Eerdmans, 1998.

---

[14] Aubrey Malphurs, *Planting Growing Churches for the 21st Century* (Grand Rapids: Baker, 2000), 44.
[15] Ibid.
[16] Timothy J. Keller, "Why Plant Churches?" (unpublished paper, New York: Redeemer Presbyterian Church, 2002), 4.

Chapter 13

Homosexuality

Grace, Truth, and the Need for Gentle Courage

ERIC REDMOND AND KEVIN DEYOUNG

The fiasco will probably seem dated by the time this book hits the shelves, but it was a big deal for a few days. On October 1, 2009, late-night TV comedian David Letterman announced to his studio audience that he had had a sexual affair with one of his female staff members. There was a mixed reaction from the public. Some thought that Letterman was receiving his just desserts and deserved to be mocked as he had mocked others. Others said it was no big deal. As Tom Shales from *The Washington Post* commented, "Letterman can continue to lampoon sleazy political figures with no real fear of hypocrisy, however, because a TV comic is not an elected official responsible for the well-being of the nation or its citizenry." So Letterman gets a pass because he's a "comic, not a cleric or a congressman."[1]

---

[1]Tom Shales, "Let's Remember That Letterman's a Comic, Not a Cleric or a Congressman," *The Washington Post*, October 6, 2009, accessed October 21, 2009, http://www.washingtonpost.com/wp-dyn/content/article/2009/10/05/AR2009100503982.html?nav=rss_email/components.

But then what do we make of Tiger Woods? After news broke of Tiger's many paramours, he lost sponsorships, public esteem, and eventually his marriage. He withdrew from upcoming tournaments and checked himself in to a sexual addiction clinic. Is Letterman okay, but Tiger not?

Anytime sex is in the news, you can count on Americans being fascinated by it. What you can't count on is the public's reaction. For one report, there are laughs. For another, gasps. Sometimes the sins are thought egregious. Other times they are mere personal indiscretions. It's as if our society wants sexual standards, but it doesn't want them standardized.

Yet, in the face of this inconsistency, evangelical Christianity maintains a theological case for a biblical sexuality that applies to all. There *is* a code of conduct defined and described by the Scriptures: a covenanted union of one man for one woman (until the death of either) as the Lord's standard for *all* people in *every* society. Given this standard, Christians need to confront a variety of sins: pornography, adultery, premarital sex, unlawful divorce and remarriage. It's not that we are killjoys, scared that people are enjoying themselves somewhere. Rather, it's because we believe the Word of God, and believe God's Word is good for us, that we feel compelled to uphold the Scripture's stance on sexuality. And this stance includes the prohibition of homosexual behavior.

How to Talk the Talk

Homosexuality is a complicated and personal topic for many people. It is often difficult to discuss. More and more, many of us have friends or family who are gay. No doubt, some individuals reading this chapter struggle with same-gender attraction. So whenever we talk about homosexuality, we are talking about something very personal, often painful, and always controversial. But we cannot avoid this issue. It demands careful thought and a careful response. Homosexuality is not the only important issue for Christians, but it is one we cannot ignore.

It is unpopular in many quarters to critique homosexuality. "Progressive" justices seek to normalize and protect the homosexual "rights," and some large denominational church bodies have approved the ordination of openly gay priests and ministers. The media presents homosexuality as acceptable and American as mom and apple pie. The Christian critique in this environment often sounds strident or bigoted. Sometimes, sadly, it is. But our attitude must be one of humility. To be a Christian is to acknowledge that we once were rebellious toward God and, in fact, are still fighting against rebellious impulses in our hearts. So we speak to those indulging in any sin from a point of meekness, as those who have been shown mercy and forgiveness, not as those worthy of God or morally superior to others. Our critique is strong, but, we hope, also humble. We have no righteousness of our own, and the only truth we speak is what we see in God's Word.

In the Beginning

God's plan from the beginning has been for one man and one woman to become one flesh in the covenant of marriage. When no suitable helper was found for Adam, the Lord God made a woman (Gen. 2:20, 22). She was bone of his bone and flesh of his flesh, and the two became one flesh (Gen. 2:23–24). God made the man and the woman to fit together, quite literally. In the creation, God intended for man and woman to exist in a state in which they could enjoy one another in an exclusive, lifelong "one flesh" union that would result in "filling the earth." This kind of union only comes about in a heterosexual marriage.

We have good reason to think this one man–one woman union was and continues to be God's design for human sexuality. For starters, marriage is given before the fall and pronounced very good (Gen. 1:31). What is good about it is not simply that Adam had a meaningful relationship, but that he was given a helper suitable for him—not an animal, not another man, but a woman, Eve. Moreover, Jesus reaffirmed God's design for a one man–one woman marriage in Matthew 19:4–5: "Have you not read that he who created them from the beginning made them male and female, and said, 'Therefore a man shall leave his father and his mother and hold fast to his wife, and the two shall become one flesh'?" Heterosexual monogamy is God's normative design for marriage. The Bible refuses to commend whatever deviates from this pattern—be it adultery, bestiality, polygamy, fornication, or homosexual behavior.

Sexuality in the context of heterosexual marriage is not only good, but exclusively good. Only heterosexual marriage relationships can show forth the complementary design of men and women. According to the apostle Paul, one of the purposes of marriage is to show forth the mystery of Christ and the church (Eph. 5:32). If marriage can be construed as a man and a man or a woman and a woman, what is left of the glorious mystery of Christ and the church? We are left with only Christ and Christ or church and church.

Similarly, only heterosexual marriage relationships can fulfill God's design in marriage to be fruitful and increase in number (Gen. 1:28). To be sure, sex is given for more than procreation. But just as surely, we cannot deny that God intends for children to be the result of the marriage union. Speaking about the covenant of marriage, Malachi 2:15 says, "Has not the LORD made them one? In flesh and spirit they are his. And why one? Because he was seeking godly offspring" (NIV). Granted, some heterosexual couples cannot have children because of barrenness, impotence, old age, or other medical reasons. Their lack of reproduction does not make their union inappropriate. But that we live in a fallen world where the gift of children does not come to all couples is beside the point. What still stands is God's design. Part of God's plan for marriage is godly offspring. The issue is not whether every couple will be able to have children, but whether the marriage union itself reflects God's original design for two people to come together who were given sexual organs to reproduce, one with the other.

Why Not Homosexuality?
The rest of Scripture confirms the Genesis design for marriage and sexual union. In particular, three clusters of passages teach that homosexual behavior is contrary to Scripture and displeasing to God.

Sodom and Gomorrah
In Genesis 19, the Lord destroyed Sodom and Gomorrah for their heinous sins (cf. Gen. 18:20). Their sins were manifold and, no doubt, went off in many different directions. Some have asserted that the sin of Sodom was social, that they were inhospitable. This is true. Ezekiel 16:49 states, "Behold, this was the guilt of your sister Sodom: she and her daughters had pride, excess of food, and prosperous ease, but did not aid the poor and needy." But part of their offense was also sexual. They committed "abominations" before the Lord (Ezek. 16:51; cf. 16:22, 58). The men of Sodom called to Lot, "Where are the men who came to you

tonight? Bring them out to us, that we may know them" (Gen. 19:5). The word in verse 5 translated "have sex" in other translations is *yada*, the Hebrew word for "know." It is the same word used in verse 8 when Lot offers his two daughters who have never "known"(*yada*) a man. Sodom's immorality showed itself, in part, in that the men of Sodom wanted to commit homosexual acts with Lot's guests.

Admittedly, this story sounds more like gang rape than gay marriage. So, could it be that the story of Sodom and Gomorrah says nothing against homosexual behavior in a monogamous committed relationship? Jude's inspired commentary on Genesis 19 points us in a different direction. Jude 7 says, "Just as Sodom and Gomorrah and the surrounding cities, which likewise indulged in sexual immorality and pursued unnatural desire, serve as an example by undergoing a punishment of eternal fire. . . ." This verse makes three important contributions to our understanding of Genesis 19.

First, we see that God takes sexual sin seriously. Sodom and Gomorrah are "an example of what is going to happen to the ungodly" (2 Pet. 2:6).

Second, we see that the sin of Sodom was not simply inhospitality or some other social negligence. They also gave themselves up to sexual immorality.

Third, their sin was also a sin of perversion. The Greek is *apelthousai opisō sarkos heteras*, which even the more progressive NRSV translates as "pursued unnatural lust." The sin of the men of Sodom was not merely gang rape, but that they desired what was unnatural: men desired to have sex with other men.

Some have suggested that the "unnatural lust" or "strange flesh" refers to Sodom's desire to sleep with angels (recall Lot's guests were actually angels). But the men of Sodom did not know they were angels. They called them men (Gen. 19:5). Besides, are we really to think that Jude condemns Sodom only because they wanted to sleep with angels unawares, but if the three men had not been angels, that would not have been "perversion"? And are we to suppose that the false teachers Jude is confronting—those "who pervert the grace of our God into sensuality"—were "ungodly people" because they encouraged Jude's audience to sleep with angels (Jude 4)? It strains credulity to think that

Sodom's sin of "sexual immorality" is only a reference to angels and not to acts of homosexual perversion.

Leviticus 18 and 20 in the Old Testament and New Testament

Leviticus 18:22 states, "You shall not lie with a male as with a woman; it is an abomination." Likewise, Leviticus 20:13: "If a man lies with a male as with a woman, both of them have committed an abomination." Any discussion of these texts will be difficult because the relationship between the Old Testament law and the New Testament is complex. While it is true that we cannot just pull verses from Leviticus and make them normative for all time, neither can we simply ignore verses in the Old Testament because they seem strange to our sensibilities or appear in conjunction with regulations or penalties that have been abrogated with the end of theocratic Israel and the coming of Christ. We must ask—and there are other questions to ask of Leviticus 18:22 and 20:13, but this may be the most crucial: Do these verses lie behind any of the New Testament prohibitions of same-sex acts? The answer is yes.

First Corinthians 6:9–10 says, "Do you not know that the unrighteous will not inherit the kingdom of God? Do not be deceived: neither the sexually immoral, nor idolaters, nor adulterers, nor men who practice homosexuality, nor thieves, nor the greedy, nor drunkards, nor revilers, nor swindlers will inherit the kingdom of God." Similarly, 1 Timothy 1:9–10 states,

> The law is not laid down for the just but for the lawless and disobedient, for the ungodly and sinners, for the unholy and profane, for those who strike their fathers or mothers, for murderers, for the sexually immoral, men who practice homosexuality, enslavers, liars, perjurers, and whatever else is contrary to sound doctrine.

The word for "men who practice homosexuality" is used in both passages. It is the Greek word *arsenokoitēs*, a compound of the word *arsen* ("man") and *koitēs* ("bed").

Arsenokoitēs is a rare Greek word; it does not appear prior to the New Testament, and it does not show up again until two centuries later. It seems as if Paul coined the word from the Septuagint (the Greek translation of the Old Testament used by first-century Jews and Christians). The Septuagint renders the texts from Leviticus:

meta arsenos ou koimēthēsē koitēn gunaikos (Lev. 18:22)
"with a man do not lie [as one] lies [with a] woman"

hos an koimēthē meta arsenos koitēn gunaikos (Lev. 20:13)
"whoever lies with a man [as one] lies with a woman"

Considering the rarity of the word before and after the New Testament, it is hard to escape the conclusion that Paul coined the word *arsenokoitēs* from Leviticus, in particular 20:13, where the two words forming that term stand side by side. Given this conclusion, Paul's use of *arsenokoitēs* yields two important points. First, Paul did not see the prohibitions in Leviticus 18:22 and 20:13 to be concerned only with ritual purity. He used them as his basis for a New Testament sexual ethic. Second, 1 Corinthians 6:9 and 1 Timothy 1:10 cannot be seen as speaking against temple prostitution or pederasty (man-boy love) alone. The word *arsenokoitēs*, drawing from Leviticus, has a broader meaning encompassing more generally same-sex acts. The New Testament, like the Old Testament, considers all forms of same-sex unions to be sinful.

Romans 1
Romans 1:24–27 states:

> Therefore God gave them up in the lusts of their hearts to impurity, to the dishonoring of their bodies among themselves, because they exchanged the truth about God for a lie and worshiped and served the creature rather than the Creator, who is blessed forever! Amen.
>
> For this reason God gave them up to dishonorable passions. For their women exchanged natural relations for those that are contrary to nature; and the men likewise gave up natural relations with women and were consumed with passion for one another, men committing shameless acts with men and receiving in themselves the due penalty for their error.

Three considerations support the church's long-held understanding that these verses prohibit homosexual behavior.

First, the fact that Paul mentions women lusting after women (and mentions it first) indicates that he is not just concerned to condemn the common man-boy relationships of the day. He has all unnatural lust in mind.

Second, Paul firmly grounds his argument in creation. Women having sex with women and men with men are "against nature" (*para physin*). Homosexual acts are contrary to God's original design for men and women.

Third, although there may be value in distinguishing between those who consciously choose homosexuality and those who, without a conscious decision, feel attracted to members of the same sex, this does not mean we can scrap Romans 1 for our modern notion of orientation. When Paul talks about that which is "against nature," he is not thinking of the self, or orientation, or any other modern notions that would have been foreign to him. His concern is not with individuals who deny their true selves, but with humanity in general, which has exchanged the truth of God for a lie. He is thinking of nature as the order of things, not in our isolated selves, but in God's universe.

In conclusion, then, Romans 1 teaches that there are many ways humanity disregards God's righteous decrees (Rom. 1:32); homosexual behavior is not singled out as a worse offense than the rest, but is prohibited along with other acts of sin and idolatry. From the first chapters of the Bible to the Torah to the New Testament, there is no hint that homosexuality is acceptable behavior for God's people. To think the Bible affirms homosexuality takes more than special pleading—it requires a denial of the plain teaching of Scripture. Listen to what Luke Timothy Johnson, a well-respected scholar from Emory University and a pro-gay advocate, says about defending homosexuality from the Bible:

> The task demands intellectual honesty. I have little patience with efforts to make Scripture say something other than what it says, through appeals to linguistic or cultural subtleties. The exegetical situation is straightforward: we know what the text says. . . . I think it important to state clearly that we do, in fact, reject the straightforward commands of Scripture, and appeal instead to another authority when we declare that same-sex unions can be holy and good. And what exactly is that authority? We appeal explicitly to the weight of our own experience and the experience thousands of others have witnessed to, which tells us that to claim our own sexual orientation is in fact to accept the way in which God has created us. By so doing, we explicitly reject as well the

premises of the scriptural statements condemning homosexuality—
namely, that it is a vice freely chosen, a symptom of human corruption,
and disobedience to God's created order.[2]

Thank God for this honest non-evangelical who sees what everyone
should be able to see: the straightforward commands of Scripture prohibit homosexual activity.

A Quick Look at Common Objections

We believe the exegetical argument against homosexuality is sound. It
certainly would have made sense to virtually every Christian everywhere
until about fifty years ago. But, still, many raise objections to this
understanding of Scripture. We only have space to deal very briefly
with a few of the most common.

1. *"Jesus didn't say anything about homosexuality."* It is true that
Jesus never used a term for homosexuality in his teachings. Jesus did not
address homosexuality because no one was thinking to condone it. But
the Judaism in which Jesus would have been raised certainly rejected
homosexuality, and he does nothing to counter this assumption. In
fact, Jesus goes out of his way to emphasize his acceptance of the Old
Testament law (Matt. 5:17). He also reaffirms the Genesis account of
marriage (Matt. 19:4–6).

2. *"The creeds and confessions of the church don't prohibit homosexuality."* To the extent this is true, it is because the church did not have to
wrestle with this issue until recently. Creeds are formed in response to
controversies. This was not a controversy earlier because no one affirmed
homosexuality. Moreover, various catechisms and confessions implicitly
reject homosexuality in their teaching of sexual immorality.

3. *"What if they discover a gay gene?"* Studies have shown that one
identical twin can be gay and the other not, even though they have the
same genetic makeup. So science has not proved a genetic causation.
At the most, there may be congenital influences that can increase the
likelihood of homosexual development, but hereditary factors play a role
in all sorts of inclinations. Some people may be more prone to struggle
with anger, adultery, or alcoholism because of their genetic makeup, but
this does not mean their behavior is biologically determined. Humans

---

[2]"Christianity and the Church: Scripture and Experience," *Commonweal*, June 15, 2007.

are responsible for sin even if some are more easily tempted than others to desire certain sins.

4. *"The Bible teaches lots of things we don't follow. Aren't you just picking and choosing what you want to believe?"* While it's true that not every command in the Bible is normative for all people in all places (e.g., we don't have to go build an ark), this doesn't mean we simply pick and choose what to believe. In studying the Bible we first try to determine the author's intent. Then we try to determine what the passage means for us by looking at the context, the type of book we are reading (law, poetry, letter, history, etc.), and if there are any clues about its abiding significance. We've tried to show that God's frequent prohibitions against homosexuality are related to transcultural factors like the order of creation and the nature of men and women.

5. *"But I know many wonderful gay people."* We are not suggesting gays and lesbians are weird or obnoxiously wicked. We know that many homosexuals have found a kind of peace in "accepting" their sexuality. Likewise, we recognize that gays and lesbians can be kind, considerate, and loving. But our ethics must be based on scriptural testimony before personal testimony. We must interpret our experiences through the lens of God's revelation, not the other way around.

Closing Considerations

This issue of homosexuality should not be ignored or sidestepped in order to get on with "more important things." Of course, we would all rather focus on evangelism and discipleship. But perhaps our prayers for renewal will be answered by taking a courageous and crystal clear stance with regard to homosexuality. Much is at stake in this debate.

Grace is at stake in the debate over homosexuality. Will we offer people the grace to change or affirm them in behavior that the Bible has said is inappropriate? And when we offer people grace in Jesus' name, will it be cheap grace that advocates mercy apart from justice, election without sanctification, and Christianity without discipleship?

Our approach to the Bible is at stake. Theologians have always recognized that God unfolds his truth in Scripture by means of progressive revelation. But does this mean we need to look for "new light" that contradicts the consistent witness of Scripture? Do we think God has changed his mind on this issue? How will we know? And what does this do to our confidence in the Bible? Are the Scriptures clear and complete, or might we need a better ethic than the New Testament?

Where we find the authority for our beliefs is at stake. Will we allow this issue to be settled by the back-and-forth debate in medical journals and psychological studies, or we will stand on the Bible alone and examine general revelation through the spectacles of Scripture?

Our pastoral approach to persons struggling with same-gender attraction is at stake. At our best, we who oppose homosexual behavior do so motivated by love—love for the hurting, the struggling, the ostracized, and the confused. We want to minister, as Jesus did, with grace and truth. No doubt, some homosexuals like to tell stories of the love and acceptance they have found in affirming churches. But many others would tell the opposite story, like this man who yearns for something more than cheap grace. We conclude with his words.

> Like many other Christians, I have struggled for years with same-sex attraction. By God's grace I know freedom from a way of life that still holds too many others captive. Yet many within the so-called affirming church would deny us that freedom. They say homosexuality is God's plan for our lives, even though the Bible clearly says that homosexual behavior is a sin. . . . Believers can act like the false physician, telling people tempted by homosexuality that same-sex orientation is part of their identity and that they should accept it. Or, we can act as judge, jury, and executioner, driving them away from the Savior who loves them. Either way, we risk the same result: spiritual death.
>
> Or we can respond like Jesus would, with grace and truth: "Come unto me, all who are weary and heavy-laden, and I will give you rest." Those words called to me, weary and heavy-laden with sin, several years ago. Shouldn't all Christians bear that message of freedom and hope?[3]

FOR FURTHER STUDY

Ash, Christopher. *Marriage: Sex in the Service of God.* Vancouver: Regent, 2005.

Heimbach, Daniel R. *True Sexual Morality: Recovering Biblical Standards for a Culture in Crisis.* Wheaton, IL: Crossway, 2004.

Schmidt, Thomas E. *Straight and Narrow.* Downers Grove, IL: InterVarsity, 1995.

---

[3] *Christianity Today*, December 2004, 50–51.

Chapter 14

Abortion

Why Silence and Inaction Are Not Options for Evangelicals

JUSTIN TAYLOR

Do you remember "Balloon Boy"? By the time you read this, the stunt may only be a little-known question in *Trivial Pursuit*. Here's the short version: a publicity-hungry amateur-scientist father of three pulled off a hoax that captured the attention of America. On October 15, 2009, Richard Heene released a large gray helium balloon that looked like a UFO from a 1950s movie, then called the authorities to report that his nine-year-old son, Falcon, was trapped inside. As the balloon floated some fifty miles across the Colorado sky, newsrooms across America sprang into action. People prayed. Emergency medical teams stood by. Police squads were mobilized. Denver International Airport was shut down. Several National Guard helicopters were in hot pursuit.

As the helium began to leak, the balloon eventually crashed in a field. Rescuers made a mad dash to lessen the blow, then to save the boy's life—if he was still alive. As it turned out, there was no one inside the balloon! A manhunt was quickly organized, thinking that perhaps Falcon had fallen out earlier. But then came word that Falcon was safe and sound at home. He had been hiding—per his father's instructions—in the family attic. He got sleepy, had fallen asleep, and awoke a few hours later to a media frenzy. He went to sleep as Falcon and awoke as Balloon Boy.

This is not a chapter about balloons, hoaxes, and men who use their children as pawns to pitch a reality TV show. It's a chapter about abortion—one of the most painful and politicized issues in our public discourse. So what exactly does the killing of a baby in the womb have to do with the boy in the balloon? I bring it up for one reason. It helps to focus our attention on a crucial question: *what's in there?* If we believe that there is a human being within that balloon, we will stop at nothing to protect and to preserve that life. No amount of money or energy or equipment is too big: we must do everything we can to protect and preserve the life of a fellow human being in distress. Likewise, if we believe that what's growing inside of a woman's womb is a living human being, should we not think the same? If the balloon is merely filled with air, or if the womb is merely occupied with a clump of cells, then no action is needed. Knowing what's inside makes all the difference in the world.

Here's another way to look at it: Greg Koukl[1] asks us to imagine a boy in the backyard calling to his dad, "Hey Dad, can I kill this?" What does the dad need to know before he can answer his son's question? Just one thing: *what is it?* If it's a cockroach, the dad will cheer his son on. If it's the neighbor's cat, it's another matter altogether! The application of this commonsensical principle is this: determining *what* is in the womb determines how you will *treat* what is in the womb.

What Is a Human Being, and When Does Life Begin?

The first thing the Bible says about human beings is that we are all created to resemble God (Gen. 1:26–27; 5:1–3). We're made in God's image and after his likeness. Humans are uniquely designed to reflect—

---

[1] See his excellent book, *Tactics: A Game Plan for Discussing Your Christian Convictions* (Grand Rapids: Zondervan, 2009).

to image forth—God's character and glory. Being human carries with it the stamp of God's image.

Being in God's image means that human beings have inherent value and that God hates and abominates "hands that shed innocent blood" (Prov. 6:16–17). Biblical ethics can at times be complicated and difficult to apply, but God's command not to "kill the innocent" (Ex. 23:7) is clear and pervasive throughout the entire Bible.

Even if the above is true, how do we know that the unborn are in this same category of human beings created in God's image and deserving protection and life?

When human life begins is a scientific question, but one that Scripture does address to some extent. Everything in the Bible points to the fact that God is working within the womb, and that what's in the womb is a human life that matters to God. In Psalm 51:5 David confesses that he has been a sinner since conception ("In sin did my mother conceive me"), which would require that he was a person upon conception, given that only persons can have moral responsibility. In Psalm 139 he praises God for forming his inward parts, knitting and weaving him together in his mother's womb (vv. 13, 15; cf. Job 31:13–15). God creates human beings at the point of conception, endows them with his image, and orchestrates their development in the womb.

When does biological science say that life begins? Princeton professor Robert P. George writes, "From a purely biological perspective, *scientists can identify the point at which a human life begins.* The relevant studies are legion. The biological facts are uncontested. The method of analysis applied to the data is universally accepted."[2] Human life begins at conception as a new, complete, living human organism is created when egg and sperm fuse together, forming a human embryo. The late Dr. Hymie Gordon, founder and director of the Mayo Clinic's world-renowned medical genetics program, submitted the following expert testimony before Congress:

> I think we can now also say that the question of the beginning of life—when life begins—is no longer a question for theological or philosophical dispute. It is an established scientific fact. Theologians and philosophers may go on to debate the meaning of life or purpose

---

[2]Robert P. George, "When Life Begins," *National Review Online*, November 2, 2008 (his emphasis).

of life, but it is an established fact that all life, including human life, begins at the moment of conception.[3]

To summarize: science tells us that life begins at conception, and Scripture tells us that that human life is created by God in his image, with grave consequences for those who shed such innocent blood.

What Is Abortion?

An elective abortion is a procedure where a living human being is removed from a woman's uterus in such a way that the unborn child's life is terminated. In the United States it is legal for a woman to have an abortion at any time of her pregnancy, for virtually any reason. Each year in the US we kill 1.37 million unborn children. That's 3,700 per day, or one baby killed every twenty-three seconds. The Guttmacher Institute, Planned Parenthood's research arm, estimates that one in three women in America under the age of forty-five has had an abortion.

Most of us have never seen an abortion, or even pictures of one.[4] But Abby Johnson has. Ms. Johnson worked as a director for a Planned Parenthood clinic in Texas for eight years. Until she witnessed an actual abortion for the first time. She explained in a television interview:

> It was actually an ultrasound-guided abortion procedure.... And my job was to hold the ultrasound probe on this woman's abdomen so that the physician could actually see the uterus on the ultrasound screen. And when I looked at the screen, I saw a baby.... I saw a full side profile. So I saw face to feet.... I saw the probe going into the woman's uterus. And at that moment, I saw the baby moving and trying to get away from the probe.... And I thought, "It's fighting for its life.... It's life, I mean, it's alive."... And then, all of a sudden, I mean, it was just over.... And I just saw the, I just saw the baby just literally, just crumble, and it was over.... I was thinking about my daughter, who's three, and I was thinking about the ultrasound I had of her, and I was thinking of just how perfect that ultrasound was when she was twelve

---

[3]Cited in Francis J. Beckwith, *Defending Life: A Moral and Legal Case against Abortion Choice* (New York: Cambridge University Press, 2007), 253n11.
[4]I encourage you to take the painful step of watching this four-minute video: www.abort73.com/HTML/I-A-4-video.html.

weeks in the womb. And I was just thinking, "What am I doing, What am I doing here?" . . . I had one hand on this woman's belly, and I was thinking, "There was life in here, and now there's not."

Abby Johnson quit her position and is now working as an advocate for life.

How Can We Persuade Others That Abortion Is Wrong?

Knowing *that* abortion is wrong is not enough. If we are to engage—and win—the argument, we need to be able to show *why* abortion is wrong and *how* that can be known.

Engaging in the public square on this issue can feel intimidating. Lots of smart folks argue against legally protecting the unborn, and they offer historical, legal, philosophical, political, moral, theological, and emotional objections. To get clarity you have to know how to cut through the fog.

Tommy the Toddler

As I mentioned earlier, science tells us that a new, whole, living human organism is formed at conception, the result of the union or fusion of an ovum and a sperm. But when was the last time somebody cited an embryology textbook during casual conversation? There's a more effective way to make the point. We can start with what everybody already knows. For example, there's no debate that a *toddler* is a human being with legal protections on his or her life. So instead of taking down a textbook, I recommend trotting out "Tommy the Toddler."[5] (You don't need to actually find a kid named Tommy; any name will do.)

There are only four differences between a toddler in the room and a baby in the womb. Tommy the Toddler is bigger, is more developmentally advanced, lives outside the womb, and is therefore more independent. But here's the crucial point: *none of these factors defines Tommy's value or who he is.*

Try thinking of these factors by the acronym SLED[6] and you'll see this even more clearly:

---

[5]For more, see Scott Klusendorf's excellent book, *The Case for Life: Equipping Christians to Engage the Culture* (Wheaton, IL: Crossway, 2009). See also the companion website, www.caseforlife.com.
[6]Ibid., following Stephen Schwartz, *The Moral Question of Abortion* (Chicago: Loyola University Press, 1990).

- *Size*. How big you are doesn't determine who you are.
- *Level of development*. How developed you are doesn't determine who you are.
- *Environment*. Where you are doesn't determine who you are.
- *Degree of dependency*. How dependent you are on another doesn't determine who you are.

We know all of this intuitively, don't we? Either you are human or you're not. It's not something that comes in degrees—like age or height or weight or beauty or intelligence. You can be older or younger, taller or shorter, fatter or thinner, prettier or uglier, smarter or dumber. But no amount of size or development or location or dependency makes you more human or less human than another.

So if a toddler and an unborn baby are equally human, then they should have the same basic human right to life. At the end of the day, any argument used to justify the killing of the unborn would equally apply to the killing of the already born.

Common Objections and Responses
Let's briefly look at a few objections that are commonly raised and try to apply what we've learned above.

I'm personally opposed to abortion—I'd never have one myself—but I can't impose my values on others. Would anyone honestly say, "I'm personally opposed to killing Tommy the Toddler, but other people disagree, and therefore I can't tell them what they can and can't do. It should be legal to kill Tommy even if I'd never do it myself." Only by presupposing that Tommy and the unborn are substantially different in kind can the argument succeed—but that's precisely the point that needs to be shown.

Perhaps you've seen the bumper sticker or T-shirt that says, "Against abortion? Don't have one." It's basically making the same point as above: if you oppose abortion, good for you—don't have one; but also don't tell other people what they can and can't do. I wonder why no one applies this to other issues:

- Against child abuse? Don't do it.
- Against slavery? Don't own one.
- Against rape? Don't do it.

The bumper stick sounds compelling at first—until you stop and think about it.

Women have a right to choose. Amen. Women have a right to choose a thousand different things: husbands, jobs, political candidates, and so on. The issue is not "choice" per se; it's the *object* of that choice that's being debated. What we need to do is to encourage people to finish that sentence. "Woman have a right to choose—what?" "An abortion." "An abortion of what?" We need to move beyond euphemism to get to the heart of the matter: does anyone have the right to choose to kill an unborn human being? If so, why not logically also have the right to kill an already-born human being?

The issue is too complex; smart people disagree, and I don't think I can say one way or the other whether abortion is the taking of a human life. A response like this is a confession of ignorance, and that is welcome. But if we don't know, shouldn't we err on the side of life? If I'm on a hunting trip and see something moving behind a tree and can't decide whether it's a fellow human being or a buck, should we conclude that shooting is thereby permissible? If there's even a chance that what's in the womb is an innocent human being, then we cannot support killing it.

A woman who conceives a baby via rape or incest should not have to be reminded of that terrible crime for the rest of her life. Rape and incest are unfathomably wicked acts of violence and violation that deserve our moral revulsion against the perpetrator and our deepest compassion for the victim. And children are indeed conceived in a very small percentage of rape and incest cases. But this child, painful though the circumstances may be, has done nothing wrong, and perpetuating another act of violence against an innocent victim is not the solution. The fact remains that *how* someone was conceived does not determine *who* he or she is. We know this intuitively, given that no one would advocate killing a child already born based upon the way he or she was conceived. We should also remember that there are many couples who are willing and eager to adopt children in such a situation.

Women who are poor should not be forced to give birth to a baby that is going to grow up in poverty, or who may end up unwanted. Let's say

Tommy the Toddler is poor and his parents are struggling to make ends meet. May we therefore eliminate Tommy? Of course not! Why not? Because Tommy is an innocent human being; even if he has a hard life or no one wants him, that doesn't justify killing him. So why would we say that a baby in the womb can be killed to prevent future suffering?

If abortion becomes illegal in the US, we will return to the days of unsterile, dangerous, back-alley abortions. This objection has become a powerful symbol for those supporting abortion choice, often represented simply by a picture of a coat hanger. Two things need to be kept in mind here: First, thirteen years before *Roe v. Wade* Planned Parenthood's medical director wrote in the *American Journal of Public Health* that 90 percent of illegal abortions were being performed by good, trained physicians, and that's why the death rate was so low. Second, the cofounder of the National Abortion Rights Action League—who later became pro-life—admitted that they used to exaggerate the deaths from illegal abortions, citing five thousand to ten thousand deaths per year. In fact, in 1972—the year before *Roe v. Wade*—the Centers for Disease Control reported only thirty-nine deaths from illegal abortions. Besides being built largely on a myth, this objection also begs the question. It assumes that the unborn aren't human. If the objector thought that the unborn *were* human beings, then the logic would be as follows: in order that some humans not die in their attempt to kill a fellow human being, the state should make the killing safe and legal. The logic fails.

Political Objections and Responses
A few years ago Douglas Groothuis, a philosophy professor at Denver Seminary, coined the term "fetus fatigue" to describe the growing evangelical lethargy on abortion. It is an apt description that hits close to home. One of the reasons some younger evangelicals have "fetus fatigue" is that they are uncomfortable with how politicized the abortion issue is, and they don't want to associate their evangelical faith with partisan politics. So it's worth pausing to look at a few objections along these lines.

Pro-life rhetoric is just a ploy to get evangelicals to support Republicans. There's some truth behind this objection. Many Republican politicians are pro-life not for passionately principled reasons but for electoral advantage. Furthermore, it's an unhealthy development that many people think that *Republican* and *evangelical* are essentially interchangeable terms—as if evangelicalism is a wholly owned subsidiary of the GOP. My own political philosophy tends to be conservative, but it would be a terrible thing for the glorious gospel of Christ and the countercultural kingdom of God to be domesticated to any political party.

But because the pro-life position is a part of the Republican platform, and because the Democrats by and large have rejected the pro-life position and have favored abortion choice as a legal and political litmus test, the perception is that to be pro-life—and to *advocate* for the pro-life position—is to endorse the entire Republican platform. And some of us would rather die than be labeled a religious right-winger. This, I think, is where we need to fight against the fear of man: even if our position is distorted, even if we are lumped in with people we disagree with, we must boldly stand up for the smallest, weakest, and voiceless members of the human race.

We shouldn't be one-issue voters. Many younger evangelicals are concerned that abortion is being portrayed as if it's the only ethical game in town, the only issue worth losing sleep over. Social justice, concern for the poor, environmental stewardship, foreign policy—surely these, too, are issues that demand the attention of Christians. Surely Christians should be engaged on more than one issue. Why should abortion be privileged above all else?

I want to *encourage* Christians to develop a biblically informed ethic on a wide range of issues, including those related to public policy and political philosophy. Yet at the same time I want to insist that abortion is in a category of its own. The question is not whether you should consider only one issue, but whether or not some issues are so significant that they have a determinative effect on how you view those who will lead and represent you. As John Piper has written:

> You have to decide what those issues are for you. What do you think disqualifies a person from holding public office? I believe that the endorsement of the right to kill unborn children disqualifies a person from any position of public office. It's simply the same as saying that

the endorsement of racism, fraud, or bribery would disqualify him—
except that child-killing is more serious than those.[7]

*Pro-life people only care about life in the womb and disregard it
outside the womb.* The claim here is that once babies are actually born,
there's little advocacy or attention for those in poverty or in abusive
situations. Such criticism was more popular several years ago and is
less so now as more evangelicals continue to rise up to serve young
mothers with children and to adopt children. But even if this is more
of a rhetorical flourish designed to score political points, we should still
take the question to heart.

If we want to see abortion eliminated in America, are we prepared
to act in response to an influx of unwanted children? Are our churches
being encouraged to follow the path of "pure religion," which involves
visiting orphans in their distress (James 1:27)? Are we following the
model of our Savior, who rebuked his confused disciples for their wrong
view of the kingdom, and who invited all the children to come to him
(Luke 18:16)? Are we mimicking the culture in simultaneously making comfort an idol and children an inconvenience? Or are we actively
seeking to cultivate a counterculture where life is prized and treasured,
and children—even those unwanted by others—are cared for and celebrated? Let us commit not only to being "pro-life," but to being "whole
life," working for the good of our neighbors and the dignity of human
life in all stages of life, from the womb to the tomb.[8]

What Then Shall We Do?

Abortion is not just an act of unjustified violence against a fellow human
being (in fact, the smallest, weakest, most defenseless among us). It is
an act of rebellious treason against our Maker (the greatest and most
powerful person in the universe). In one act we simultaneously destroy
the weak and dishonor the Almighty. If we take Jesus' double love
command seriously—to love God with all our heart, soul, and mind;

---

[7]John Piper, "One-Issue Politics, One-Issue Marriage, and the Humane Society" (January 1, 1995), available
online at www.desiringGod.org.
[8]Abortion is the most dramatic and pervasive attack upon the sanctity of human life in our day. But it
would be misleading to imply that it is the only attack upon the dignity and sanctity of human life. For a
good discussion of embryonic stem-cell research and how it can destroy living embryos, see Klusendorf,
A Case for Life, chapter 4.

and to love our neighbor as ourselves—we cannot be indifferent to abortion.

Scripture has something to say about our required response:

> *Rescue* those who are being taken away to death;
> *hold back* those who are stumbling to the slaughter. (Prov. 24:11)

What kind of death and slaughter is the proverb referring to? It doesn't say. What kind of rescuing and holding back are we required to perform? It doesn't say. It's a general principle with multiple applications.

What should such rescue look like in your own life? It may mean many different things, including the giving of time, talent, and treasure. It may mean public advocacy. It may mean counseling young women who are abused or confused and not sure what to do. It may mean opening your home for foster care or adoption. It may mean donating to a crisis pregnancy center that serves women considering abortion. It may mean a spiritual investment in secret that no one will see: fasting and prayer. But one thing is clear: inaction is not a biblically permissible option.

One first step is to consider praying this prayer to the Father in the name of Jesus and in the power of the Holy Spirit, confessing our helplessness but pleading for him to work:

We are not able in ourselves to win this battle.

We are not able to change hearts or minds.

We are not able to change worldviews and transform culture and save [1.37] million children.

We are not able to reform the judiciary or embolden the legislature or mobilize the slumbering population.

We are not able to heal the endless wounds of godless ideologies and their bloody deeds.

But, O God, you are able!

And we turn from reliance on ourselves to you.

And we cry out to you and plead that for the sake of your name, and
for the sake of your glory, and for the advancement of your saving
purpose in the world, and for the demonstration of your wisdom
and your power and your authority over all things, and for the sway
of your Truth and the relief of the poor and the helpless, act, O God.
This much we hunger for the revelation of your power. With all our
thinking and all our writing and all our doing, we pray and we fast.
Come. Manifest your glory.[9]

God is not calling you to sign up for a political agenda. He is not
calling you to care about only one issue. And since I don't know you,
and I don't know God's will for your life, I don't know *how* he wants to
use you to become an advocate and agent for truth on behalf of life.
But I do know one thing: he does not give us the option of sitting this
one out. May God give us the grace not to grow weary in doing good
(Gal. 6:9; 2 Thess. 3:13).

FOR FURTHER STUDY

Alcorn, Randy. *Pro-Life Answers to Pro-Choice Arguments*. Rev. ed.
    Sisters, OR: Multnomah, 2000.
Beckwith, Francis J. *Defending Life: A Moral and Legal Case against
    Abortion Choice*. New York: Cambridge University Press, 2007.
Klusendorf, Scott. *The Case for Life: Equipping Christians to Engage the
    Culture*. Wheaton, IL: Crossway, 2009.
See also the websites www.caseforlife.com and www.abort73.org.

---

[9]John Piper, *A Hunger for God* (Wheaton, IL: Crossway, 1997), 171.

Chapter 15

Gender Confusion and a Gospel-Shaped Counterculture

DENNY BURK

"I Kissed a Girl, and I Liked It" was the title of a song that dominated the pop music airwaves during the summer of 2008.[1] Even as the lyrics scandalized many listeners, adolescents across the nation embraced the rollicking tune as an anthem for a new generation. Katy Perry wrote and performed this ditty about a girl who goes to a party, has a little bit too much to drink, and decides to experiment with her sexuality. Perry narrates the experience in the first person and describes her ambivalence about the whole event, saying "It felt so wrong, it felt so right." She worries out loud about whether or not her boyfriend will be offended by the behavior. Apparently not declaring herself to be lesbian, she simply says that she did what she did "just to try it."

This essay is an expansion of an editorial written in 2009 for *The Journal of Biblical Manhood and Woman-hood*. See Denny Burk, "Editorial: A Collision of Worldviews and the Complementarian Response," *JBMW* 14, no. 1 (2009): 2–5.

[1] I first heard the story of Katy Perry in a sermon by Dr. Hershel York titled, "I Kissed a Girl and I Liked It." It was delivered in the chapel of the Southern Baptist Theological Seminary, February 26, 2009.

Almost anyone tuned in to pop culture at all in 2008 knew who Katy Perry was. What many people did not know is that Katy Perry was formerly known as Katy Hudson and that she was raised by parents who were copastors of a charismatic church in Southern California. The evangelical subculture knew her in 2001 as a sixteen-year-old rising star of Christian pop music. In that year, she released a self-titled album that included a song titled "Faith Won't Fail." In that song, she proclaims that no matter what comes her way—trials, tribulations, suffering, temptations, failures—her faith will never falter. The song was an unflinching declaration of her permanent commitment to Christ.

Obviously, the subject matter of Perry's music changed dramatically from 2001 to 2008. The question is, what happened? In the liner notes of her 2008 CD, she says, "I'm happy to know there's someone else out there bigger than me controlling things. I recognize my talents are God-given . . . and for this, I thank you." But in an interview with *Entertainment Weekly*, Perry sounds an uncertain note, saying:

> I'm not exactly the poster child for anything religious and I'm definitely not what I grew up in. But I got this Jesus tattoo on my wrist when I was 18 because I know that it's always going to be a part of me. When I'm playing, it's staring right back at me, saying, "Remember where you came from." After seeing some of the world, my brain has a little bit of a question mark about what I believe. I'm still searching.[2]

I tell this story not to run down Katy Perry. If anything, evangelicals would do well simply to pray for her. I tell her story because in many ways it is a parable of the gender confusion both in the wider culture and within some sectors of the evangelical subculture. There is for many still a "bit of a question mark" over what they believe about what it means to live as male or female.

Such confusion, however, is not merely the domain of pop-culture mavens. The Lesbian-Gay-Bisexual-Transgender/Queer Hermeneutics Section is a regular part of the program at the annual meeting of the Society of Biblical Literature (SBL).[3] The average layperson would likely

---

[2] Leah Greenblatt, "Katy Perry's Long Road: How the 'I Kissed a Girl' Songstress Finally Hit It Big," *Entertainment Weekly*, August 1, 2008.
[3] "The Society of Biblical Literature is the oldest and largest international scholarly membership organization in the field of biblical studies. Founded in 1880, the Society has grown to over 8,500 international members including teachers, students, religious leaders and individuals from all walks of life who share a mutual

be astonished by the existence of such a group, but it is no surprise at all to those who have been following recent developments in the academic study of Scripture. It merely follows a trend that has become standard fare for a whole sector of biblical and religious studies. Among other things, the LGBT/Queer Hermeneutics Section aims to explore "the intersections between queer readers and biblical interpretations."[4] In general, participants in this section support the normalization of homosexual orientation and practice in spite of what the Bible teaches. They seek to read the Bible as those who would "interrogate" traditions (biblical and otherwise) that they deem to be oppressive.[5]

I sat in for a portion of the LGBT/Queer Hermeneutics Section at the 2008 annual SBL meeting in Boston.[6] What I heard there was both startling and sobering. The presentation that I attended featured a female theologian from a small seminary in Atlanta. She delivered a paper on Paul's first letter to the Thessalonians—a presentation that included a variety of vulgar double entendres involving the text of Scripture and that would hardly be useful to repeat here. What was noteworthy, however, was her stance toward the apostle Paul, which was decidedly antagonistic. She complained that Paul's letters reveal an attempt not to undermine empire but to substitute one empire for another (the Christian empire in place of the Roman Empire). Thus Paul's politics were as flawed as Rome's. The apostle's flawed political views were no doubt informed by his flawed views of gender and his embrace of patriarchy.

This theology professor pulled out from this text one particularly important implication. She argued that the current American political system is also flawed because it is organized on the basis of a patriarchal definition of the family. The traditional definition of the family (with one man and one woman in covenanted union at the center) is a structure that oppressively limits who can have sex with whom. Thus

interest in the critical investigation of the Bible." "About SBL" [cited March 23, 2009]. Online: http://www.sbl-site.org/aboutus.aspx.
[4]"Meeting Program Units," accessed March 23, 2009, http://www.sbl-site.org/meetings/Congresses_Call ForPaperDetails.aspx?MeetingId=15&VolunteerUnitId=350.
[5]Peter Jones argues that the "queer hermeneutics" project works "in cooperation with feminist biblical interpretation." He describes it this way: "Queer readings merely seek to take one more step in the hermeneutics of suspicion and expose the 'heterosexist bias' of the Bible and Bible interpreters. Identifying exegesis as an exercise in social power, queer theorists reject the oppressive narrowness of the Bible's male/female binary vision and boldly generate textual meaning on the basis of the 'inner erotic power' of the gay interpreter." Peter Jones, "Androgyny: The Pagan Sexual Ideal," *Journal of the Evangelical Theological Society* 43 (2000): 444.
[6]The following story also appeared in Denny Burk, "Why Evangelicals Should Not Heed Brian McLaren: How the New Testament Requires Evangelicals to Render a Judgment on the Moral Status of Homosexuality," *Themelios* 35, no. 2 (2010): 215–16.

the traditional definition of the family has become an obstacle to liberty, and the American political system is flawed because it is organized around a notion of family that restricts individual liberty. In effect, she was arguing that a just society would not recognize any definition of the family that limits who can have sex with whom.

From pop-culture idols to professors publishing books on human sexuality, contemporary Western culture confronts Christians with a worldview in conflict with the Bible's teaching about manhood and womanhood. This worldview has implications for almost every sector of society, and Christians can hardly declare these matters outside the purview of their gospel concern. Indeed, in the midst of a gender-confused culture, Christians are needed more than ever to embody a gospel-shaped counterculture. In other words, Christians should be in the world, not of the world, for the sake of the world on questions of gender and sexuality.

Living in the world requires Christians to be like the men of Issachar, who understood the times and knew what the people of God were to do (1 Chron. 12:32). For it is, after all, the church that is the pillar and foundation of the truth (1 Tim. 3:15). It is the church that God has appointed to evangelize the world (Matt. 28:19–20). And it is the church that must see the gender-confused culture for what it is so that a gospel counterculture might flourish in it.

The Gender-Confused Culture
Whether it's the normalization of homosexuality or open antagonism toward the nuclear family, there are countless ways in which modern people express confusion about gender. Both secular and religious expressions of this confusion hold in common at least three characteristic beliefs.

Myth 1: Gender Is Something You Learn, Not Something You Are
What does it mean to say that gender is something you learn, not something you are? It means that "male and female" is not a description of humanity as God created it. Nor does "male and female" designate a universal, innate distinction among humans. Rather, the terms *male* and *female* comprise stereotypes that we absorb from our culture. Thus gender is merely a social construct. Except for obvious biological differences, all other social distinctions between males and females

are purely conventional. If there are any psychological distinctions between males and females, they are learned, and they can and need to be unlearned so that there can be a total equality between the sexes. This worldview is so entrenched in today's culture that one can hardly suggest that there might be innate differences between men and women without being dismissed as a sexist and a bigot.

The former president of Harvard University learned this the hard way after giving a speech in 2005 to a group of scientists.[7] In his speech, President Lawrence Summers tried to account for the fact that there is a "shortage of elite female scientists." He attributed the shortage in part to what may be "innate" differences between men and women. He shared an anecdote about his daughter to illustrate the point. In an effort at "gender-neutral parenting," he once set before his daughter two toy trucks. In almost no time at all, his daughter began referring to one of the trucks as "daddy truck" and the other as "baby truck." The event led him to ponder whether there was any truth to the notion that certain neurological inclinations might be connected to gender. For his daughter, at least, her playtime activity matched a feminine stereotype that she had not learned from him. In fact, he was conscientiously working against such stereotypes.

A firestorm of controversy ensued after Summers's remarks. One female biology professor from MIT who attended the speech said, "I felt I was going to be sick. My heart was pounding and my breath was shallow. I was extremely upset." She got up and walked out of the event. After that speech, Summers was impugned as a sexist and was reprimanded by the faculty of Harvard. He was on the outs with the faculty from then on and eventually had to resign. Summers found that there was a steep price to pay in our culture for suggesting that gender differences may be more than mere human convention.

Myth 2: Sex Is for Pleasure, Not for God

We might call this the Sheryl Crow philosophy on sexuality. If it makes you happy, it can't be that bad. This worldview affirms any and all attempts to get sexual pleasure so long as such attempts do not harm others. If it feels good and you're not hurting anyone, then how could

---

[7]Michael Dobbs, "Harvard Chief's Comments on Women Assailed," *Washington Post*, January 19, 2005, A02.

it possibly be wrong? The encroachment of this worldview explains to some extent why only 74 percent of evangelical "Christian" teenagers say that they believe in abstaining from sex before marriage,[8] and why 36 percent of white evangelical Protestants make their "sexual debut" shortly after turning sixteen.[9] This libertine worldview has had its influence on Christian mores with devastating effect.

This worldview also accounts for the normalization of homosexuality in the wider culture. If the goal of sex is pleasure, and if gender is merely something we learn, not something we are, then same-sex attraction is okay (so long as it's between consenting adults and you don't hurt anybody). This mind-set is not merely a feature of the secular culture, but there are even some "evangelical" Christians who are revisiting the issue. In his 2010 book *A New Kind of Christianity*, Brian McLaren seeks to redefine the Christian faith for a new day, and in one chapter in particular he argues that traditional evangelicals need to abandon their two-thousand-year-old ethic on homosexuality.[10] He pillories their beliefs as "fundasexuality," which he defines as a "reactive, combative brand of religious *fundamentalism* that preoccupies itself with *sexuality*. . . . It is a kind of *heterophobia*: the fear of people who are different."[11] All of this comes from a man who was selected by *Time* magazine in 2005 as one of the twenty-five most influential evangelicals.[12]

Likewise in the fall of 2008, Tony Jones, the former national coordinator of Emergent Village declared:

> Gay persons are fully human persons and should be afforded all of the cultural and ecclesial benefits that I am. . . . I now believe that GLBTQ can live lives in accord with biblical Christianity (at least as much as any of us can!) and that their monogamy can and should be sanctioned and blessed by church and state.[13]

[8]Margaret Talbot, "Red Sex, Blue Sex: Why Do So Many Evangelical Teen-agers Become Pregnant?," *The New Yorker*, November 3, 2008, accessed April 6, 2009, http://www.newyorker.com/reporting/2008/11/03/081103fa_fact_talbot?printable=true.

[9]Mark Regnurus, *Forbidden Fruit: Sex and Religion in the Lives of American Teenagers* (New York: Oxford University Press, 2007), 123, 127.

[10]For more on this, see Burk, "Why Evangelicals Should Not Heed Brian McLaren," 212–26.

[11]Brian McLaren, *A New Kind of Christianity: Ten Questions That Are Transforming the Faith* (New York: HarperOne, 2010), 174–75.

[12]"The 25 Most Influential Evangelicals in America," *Time*, February 7, 2005, 45. The article in *Time* reports that when McLaren was asked to comment on gay "marriage," he replied, "You know what, the thing that breaks my heart is that there's no way I can answer it without hurting someone on either side."

[13]Tony Jones, "How I Went from There to Here: Same Sex Marriage Blogalogue," November 19, 2008, http://blog.beliefnet.com/tonyjones/2008/11/same-sex-marriage-blogalogue-h.html.

Jones's pronouncement shows that at least some sectors of the evangelical movement are being shaped more by the culture than by the Bible. And that leads us to the third feature of this worldview.

Myth 3: Marriage Is Cultural, Not Universal

In other words, marriage is something that comes to us from human culture, not from God. It has a human origin, not a divine one. With God out of the picture, humans are free to make marriage into whatever they want. This final piece accounts for much of the confusion and conflict surrounding the so-called culture war on the issue of marriage in our society. Not only is this worldview evident in sky-high divorce rates and in legal outrages such as "no fault" divorce; it also undergirds the current push in our society for states to recognize same-sex "marriage." If gender is something you learn and not something you are, and if sex is for pleasure and not for God, then same-sex relationships should not be treated any differently than heterosexual relationships. Once a society divorces maleness and femaleness and their respective sexualities from their Creator's design, there is no moral basis for privileging heterosexual unions over any other kind of union (homosexual or otherwise). The heterosexual norm of Scripture is regarded merely as a social convention forced on the masses to limit who can have sex with whom—a convention that must be cast off in a just society. Already in some sectors of our society, to privilege the heterosexual ideal of Scripture over homosexual sin is to engage in bigotry and hatred.

The Gospel-Shaped Counterculture

A gospel-shaped counterculture must *proclaim* and *embody* the gospel of Jesus Christ in such a way that God's design for gender, sex, and marriage is clear and compelling. That will require both a countercultural *message* from churches and countercultural *living* among individuals and families in those churches. Let me briefly outline three counterpoints to the aforementioned worldview that must be at the core of an evangelical witness on these matters.

Truth 1: Gender Is Something You Are before You Learn Anything

The distinctions between male and female find their origin in God's good creation, not in what we learn from culture. That is not to deny that people absorb ideas about gender from the culture, some of which are quite unhelpful. But that fact should not be used to suppress the truth that in the beginning God differentiated humankind as male and female in his original creation design. Nor should it obscure the fact that God unambiguously called this differentiation "good" (Gen. 1:27, 31). The union of the first man and the first woman was the most healthy, wholesome, and satisfying union that has ever existed, and it involved a man leading his wife and a wife following the leadership of her husband (Genesis 2; 1 Cor. 11:3; Eph. 5:21–33). And though no other marriage will reach this perfection this side of glory, evangelicals need to strive with integrity toward this ideal. And they need to do so even when it grates against the ingrained mores of the wider culture.

Truth 2: Sex Is for God before There Is Any Lasting Pleasure

God is not a cosmic killjoy when it comes to sex. God intends for his creatures to enjoy this great gift for his sake. But when people treat pleasure as the *goal* of sex, not only do they end up in immorality, but they also end up with less pleasure. The only way to maximize the pleasure that God intends for our sexuality is to live in light of the truth that our bodies are not for immorality but for the Lord.

To this end the apostle Paul once confronted a group of sex addicts in the Corinthian church who had been visiting prostitutes (1 Cor. 6:15). Paul explained to them that the Holy Spirit dwells within the believer's body and thus makes the physical body of utmost importance in the present age. Because the Holy Spirit resides within the temple of the believer's body, the believer has no ultimate claim to ownership over his body, "For you were bought at a price" (1 Cor. 6:20, AT). In this way, Paul reminds us that we do not own ourselves. God owns us because he bought us at the cost of his Son and because God's Spirit dwells in us as a guarantee of final redemption. As Paul has argued elsewhere, the presence of the indwelling Spirit is the ground of our hope that God will resurrect our physical bodies from the grave (Rom. 8:11).

Thus what we do with our bodies vis-à-vis sex matters to God. That is why Paul concludes 1 Corinthians 6 with an emphatic imperative, "Therefore, glorify God with your body" (1 Cor. 6:20, AT). When Paul speaks of glorifying God with the body, he specifically has in mind how the body is used sexually. We might even paraphrase Paul to be saying in effect, "Glorify God with your sex." This means that the covenanted union of marriage is the most pleasurable and the most God-glorifying context in which to enjoy our sexuality. The Christian sexual ethic does not call people away from joy, but toward it.[14]

Truth 3: Marriage Is Universal, Not Cultural

The Bible teaches that marriage was designed and created by God, not by human culture. In fact, it is interesting to see how the New Testament proves this fact in light of the Old Testament. When Jesus and Paul set out new covenant marital norms, they do not appeal to polygamist kings like David or Solomon or to polygamist patriarchs like Abraham, Isaac, or Jacob. For all the importance these Old Testament figures have in the history of redemption, Jesus and Paul do not look to any of them as the paradigm for understanding marriage. Instead, Jesus and Paul look back without exception to the prefall monogamous union of Adam and Eve in Genesis 2 as the norm of human sexuality and marriage. "For this cause a man shall leave his father and his mother and shall cling to his wife; and they shall become one flesh" (Gen. 2:24, AT; cf. Matt. 19:5; Mark 10:7–8; 1 Cor. 6:16; Eph. 5:31).

The apostle Paul says that the great "mystery" of the Genesis 2 norm of marriage (one man and one woman in covenanted union) is that God intended it all along to be a shadow of a greater reality. From the garden of Eden forward, God intended marriage to be an enacted parable of another marriage: Christ's marriage to his church (Eph. 5:31–32). Thus, marriage is not defined by the culture, but by the gospel itself. Jesus loves his bride exclusively and self-sacrificially; and Jesus' bride is to respect and to submit to her husband. In this way, marriage is meant to portray a gospel archetype that is rooted in the eternal purposes of God. The gospel that shapes this archetype is also the hope for humanity and the context in which human happiness reaches its fullest potential. Here is the innermost meaning of marriage, and faithful churches will engage the culture with proclamation and living that bears out this truth.

Conclusion

The presentation that I heard at SBL reveals just how much the ambient culture stands in opposition to a Christian worldview. But the response of

---

[14]Denny Burk, "Discerning Corinthian Slogans through Paul's Use of the Diatribe in 1 Corinthians 6.12–20," *Bulletin for Biblical Research* 18, no. 1 (2008): 99–121.

Christians to that opposition should not be simply to curse the darkness and to retreat from culture. Rather, what the culture needs more than anything else is for the Christian church to engage it with proclamation and a wholesome living out of God's design for human sexuality and marriage. The Christian church should be a counterculture that images forth an alternative set of priorities. In other words, the church should be a place where marriage is held in high esteem both in living and in teaching and discipline, and the church should be that way because of its commitment to the gospel.

In the end, Katy Perry and papers delivered at SBL are not the main problem. They are but a symptom of a larger system set against Christ and his purposes in the world (1 John 2:15–17). And what our friends and neighbors need more than anything else is for Christians and their churches to set forth a faithful counterwitness on these issues. The messages coming from the culture are clear. The church's should be even more so.

FOR FURTHER STUDY

Gagnon, Robert A. J. *The Bible and Homosexual Practice: Texts and Hermeneutics.* Nashville: Abingdon, 2001.

Köstenberger, Andreas J., and David W. Jones. *God, Marriage, and Family: Rebuilding the Biblical Foundation*, 2nd ed. Wheaton, IL: Crossway, 2010.

Piper, John, and Wayne Grudem, eds. *Recovering Biblical Manhood and Womanhood: A Response to Evangelical Feminism.* Wheaton, IL: Crossway, 1991.

Chapter 16

The Local Church

Not Always Amazing, but Loved by Jesus

THABITI ANYABWILE

Today there rages an ongoing debate among Bible-believing Christians about the nature and the necessity of the local church. With the plethora of voices and opinions, it can be a confusing time to be a Christian.

One side has a tendency to emphasize the spiritual or universal church to the minimizing of the local church. The local church is something people can be committed to if they like, but they need not be. When those who hold this view commit to a local church, they often choose a church composed of people with like experiences and interests, affinity clusters based on common culture, age, and so on. Membership is already settled because every Christian is a member of the body of Christ. There are few if any further formal requirements, which are often seen as holdovers from a bygone era or borrowed from civic and social groups like Rotary and country clubs. Local church member-

An earlier form of this chapter was given as an address of the 2009 Worship God conference.

ship might even be viewed as divisive, contrary to a needed and good catholicity.[1]

On the other side are Christians who emphasize the visible, local nature of the church while minimizing the universal or spiritual church. Membership in the universal church is assumed, but must be demonstrated in the local church. Some add that New Testament Christianity makes little sense apart from an active practice of local church membership.

People arrive at these two poles in different ways. Some arrive there theologically. The way they read their Bibles and the assumptions they make push them to one pole or the other. Some arrive there out of experience. They have been hurt by the church in some way, or they have had a very positive time in a local church. Still others arrive there by evaluating the church. The church either does a good job and should be supported or fails in its mission and ought to be abandoned or completely rethought.[2]

Given such radically different conceptions of the local church and its importance, we must develop a biblical understanding of the church and our part in it. Does the local church and membership in it matter to us? If so, why and how? If not, why not? Does our approach to the local church square with the Scriptures? Do we see any connection between our personal spiritual life and our involvement in the local church?

In this chapter, I want to persuade you—if you're not already persuaded—that the local church and your active membership in it are essential to your spiritual well-being and that of the entire congregation. Two things prosper when we make the local church central to our understanding of the Christian life: our individual souls and the souls of other Christians in the congregation.

To put it another way, if membership in a healthy local church is not central to your understanding of the Christian life and your daily living, you are slowly, perhaps imperceptibly, starving, shriveling, and loveless—even if you don't feel it yet. The local church is that vitally important.

---

[1] By "catholic" or "catholicity," I'm referring to the recognition of the universal church, the church as it exists at all times and all places, across culture, denominations, and other boundaries.
[2] For an insightful, friendly, and witty overview of much of this debate, see Kevin DeYoung and Ted Kluck, *Why We Love the Church: In Praise of Institutions and Organized Religion* (Chicago: Moody, 2009).

What Is the Church?

Let's start with definitions. Much of the confusion and disagreement begins here. When we say "church," what do we mean?

People use the word *church* to refer to a number of things, including buildings where Christians gather and denominations in which individual churches cooperate. While we understand these common uses, the Bible never uses the term *church* in these ways.

The Greek word we translate "church" is *ekklēsia*, which means "called out ones" or "those called together." We might use the words "gathering" or "assembly" to express the same idea. A church is an assembly, a gathering, those called together. But it's not just any gathering or assembly.

Both the English word *church* and the Scottish *kirk* have their root in the Greek word *kyrios*, meaning "lord." If we put these two meanings together, "assembly" and "lord," we get a good definition of the word *church*. The church is "that assembly of people who belong to the Lord, who are gathered together for Him."[3] The gospel of Jesus Christ calls individuals out of the world of sin and death and into eternal light and life; it takes people who were no people and turns them into a special people for God (1 Pet. 2:9–10). That's what the church is. It's the assembly of people living under the rule of Jesus and committed to each other in the faith.

But the Bible speaks of the church in at least two ways. First, there are passages where all of God's people throughout all of time are in view (e.g., Eph. 1:22–33). This is the "universal" church. Second, the Bible speaks of the church as an assembly of believers in a particular place and time (e.g., Gal. 1:2). This is the "local" church. The vast majority of instances where the Bible mentions the church are references to local assemblies of believers living under the lordship of Jesus Christ.

We should not make the universal and local churches to be enemies, antagonists in the spiritual life. It's a great confusion to pit these two aspects of the church against one another. When we speak of the universal and local church, we're speaking of different perspectives on the same thing. There is only one church, but we may view her from varying altitudes—like one painter who paints a forest scene elevated on a cliff

---

[3]D. Martyn Lloyd-Jones, *Great Bible Doctrines*, vol. 3, *The Church and the Last Things* (Wheaton, IL: Crossway, 2003), 4–5.

while another paints from within the forest itself. The perspectives are different, but they are fundamentally the same subject. The glorious elevated vision of God's universal church is meant to deepen and enrich our participation in the visible, local aspect of the church.

Where Did the Church Come From?

Some Christians think of the church as just another institution. Beneath so much criticism of the church lurks this basic misconception of how the church came into being. We're not surprised, then, that so many people—even Christians—can be as negative toward the church as they are toward political parties or rival sports teams. But is the church just another human invention with all the warts of human social organizations?

The Bible holds out a very different view. First Corinthians 12:12–18 teaches that the church is a Trinitarian creation. Each member of the Godhead plays a specific and active part in crafting and assembling the body of Christ.

Jesus Christ, God the Son, incorporates us as members or parts of his own body. "For just as the body is one and has many members, and all the members of the body, though many, are one body, so it is with Christ" (1 Cor. 12:12). Jesus joins us to himself. When we are born again by the sovereign work of God's Spirit, we are united together with Jesus as part of the Lord's body. We become "members" or "parts" of Jesus' body.

When Christians speak of a "member" of a church, we're not borrowing language from secular organizations. The term *member* or *part* is uniquely christological. Its use is over two thousand years old—much older than civic organizations—and it reminds us of something about Jesus himself. The Lord Jesus is the only ruling Head of his body, the church, of which we are members or parts. So, our union with Christ through faith becomes the theological and spiritual reality that warrants our active participation in the local church. When we join a local church, we give visible testimony to our being joined to Jesus. We say, "I'm a part of Jesus' body."

God the Holy Spirit baptizes us into the body of Christ. This baptism is common to all Christians, whatever ethnic background or social standing. "In one Spirit we were all baptized into one body . . . and all were made to drink of one Spirit" (1 Cor. 12:13). I take this to mean that a gathering of all-white, khaki-wearing, Starbucks-drinking folks, if culturally homogeneous by design, may be called a lot of things, but should not be called a church. And whatever an all-black, traditional-gospel-singing, whoopin'-preacher assembly may be called, if it occurs by design, it is short of the Bible's vision of a Spirit-baptized church. Intentionally organizing a church where all the members are alike may be a great work of man, but it's not a great work of God. As one theologian put it, it may be little more than self-love spread over a wider area. But God creates a Spirit-wrought unity that eclipses ethnicity, gender, and class divisions (Gal. 3:26–28; Eph. 2:14–15; Col. 3:11).[4]

God the Father arranges members in the body—"each one of them, as he chose" (1 Cor. 12:18). The Father hand-selects each individual member—each individual Christian—and thoughtfully, skillfully, purposefully, assuredly places each member exactly where he would have him or her be. There is sovereignty, design, and wisdom on display in the Father's construction of the church.

It's as though before the foundation of the world God sees persons rushing over the brink of destruction, their souls singed with the fires of hell. He says, "I want that one. She will play a key role in what I'm building here." And the Son says, "Okay, Father, I'll rescue her for you." So, the Lord Jesus comes, takes our place, suffers our wrath on the cross, and with his own blood redeems us for eternal life and eternal love with the Father. God the Spirit replies, "All those you redeem, I'll seal and guarantee until all the pieces are purchased and the whole is complete." Each person in the Trinity does his part to create and secure the church.

At the very least, we must affirm from 1 Corinthians 12:12–18 three things about the church and our part in it. First, every individual in the church is handpicked by the Father to play a vital part in the body. So, we cannot think lightly of our assignment as a member. Second, our inclusion in the body is not only intentional but costly, purchased by

---

[4]In saying that our union with Christ and common baptism in the Spirit create a unity that transcends ethnic, gender, and social distinctions, I do not, therefore, mean that such distinctions no longer exist or that roles associated with gender no longer apply. The Bible teaches both our equality in Christ ("neither male nor female") and that God has appointed particular roles in the family and the church (Eph. 5:22–33; Col. 3:18–4:1; 1 Tim. 2:12; 3:2–5; 1 Pet. 3:1–7). For a more complete treatment of this subject in this volume, see the previous chapter, by Denny Burk, "Gender Confusion and a Gospel-Shaped Counterculture."

nothing less than the blood of Christ. Our membership is expensive. Third, we are now more than the sum of our parts. We are parts, but we are also one new body, all baptized into spiritual union with Christ. The church is far from being just another human agency. It's everything but that. And it is precious.

But we may have to address and adjust some wrong attitudes before we can love the church as the handiwork of God.

What's Our Attitude toward the Church?

Before we were Christians, perhaps we rejected God and his work because we blamed him for the problems of the world. If suffering exists, then God must not exist, or he is not really good. Or, since evil exists, God cannot be good or powerful enough to stop it. As sinful people, we hear the echoes of our fall as an indictment against God and not ourselves.

There is a Christian equivalent to those attitudes. We don't so much blame God anymore for evil or suffering. We've perhaps come to terms with God's goodness and power in the presence of evil and suffering. Now, however, many Christians blame and indict God for the church.

- The church doesn't do this correctly.
- The church has these problems.
- Christians are hypocrites.
- The church doesn't really have any life; I don't get anything out of it.

Sometimes these complaints have validity. But many of us are saying, though we'd never be so crass, "God, you don't know what you're doing. Look at this junk you've made! I've got a better way than this!"

In 1 Corinthians 12, we find this basic attitude expressed in two ways. There are those who say, "I have no need of you" (v. 21). They are the spiritual independents who think they can go it alone. They are Lone Ranger Christians happy to hang out with a Tonto or two, but their anthem is, "Me, kemosabe. No need the church."

And then there are the spiritually insignificant—those who believe they are unworthy of the church (vv. 15–16). These Christians think their insignificance an impediment to fruitful involvement in the church. "I don't have this or that prominent gift, so I can't take part. I can't sing solos, so there's nothing for me to do on Sundays. I can't teach or open the Scripture, so I have nothing to offer those needing counsel."

Both of these attitudes come from a heart that fails to see that the church is God's handiwork and that God has not failed to make something wonderful with his church—including our parts in it. These attitudes fail to recognize our deep need for the church.

Why Do We Need the Church?

We can agree that the gospel redeems individuals from sin and wrath to make of them a new community, a new people. And we can agree that this new people—the church—is the work of God. And yet, there may still be a lingering feeling that the church is not really all that necessary. To the extent that we think of the Christian life as solely a "personal relationship with Jesus" and not also a public and communal relationship with his people, to that extent we may act as though we don't need the church.

But being a part of the body of Christ means we have a part to play in serving others, and others have an important responsibility to serve us. In 1 Corinthians 12:12–27 and Ephesians 4:11–16, the Bible uses the body analogy to describe our spiritual union with Christ and with one another, and it does so in a way that actually emphasizes and heightens the importance of local church membership.

From these two texts, we discover at least three ways in which we absolutely need the local church.

We need the local church because we need to be cared for.

God designed the church to be a mutual-care society. The church is a place where people in need receive care from other people in need. The church is a co-op of caregiving.

First Corinthians 12:24b–27 reads:

> But God has so composed the body, giving greater honor to the part that lacked it, [25]that there may be no division in the body, but that the members may have the same care for one another. [26]If one member suffers, all suffer together; if one member is honored, all rejoice together.
> [27]Now you are the body of Christ and individually members of it.

God arranges us in the body of Christ to prevent division, and in preventing division to create interrelatedness where we "have equal concern for each other." Put another way, the antidote to division in the church is every member caring equally for every other member.

Do we think that this equal care and concern by each member for every other member is a low-level, passing concern? If God expends his Son's blood and individually and specifically arranges each member where he wishes, do we think our concern for one another could ever be a ho-hum, nonchalant concern? Or is it intended to be a great, intense, active, deep, growing love from the heart?

Verse 25 is a powerful vision statement and challenge for a local church. Can you imagine and grasp the grandeur of being a member in a local church where all commit to showing the same concern each member for the other?

Now we must ask ourselves, is it our personal goal to show this kind of impartial concern for every member of our local church? That's the difference between our being a church split up into hundreds of little cliques, where love and concern are shared with a tiny few, and our being the body of Christ, where no one slips through the cracks of our attention. A million church splits happen every Sunday. Not the kind of church splits that involve arguing and strife, but the quiet, subtle splits that come from partiality, party spirit, loving some but not others, and being comfortable with that state of affairs.

Paul's vision of the church caring for itself says two things about each of us. First, we need to be cared for, and we need a lot of people doing it. In fact, we need an entire church caring for us. Dare I say it: It takes a whole church to raise a Christian. Second, God made us to care for others. We're not only receptors but also conduits. It's as we give ourselves to caring for every other member, and others do the same, that in God's economy we're all watched over and nurtured.

Too many Christians lead spiritually isolated and vulnerable lives because they don't realize that the spiritual care we all need is to be found through committed, active membership in the local church. If that describes us, we must repent. We must repent for not caring for all the other members with the same concern, and we must repent for thinking that we don't need the care and nurture of other members. One is the sin of lovelessness, and the other is the sin of proud self-reliance.

We need the local church because we need to be equipped and matured in the Christian life (Eph. 4:11–16).

I remember conducting a membership interview with a very spirited young woman named Jennifer. She shared with me the work of God's grace in her life—how, right after she married, God opened her eyes to see her sin, her need, his grace, and his love. So, she and her husband joined a local church with great enthusiasm.

I asked her to describe her experience in that church. Her face fell into her lap in sadness. "I thought someone would teach me what it meant to be a Christian, how to live out the faith," she said. "But it was like they were happy we were Christians and then just left us in a corner somewhere."

I wonder how many have that experience in their local church families. I fear it's all too common. It's as though we've forgotten that the church exists to make disciples, not decisions. And disciple making requires equipping people for the Christian life and maturing them in the faith. This is one reason we need the church.

Ephesians 4:11–16 uses body imagery to describe how the local church produces spiritual maturity in its members. Paul tells us that the reason God gives the church gifted leaders is to prepare the saints for "the work of the ministry, for building up the body of Christ" (vv. 11–12). We need the church because we need this equipping and edification, this preparation and maturing.

Spiritual maturity is the opposite of infancy, where like children we're tossed around by every teaching and deceitful scheme (v. 14). Leaders equip and build up the body until we reach "mature manhood" (v. 13) or become "a full-grown man" (v. 13, ESV mg.) God intends for this equipping work to go on until we reach "the measure of the stature of the fullness of Christ" (v. 13) until we "grow up in every way into him who is the head, into Christ" (v. 15). And this is a community project. The entire church must grow up into the Head, into Christ, "from whom the whole body, joined and held together by every joint with which it is equipped, when each part is working properly, makes the body grow so that it builds itself up in love" (v. 16).

God has no other plan for our discipleship besides the local church. In the words of John Stott, an "unchurched Christian" is a "grotesque anomaly." Stott contends, "The New Testament knows nothing of such a person. For the church lies at the very center of the eternal purpose of God. It is not a divine afterthought. It is not an accident of history. On the contrary, the church is God's new community."[5]

If you're disconnected from the body, you will not grow up into the Head. It's that simple. Kevin DeYoung and Ted Kluck have coined a wonderful term for describing the "grotesque anomaly" Stott rejects. They write, "If *decapitation*, from the Latin word *caput*, means to cut off the head, then it stands to reason that *decorpulation*, from the Latin word *corpus*, should refer to cutting off the body."[6] We now live in a Christian culture where many people want the Head but not the body. They want Christ but not the members of his body. They'd rather be "decorpulated."

But a decorpulated member—an amputated foot or hand or arm, that grotesque anomaly—does not grow. It does not mature. It does not have life. It decays and it dies. To be an active part of the body, to live and grow as God intends, we need the church.

We need the local church because we need God's love (John 13:34–35). Is there anyone living who does not need love? Of course not; we all need to know, experience, celebrate that wonderful and ineffable thing called love. While the world chases after love in all the wrong places, like Indiana Jones searching for lost treasure, Christians are told precisely where to regularly find God's love: "A new commandment I give to you, that you love one another: just as I have loved you, you also are to love one another. By this all people will know that you are my disciples, if you have love for one another" (John 13:34–35). We find Jesus' love when we love one another "as Christ loved us" (Eph. 5:1–2). We find the Savior's love in and through the love we share as his disciples.

Moreover, the world needs to know the love of God, too. The world perishes without knowing this love. The best way to be for the world's redemption is to be for the church, actively loving other Christians to such an extent that our love is obvious and distinctive in the eyes of the unredeemed. Our friends and relatives who are not Christians will know what Jesus' love is like as they watch the visible, practical, almost tangible, compelling love shared and spread in the family of God. That

---

[5]John Stott, *The Living Church: Convictions of a Lifelong Pastor* (Nottingham, UK: Inter-Varsity, 2007), 19.
[6]DeYoung and Kluck, *Why We Love the Church*, 13.

love will take both the form of encouragement and care and the form of gentle correction and restorative discipline.

What's more, sharing the love of God with our fellow members in the church is not optional. It's mandatory. It's a command. Whether we love our brothers and sisters evidences whether we genuinely love God. The apostle John writes, "We love because he first loved us. If anyone says, 'I love God,' and hates his brother, he is a liar; for he who does not love his brother whom he has seen cannot love God whom he has not seen. And this commandment we have from him: whoever loves God must also love his brother" (1 John 4:19–21).

A person who does not love his brethren—all of them—does not love God. But a man who loves God loves the church and is loved by the church with the love of God.

Conclusion

The church is God's marvelous handiwork demonstrating his manifold wisdom to the universe (Eph. 3:10). Whatever her limitations and weakness, she is still gloriously more wonderful than any alternatives we can imagine.

And we desperately need the church for love, for maturity and preparedness, for spiritual care. It is arrogant, rebellious, self-reliant, God-indicting pride to conclude that the church is an optional extra to the Christian life. We need everything God designs for us. Everything. To reject what God designs for his glory and our good is spiritual suicide. To reject the church is to take your own spiritual life.

Don't do it. Make the church central to your life, and live as the Lord intends, in the covenant community and love of his people.

FOR FURTHER STUDY

Clowney, Edmund P. *The Church.* Downers Grove, IL: InterVarsity, 1995.

Dever, Mark. *What Is a Healthy Church?* Wheaton, IL: Crossway, 2005.

DeYoung, Kevin, and Ted Kluck. *Why We Love the Church: In Praise of Institutions and Organized Religion.* Chicago: Moody, 2009.

Harris, Joshua. *Stop Dating the Church: Fall in Love with the Family of God.* Sisters, OR: Multnomah, 2004.

Chapter 17

Worship

It's a Big Deal

TULLIAN TCHIVIDJIAN

At sixteen I dropped out of high school.[1] And because my lifestyle had become so disruptive to the rest of the household (I'm the middle of seven children), my grieving parents had no choice but to kick me out of the house.

Having successfully freed myself from the constraints of teachers and parents, I could now live every young guy's dream. No one to look over my shoulder, no one to breathe down my neck, no one to tell me what I could and couldn't do. I was finally free—or so I thought.

My newfound freedom had me chasing the things of this world harder than most others my age. I sought acceptance, affection, meaning, and respect behind every worldly tree and under every worldly rock. The siren song of our culture promised me that by pursuing the

---

[1] This personal story is adapted from *Unfashionable: Making a Difference in the World by Being Different*, by Tullian Tchividjian, copyright © 2009 by William Graham Tullian Tchividjian. Used by permission of WaterBrook Multnomah, an imprint of the Crown Publishing Group, a division of Random House, Inc.

right people, places, and things, I'd find the satisfaction, security, and significance I craved. If I could look, act, and talk a certain way, my deep itch to matter would finally get scratched.

But it didn't work out that way. The more I pursued those things, the more lost I felt. The more I drank from the well of worldly acceptance, the thirstier I became. The faster I ran toward godless pleasure, the further I felt from true fulfillment. The more I pursued freedom, the more enslaved I became. At twenty-one I found myself painfully realizing that the world hadn't satisfied me the way it promised, the way I'd anticipated. The world's message and methods had, in fact, hung me out to dry.

I felt betrayed. Lied to. I desperately longed for something—Someone—out of this world.

One morning I woke up with an aching head and a sudden, stark awareness of my empty heart. Having returned to my apartment after another night of hard partying on Miami's South Beach, I'd passed out with all my clothes on. Hours later, as I stirred to a vacant, painful alertness, I realized it was Sunday morning. I was so broken and longing for something transcendent, for something higher than anything this world has to offer, that I decided to go to church. I didn't even change my clothes. I jumped up and stumbled out the door.

I arrived late and found my way to the only seats still available, in the balcony. It wasn't long before I realized how different everything was in this place. I immediately sensed the distinctiveness of God. Through both the music and the message, it was clear that God, not I, was the guest of honor there. Having suffered the bankruptcy of our society's emphasis on "self-salvation," I was remarkably refreshed to discover a place that joyfully celebrated our inability to save ourselves.

Inescapable Presence

I didn't understand everything the preacher said that morning, and I didn't like all the songs that were sung. But the style of the service became a nonissue as I encountered something I couldn't escape, something more joltingly powerful than anything I'd ever experienced, something that went above and beyond typical externals. Through song, sermon, and sacrament, the transcendent presence of God punctured the roof, leaving me—like Isaiah when he entered the temple—awestruck and undone.

I was on the receiving end of something infinitely larger than grand impressions of human talent. God and his glorious gospel were on full display. It was God, not the preacher or the musicians, who was being lifted up for all to see. It wasn't some carefully orchestrated performance (which, believe me, I would have seen right through). Rather, I was observing the people of God being wrecked afresh by God's good-news announcement that in the person of Jesus, he had done for them what they could never do for themselves. In and through the praising, praying, and preaching, the mighty acts of God in bringing salvation to our broken world were recited and rehearsed.

I was a "seeker" being reached, not by a man-centered, works-filled, trendy show, but by a God-centered, gospel-fueled, transcendent atmosphere. I was experiencing what Dr. Ed Clowney, the late president of Westminster Theological Seminary, used to call "doxological evangelism." It was, quite literally, out of this world.

I tell you this personal story as a way to illustrate just how important a church's corporate worship is—God used a worship service to save my life.

I view my story as proof that the way a church worships is a big deal. Paul made it clear to the Corinthian church that worship is not to be taken lightly—that when Christians are gathered by God to worship, they should worship in such a way that non-Christians in their midst leave saying, "God is really among you."

A church's worship, in other words, ought to be God-centered and gospel-fueled.

By the Book

Contrary to what many modern people believe, we can't approach God any way we please. Trying to do so is extremely dangerous, as the Bible makes clear (see Cain, Nadab, and Abihu, for example). In the Bible, God provides us with commands, instructions, examples, and stories to illustrate how he wants us to worship him. Our worship, therefore, is to be regulated by God himself through his Word.

The often-misunderstood "regulative principle" of worship simply means we must worship by the Book—that everything we do in worship must be divinely approved.

During the Protestant Reformation, two views emerged regarding how *sola Scriptura* ought to be understood when it comes to worship practices. Martin Luther believed we may do anything we want in worship as long as the Bible doesn't say no—whatever is not prohibited is permitted. John Calvin believed we shouldn't do anything in worship unless the Bible says yes—only those elements that are appointed by God in Scripture are permissible.

Because Scripture is the all-sufficient word of God, I believe with Calvin that everything we do in worship must be prescribed in the Bible. But the *application* of the regulative principle does not need to be narrow, as is often assumed. Because the Bible instructs us with its *methods* as much as with its *material*, our scope regarding what God commands in worship is deep and wide. For instance, recognizing the various literary genres of Scripture—history, story, poetry, prophecy, epistle, and so on—should demonstrate that stylistic diversity is something God himself employs and enjoys. Therefore, shouldn't stylistic diversity be something we celebrate in worship? In other words, God is telling us something about how to worship him by the *way* he communicates, not just *what* he communicates—both style and substance are prescriptive. Understood this way, the regulative principle allows for much more variety in worship than some have concluded.

While the entire Bible ought to inform and regulate our approach to God, Isaiah 6:1–8 especially captures what it looks like to worship God in spirit and in truth. For me, this passage has become a "go to" passage on worship, and I believe our corporate worship experience ought to mirror the experience we see here.

Our Worship Is to Be God-Centered

In the opening verses of Isaiah 6, what the prophet encounters first in the house of God is the glory of God: "I saw the Lord sitting upon a throne, high and lifted up; and the train of his robe filled the temple" (v. 1). It doesn't first say he encountered well-dressed people or hot coffee or influential power brokers or a booming sound system or a great organ. What he caught sight of first was God's glory.

There's a growing trend in some churches to offer door prizes to any returning visitor. One church visited recently by a friend of mine promised him a ten-dollar Starbucks gift card if he came back the following week.

Isaiah shows us the door prize that awaited him when he walked into the house of God—the uncomfortable, wrecking presence of God's glory: "Woe is me!" (v. 5).

In the Bible, the glory of God refers to God's "heaviness," his powerful presence. It's God's prevailing excellence on display. The glory of God is the "augustness" of God—an old term conveying his awe-inspiring majesty. In fact, one reason why Christians in the Roman Empire were persecuted is that they refused to use the word *august* for the emperor— such a description belonged to God alone, they said. They understood that there is a transcendent majesty unique to God. This high and lifted- up greatness of God is what Isaiah encountered—a God who is majesti- cally and brilliantly in command.

All this means we ought to come to worship expecting first and foremost to see God. We come to encounter his glory, to be awestruck by his majesty. A worship service isn't the place to showcase human talent but the place for God to showcase his divine treasure. We gather not to be impressed by one another—how we sound, what we wear, who we are—but to be impressed by God and his mighty acts of salvation. We come to sing of who he is and what he's done. We come to hear his voice resounding in and through his Word. We come to feel the grief of our sin so that we can taste the glory of his salvation. We gather to be magnificently defeated, flattened, and shrunk by the power and might of the living God.

This is in stark contrast to the world's insistence that the bigger we get and the better we feel about ourselves, the freer we become. That's why many worship services have been reduced to little more than motivational, self-help seminars filled with "you can do it" songs and sermons. But what we find in the gospel is just the opposite. The gospel is good news for losers, not winners. It's for those who long to be freed from the slavery of believing that all of their significance, meaning, purpose, and security depend on their ability to "become a better you." The gospel tells us that weakness precedes usefulness—that, in fact, the smaller you get, the freer you will be. As G. K. Chesterton wrote, "How much larger your life would be if your self could become smaller in it."[2] Nothing makes you more aware of your smallness and life's potential bigness than encountering the glory of God in worship. Corporate worship services in the church today desperately need to recover a sense of God's magnitude!

Not long ago I was in desperate need for God to liberate me from the slavish pressure to perform by reminding me of my smallness and his bigness. And since God has used the preaching of the late Dr. D. Martyn Lloyd-Jones throughout my Christian life to bring great perspective and reorientation to my troubled soul, I went back to one of his 1959 sermons on revival. With great unction, Lloyd-Jones delivered the reminder I craved:

> Our supreme need, our only need, is to know God, the living God, and the power of his might. We need nothing else. It is just that, the power of the living God, to know that the living God is among us and that nothing else matters. . . . I say, forget everything else. Forget *every*thing else. We need to realize the presence of the living God amongst us. Let everything else be silent. This is no time for minor differences. We all need to know the touch of the power of the living God.[3]

"The touch of the power of the living God"—that's what Isaiah experienced. He was freed by realizing that God is big and he was small—that God was God and he was not. And this is what God intends for us to experience when he gathers us in worship. Isaiah didn't leave the temple thinking, "What a great angelic choir" or "What a great temple." He left thinking, "What a great God."

As pastor of Coral Ridge Presbyterian Church, I'll be the first to admit that we are blessed with great music and a world-class facility. But, as I often remind our church, if people don't leave our church thinking first, "What a great God," then our music and facilities mean nothing. Whatever else we may see in worship, we must see God first and best.

---

[2]G. K. Chesterton, *Orthodoxy* (London: John Lane, 1909), 34–35.
[3]D. Martyn Lloyd-Jones, *Revival* (Wheaton, IL: Crossway, 1987), 127–28.

A Full Encounter

Isaiah 6:4 tells us that along with this encounter the prophet had with God's glory, the temple's foundation shook. For us, it's the glory of God alone that can shake the foundations of our life so that we become more aware of his presence and more dependent on his power. A God-centered, gospel-fueled worship service is a service that leads people to conclude that Jesus plus nothing equals everything and everything minus Jesus equals nothing.

All too common today are polarizing tendencies in worship that fail to reach the whole person. For instance, in some churches, how a Christian thinks is important, but not how a Christian feels. Worship in these churches is primarily geared to informing the mind. But when it comes to feeling God, they remain stoic. These churches turn worship into a classroom for learning.

Other churches do well at feeling in worship but do poorly at thinking. In these churches, worship is primarily geared to engaging the emotions—thinking is far less important than feeling. These churches turn worship into a therapist's couch for emotional highs and healing.

Still other churches conclude that neither our thoughts nor our feelings toward God are as important as what we *do* for God. In these churches, worship is primarily geared to the will—the goal of worship is to get congregants to give more, serve more, or take some other action.

But notice Isaiah's multifaceted response to his encounter with the glory of God. He responds intellectually to God's presence—there's no question in Isaiah's *mind* that God is who he is: "My eyes have seen the King, the LORD of hosts!" (v. 5). In the same verse, there's also an emotional response—he feels the presence of God in his *heart*: "I'm undone." Finally, there's a volitional response—having encountered the living God, Isaiah is ready and *willing* to do God's will with his entire being: "Here am I! send me" (v. 8).

We, too, ought to experience God with the totality of our being in worship. Worship services ought to inform the mind intellectually, engage the heart emotionally, and bend the will volitionally. God wants thoughtful worshippers who believe, emotional worshippers who behold, and obedient worshippers who behave. God-centered worship produces people who think deeply about God, feel passionately for God, and live urgently in response to God. Therefore, when we meet God in worship, we should expect a combination of gravity and gladness, depth and delight, doctrine and devotion, precept and passion, truth and love.

Not only here in Isaiah, but throughout Scripture we see people in the presence of God weeping over their sin, celebrating their forgiveness, and exalting in God's bigness. People feel their desperation, cry out for deliverance, celebrate their pardon—and in many other ways respond in fullness to the thick presence of God's glory.

Our Worship Is to Be Gospel-Fueled

Isaiah's many-sided response to God's revealed glory is anchored ultimately in the multifaceted beauty of the gospel—the good news that in the person of Jesus Christ, God came down to recover and repair a world lost and broken by sin.

Contrary to what many Christians have concluded, the Bible does not tell two stories: one about Israel in the Old Testament, another about the church in the New Testament. The Bible tells one story and points to one figure. It narrates how God rescues his world that we wrecked, and exalts Christ as the one who accomplishes the rescue. In the Old Testament God revealed himself through types and shadows, promises and prophecies. In the New Testament God reveals himself in Christ, who is the substance of every shadow and the fulfillment of every promise and prophecy. The Old Testament *predicts* God's Rescuer; the New Testament *presents* God's Rescuer. Therefore, the whole Bible—both the Old and New Testaments—is all about God's Rescuer. A gospel-fueled worship service tells and retells this unified story—highlighting the story's infallible Hero—through song, sermon, and sacrament.

If our worship is genuinely gospel-fueled, then we, like Isaiah, will go through a range of expressions when we're together. The experience of the worshipper should be multifaceted because God's story—the gospel—is multifaceted. Our worship should have many parts because the gospel has many parts and is neither one-dimensional nor stagnant.

The cradle, the cross, and the crown of God's Rescuer are to be rehearsed and in some way felt. For instance, the gospel takes us from a sense of gratitude when pondering the *incarnation*, to a sense of grief when pondering the *crucifixion*, and to a sense of glory when pondering the *resurrection*.

God's story takes us low and brings us high, and gospel-fueled worship services should in some way reflect those ups and downs in their style and substance, context and content. With our Hero, we should experience something of the darkness of the garden of Gethsemane *and* the daylight of the garden tomb. We cannot ponder the cross without feeling our sin. And we cannot ponder the empty tomb without feeling our salvation.

Our worship should include moments of praise, lament, and thanksgiving—or, in the words of Old Testament scholar Walter Brueggemann, "orientation, disorientation, and reorientation."[4] It should involve a sense of guilt *and* gratitude, desperation *and* deliverance, somber contemplation *and* joyous celebration. It should contain silence *and* singing, confession *and* cleansing, commendation of God *and* conviction from God.

The Gospel, Always for All

A gospel-fueled worship service is a service where God serves the gospel to sinners in need of rescue—and that includes both Christians and non-Christians. Churches for years have struggled over whether their worship services ought to be geared toward Christians (to encourage and strengthen them) or non-Christians (to appeal to and win them). But that debate and the struggle over it are misguided. We're asking the wrong questions and making the wrong assumptions.

Like many others, I once assumed the gospel was simply what non-Christians must believe in order to be saved, and after they believe it, they advance to deeper theological waters. But, as Tim Keller explains, the gospel isn't simply the ABCs of Christianity, but the A through Z. The gospel doesn't just ignite the Christian life; it's the fuel that keeps Christians going and growing every day. Once God rescues sinners, his plan isn't to steer them beyond the gospel but to move them more deeply into it. After all, the only antidote to sin is the gospel—and since Christians remain sinners even after they're converted, the gospel must be the medicine a Christian takes every day. Since we never leave off sinning, we can never leave the gospel.

To describe his condition as a Christian, Martin Luther employed the phrase *simul justus et peccator*—"simultaneously justified and sinful." Luther understood that while he'd already been saved from sin's penalty, he was in daily need of salvation from sin's power.

---

[4]See Walter Brueggemann, *The Message of the Psalms* (Minneapolis: Augsburg, 1984).

Paul calls the gospel "the power of God for salvation" (Rom. 1:16), and contrary to what some have concluded, he didn't simply mean the "power of God for conversion." The gospel remains the power of God unto salvation until we are glorified because we're all "partly unbelievers until we die," as Calvin put it. We need God's rescue every day and in every way.

In his book *The Gospel for Real Life*, Jerry Bridges picks up on this theme—that Christians need the gospel just as much as non-Christians—by explaining how the spiritual poverty in so much of our Christian experience is the result of an inadequate understanding of the gospel's depths. The answer isn't to try harder in the Christian life but to comprehend more fully and clearly Christ's incredible work on behalf of sinners and then to live in a more vital awareness of that grace day by day. Our main problem in the Christian life, in other words, is not that we don't try hard enough to be good, but that we haven't thought out the deep implications of the gospel and applied its powerful reality to all parts of our life. Real spiritual growth happens as we continually rediscover the gospel.

The same dynamic explains the primary purpose of corporate worship: to rediscover the mighty acts of God in Christ's coming to do for us what we could never do for ourselves. We gather in worship to celebrate God's grip on us, not our grip on God.

A gospel-fueled worship service is a service where God's rescue in Christ is unveiled and unpacked through song, sermon, and sacrament in such a way that it results in the exposure of both the idols of our culture and the idols of our hearts. The faithful exposition of our true Savior in every element of worship will painfully, but liberatingly, reveal the subtle ways in which we as individuals and as a culture depend on lesser things than Jesus to provide the security, acceptance, protection, affection, meaning, and satisfaction that only Christ can supply.

The praising, praying, and preaching in such a service should constantly show just how relevant and necessary Jesus is. They must serve the gospel to sinners by telling and retelling the story that while we are all great sinners, Christ is a great Savior.

Rehearsal for the Future

When we gather together for worship, we ought to come reaching up, starved for God, ready to feast together on the good news that, in the person of Jesus Christ, God has descended to us because we could never ascend to him. Feasting on God's gospel together through prayer and preaching, sacrament and singing, provides us with the faith, hope, and love we need to be good-news people in a bad-news world.

And we'll not only look back to what Christ has done; we'll look ahead to what Christ will do. We'll remember the past, but also rehearse the future. For when Christ comes again, the process of reversing the curse of sin and recreating all things will be complete (1 Cor. 15:51–58). The peace on earth that the angels announced the night Christ was born will become a universal actuality. God's cosmic rescue mission will be complete. The fraying fabric of our fallen world will be fully and perfectly rewoven. Everything and everyone "in Christ" will live in perfect harmony. *Shalom* will rule.

Isaiah 11:6–9 pictures it this way:

> The wolf shall dwell with the lamb,
>   and the leopard shall lie down with the young goat,
> and the calf and the lion and the fattened calf together;
>   and a little child shall lead them.
> The cow and the bear shall graze;
>   their young shall lie down together;
>   and the lion shall eat straw like the ox.
> The nursing child shall play over the hole of the cobra,
>   and the weaned child shall put his hand on the adder's den.
> They shall not hurt or destroy
>   in all my holy mountain;
> for the earth shall be full of the knowledge of the LORD
>   as the waters cover the sea.

For those who've found forgiveness of sins in Christ, there will one day be no more sickness, no more death, no more tears, no more division, no more tension. The pardoned children of God will work and worship in a perfectly renewed earth without the interference of sin. We who believe the gospel will enjoy sinless hearts and minds along with disease-free bodies. All that causes us pain and discomfort will be destroyed, and we will live forever.

Until that day comes, we gather for worship not to escape the world's present reality, but to be reminded by God that this world isn't all there is. The Bible makes it clear that even though we enjoy one day in seven to rest from our earthly activities, there is still a rest that remains to be fulfilled (Heb. 4:9). It is the final rest when every day will be a holy day and a heavenly day.

Until the glory of the Lord fills the earth as the waters fill the sea, until the kingdom of this world becomes the kingdom of our Lord and his Christ, not every day is holy. This is why we need Sunday—to give us a one-day taste of our future destiny so we can persevere through the rest of the week.

When we worship together, we enjoy and experience an intrusion of heaven into the real world—the end-time into time. It's the future being brought into the present. In our worship together, we enter into the very outskirts of heaven and get a weekly taste of what will eventually be permanent and eternal.

I look forward to corporate worship more than any other time of the week because when I am worshipping *together* with other sinner-saints, my anticipation for the Great Gathering on the last day intensifies. What we do *together* in worship is nothing less than a glorious rehearsal of what we will experience when the "ultimate assembly" is fully and finally brought together by Christ. Our weekly worship is a foretaste of that day when our feasting will be permanent and our fasting will be over—when we will finally be able "to enjoy what is most enjoyable with unbounded energy and passion forever."[5]

For Further Study

Carson, D. A., ed. *Worship by the Book.* Grand Rapids: Zondervan, 2002.

Chapell, Bryan. *Christ-Centered Worship: Letting the Gospel Shape Our Practice.* Grand Rapids: Baker, 2009.

Frame, John M. *Worship in Spirit and Truth.* Phillipsburg, NJ: P&R, 1996.

---

[5]John Piper, *The Pleasures of God* (Portland, OR: Multnomah, 1991), 24.

Chapter 18

Missions

The Worship of Jesus and the Joy of All Peoples

DAVID MATHIS

Missions is about the worship of Jesus. The goal of missions is the global worship of Jesus by his redeemed people from every tribe, tongue, and nation. The outcome of missions is all peoples delighting to praise Jesus. And the motivation for missions is the enjoyment that his people have in him. Missions aims at, brings about, and is fueled by the worship of Jesus.

Another way to say it is that missions is about Jesus' global glory. From beginning to end—in target, effect, and impetus—missions centers on the worldwide fame of Jesus in the praises of his diverse peoples from every tribe, tongue, and nation. What's at stake in missions is the universal honor of the Father in the global glory of his Son in the joy of all the peoples.

What Is Missions?
Rooted in the Latin *mitto* (meaning "send"), *missions* is the half-millennium-old term signifying the *sending* of Jesus' followers into

his global harvest of all peoples. For nearly three hundred years, the term *missions* has been used in particular for world evangelization, for pioneering the gospel among the peoples to whom it has yet to advance.

Two passages in the Gospel of Matthew get to the heart of missions. Jesus says to his disciples in Matthew 9:37–38, "The harvest is plentiful, but the laborers are few; therefore pray earnestly to the Lord of the harvest to *send out* laborers into his harvest." Missions means *sending out* workers into the global harvest.

A second passage is Jesus' sending out of his disciples in Matthew 28:18–20, the epic-making summons called the Great Commission. Here Jesus' main command "disciple all nations" follows the charge to "go"—to be *sent out*. Sending out and going are two sides of the same coin. Jesus and his established church send out, and those who go are "the sent ones," or "missionaries." So *missions* is the church's sending out of missionaries (the sent ones) to pioneer the church among peoples who otherwise have no access to the gospel.

Jesus' Commission

Perhaps the best way forward in this chapter is to walk through this Great Commission, which gets at the heart of the missionary enterprise.

> And Jesus came and said to [his disciples], "All authority in heaven and on earth has been given to me. Go therefore and make disciples of all nations, baptizing them in the name of the Father and of the Son and of the Holy Spirit, teaching them to observe all that I have commanded you. And behold, I am with you always, to the end of the age."

Jesus Has All Authority (Matt. 28:18)

First, Jesus says that "all authority" in heaven and on earth has been given to him. From all eternity, the divine Son had "all authority" as God, but now, by virtue of his taking our humanity and accomplishing our redemption, the Son comes into "all authority" as human, as the God-man. He has fulfilled the destiny of humanity (Ps. 8:3–8; Heb. 2:5–10) and rules the globe with the very sovereignty of God, ensuring the success of his global mission.

He will not be thwarted in carrying out his promise, "I will build my church" (Matt. 16:18). The God-man most certainly will make good on his pledge that his gospel "will be proclaimed throughout the whole world as a testimony to all nations, and then the end will come" (Matt. 24:14). He guarantees the fulfillment of Habakkuk 2:14, that

> the earth will be filled
>> with the knowledge of the glory of the LORD
>> as the waters cover the sea.

Is It Megalomania—or Love?

Is it megalomania for Jesus to use "all authority" to make himself the most famous person in the universe? If knowing Jesus were anything less than the greatest of enjoyments, then his pursuit would be unloving. But he *is* the most valuable reality in the universe. Knowing him is "the surpassing worth" that makes it gain to count all else loss (Phil. 3:8). Therefore, it is profoundly loving for Jesus to exalt himself. He cannot love the nations without putting himself on display because it is he alone who truly satisfies the human soul. This makes God's heart for God the deepest foundation for missions.

So the bedrock of the Great Commission is most ultimately not God's heart for the nations—amazing as that is—but God's heart for God. And God's pursuit of his glory makes the cause of missions unstoppable. As surely as he will not give his glory to another (Isa. 48:11), so the commission will not fail. His honor is at stake. When we pursue the glory of God in the worship of Jesus in the global cause of missions, we get on board with a mission that will not abort. Jesus will build his church. The task of missions will finish.

Disciple All Nations (Matt. 28:19)

In view of his unmatched authority, Jesus draws out an implication for his followers—one of the most important *therefores* in the history of the world: "Go *therefore* and make disciples of all nations."

The two commands translated "go" and "disciple all nations" work together as one charge in Matthew's original Greek. A literal translation would be "having gone, disciple all nations." The main emphasis falls on discipling, but the going is the necessary path. In order to engage in this worldwide task of discipling all nations, there must be going. Jesus does not promise that all nations will come to Jerusalem while his disciples continue to invest where they are. They will need to go. Oceans and borders must be crossed. Like Paul and Barnabas in Antioch, they will need to be "sent" out (Acts 13:3). There must be missionaries.

But even in our current global context, with unreached peoples clustering in cities where churches are already established, another kind of going must happen: learning a language and new culture and being sent out from ordinary, everyday life among people just like us. Even where geography isn't an issue, culture and language are. The Great Commission necessitates "goings" of all sorts.

Disciple *Is a Verb*

So if Jesus' charge to "disciple all nations" is the heart of the commission, what does he mean by this discipling? He does not mean the mere pursuit of conversion. That won't work with what follows: "baptizing them in the name of the Father and of the Son and of the Holy Spirit, teaching them to observe all that I have commanded you." Teaching the nations "to observe all that I have commanded you" is not the mere pursuit of conversion. And if discipling all nations doesn't mean simply classroom-information transfer, but "teaching to observe," what must it entail?

At least, it must entail spiritual maturity. And so this is how many well-meaning Christians today use the term *discipleship*—as a term for pursuing spiritual maturity. Being a "disciple," they say, means being a serious, rather than casual, follower of Jesus. "Discipleship programs" are designed for those intentionally seeking Christian growth, so it goes. Maybe. But something seems to be lacking here.

Jesus' Example

Within the context of Matthew's Gospel, is there not more to say? Does "disciple all nations" not call to mind how Jesus himself "discipled" his men? They were, after all, his "disciples." And when they heard him say, "disciple all nations," would they not think this discipleship is what he did with them—investing prolonged, real-life, day-in, day-out, intentional time with younger believers in order to bring them to maturity as well as model for them how to *disciple* others in the same way?

This sounds like what Paul is getting at in 2 Timothy 2:2, when he instructs his disciple Timothy, "What you have heard from me in the presence of many witnesses entrust to faithful men who will be able to teach others also." *Timothy, my disciple, disciple others to disciple others*. Four spiritual generations get explicit mention here: Paul, Timothy, "faithful men," and "others also"—with the implication that further generations are to follow.

Discipleship, seen in this light, entails not merely the pursuit of spiritual maturity but also the need for personal connection and substantial intentional investment of time, the kind of investment for which there must be *going* to accomplish. Jesus spent over three years with his twelve disciples. He called them to be discipled at the outset of his ministry (Matt. 4:19), and he gave them the lion's share of his life until his departure in Matthew 28. He invested his life in his men. It is amazing to track in the Gospels how much Jesus gave of himself to his disciples. The crowds pursued him, but he pursued his disciples. He was willing to bless the masses, but he invested in the few.

All Nations

But if "disciple" refers not merely to conversion but also to spiritual maturity, even the personal investment of the discipler's life, what about "all nations"? Here Jesus has struck a note that is part of a biblical symphony spanning the Scriptures from Genesis to Revelation.

From creation, God has been concerned with "all the nations." The genealogies of Genesis trace the origin of all nations to Adam through Noah and his sons (Genesis 10).[1] And with his blessing of all nations in mind, God called a moon-worshipper named Abram to "go from your country . . . to the land that I will show you. And I will make of you a great nation . . . and in you all the families of the earth shall be blessed" (Gen. 12:1–3). Note the word *all*.

From Abram (renamed Abraham, "the father of a multitude of nations," in Gen. 17:4–5) would come God's chosen nation Israel. This nation's special relationship with God was to bring about blessing to the rest of the world's nations, who were separated from their Creator going back to their father Adam.

For the sake of the nations, God worked on this one nation for two thousand years. He multiplied her number, delivered her from slavery, led her through the wilderness, defeated her enemies, established her in his Promised Land, and brought her to her highest point of peace and prosperity under the kingship of David and his son, Solomon. With the

---

[1]Acts 17:26 confirms that God "made from one man every nation of mankind."

temple completed under Solomon, it looked as if God's blessing now was poised to come to the nations through Israel's flourishing and the nations' submission to her.

Come and See

In 1 Kings 4, Israel has become "as many as the sand by the sea" (v. 20). Solomon is ruling "over all the kingdoms from the Euphrates to the land of the Philistines and to the border of Egypt" (v. 21) and is said to have "dominion over all the region west of the Euphrates" (v. 24). Is this the fulfillment of God's promises to Abram in Genesis 12:3 and 15:5, to make his descendants as numerous as the stars and to bless the nations through his offspring? Has God brought all his purposes to pass in Israel's prosperity so that now climactically "all the peoples of the earth may know that the LORD is God" (1 Kings 8:60)?

But the sin problem that began with Adam still remained, with Israel herself suffering from the same sinful condition as all the nations. Just as the nations needed the blessing of forgiveness, a new heart, removal of divine wrath, and restoration to God himself, so also did Israel. And 1 Kings 11—2 Kings 25 catalogs how sin destroyed Israel in less than half a millennium as she fell from the height of Solomon's reign to the utter depths in the destruction of Jerusalem and in exile under the Babylonians.

But the prophets, even amid their strong denunciations, promised stunning hope beyond the exile for the remnant who would return to God. And it wouldn't be the mere restoration to Israel's former days, for as the prophet Isaiah announced,

> It is too light a thing that you should be my servant
>   to raise up the tribes of Jacob
>   and to bring back the preserved of Israel;
> I will make you as a light for the nations,
>   that my salvation may reach to the end of the earth. (Isa. 49:6)

God had more in mind for the blessing of the nations than, "Come and see Israel and eat from her scraps." In the Great Commission, we find Jesus' monumental revelation to his followers—and through them to the world—of the mission for world blessing that God had in store from the beginning: God's people knowing and enjoying him in Jesus and going and telling all the nations about him.

As Jesus prepares to go to the cross, he is the one who promises, "This gospel of the kingdom will be proclaimed throughout the whole world as a testimony to all the nations." And Jesus is the one who charges his disciples to "disciple all nations" and promises them, "You will receive power when the Holy Spirit has come upon you, and you will be my witnesses in Jerusalem and in all Judea and Samaria, and to the ends of the earth" (Acts 1:8).

Go and Disciple

Jesus has ushered in a new season of world history in which God is no longer focusing his preparatory redemptive action on Israel in a come-and-see fashion (when "in past generations he allowed all the nations to walk in their own ways," Acts 14:16). But now with the full accomplishment of the gospel of his Son, God has widened his scope, so to speak, to all the nations and inaugurated the Spirit-empowered age of *go and tell*—or better yet, *go and disciple.*

And so the apostle Paul says that the essence of his ministry is "to bring about the obedience of faith for the sake of [Jesus'] name among *all the nations*" (Rom. 1:5) and that the gospel is now being "made known to *all nations*" (Rom. 16:26). God's global purpose, being exercised through the authority of the risen and reigning God-man, is to make worshippers of his Son among *all the nations*—every tribe and tongue and people.

When Jesus grants the apostle John a glimpse of the end, John hears a new song:

> Worthy are you to take the scroll
>   and to open its seals,
> for you were slain, and by your blood you ransomed people for
>   God
>   *from every tribe and language and people and nation.*
>   (Rev. 5:9)

Two chapters later, John sees "a great multitude that no one could number, *from every nation, from all tribes and peoples and languages,* standing [in worship] before the throne and before the Lamb" (Rev. 7:9–10).

The Post-Christian West and the Global South

In pursuit of all nations, Paul brought the gospel to Philippi in Acts 16, and for the next seventeen-plus centuries, Christianity took root in particular in the West (Europe and eventually North America). The sixteenth-century Reformation deepened the roots in many respects, but the horrific seventeenth-century religious wars fed the eighteenth-century "Enlightenment" and, with it, modernism and secularism.

Today the West, once the stronghold of global Christianity, is becoming increasingly (and quickly) post-Christian. There are pockets of significant blessing and great hope for advance in the days ahead, but by and large, the church that once stood at the center of Western society is finding itself at the periphery (which, in God's economy, may be a very good thing for the Western church).

But the slow decline of Christianity in the West has not meant global decline for the gospel. Jesus will build his church. The last fifty years have produced a stunning and historic global development as Christianity has blossomed in Africa, Latin America, and Asia—in what many are calling "the Global South." The figures can be misleading, since they can report only *professing* Christians, but even allowing for significant inflation, the general trend is astonishing:

- Europe was home to over 70 percent of the world's professing Christians in 1900, but by 2000, it was less than 30 percent. In the meantime, Latin America and Africa had become home to over 40 percent.
- Africa had ten million professing Christians in 1900—about 10 percent of the population. But by 2000, the number was 360 million—about half the African population. This may mark the largest shift in religious affiliation in world history.[2]
- "The number of practicing Christians in China is approaching the number in the United States."[3]
- "Last Sunday . . . more Christian believers attended church in China than in all of so-called 'Christian Europe.'"[4]
- "In a word, the Christian church has experienced a larger geographical redistribution in the last fifty years than in any comparable period

---

[2]Philip Jenkins, "Believing in the Global South," *First Things*, December 2006, 13.
[3]Mark Noll, *The New Shape of World Christianity: How American Experience Reflects Global Faith* (Downers Grove, IL: InterVarsity, 2009), 10.
[4]Ibid.

in its history, with the exception of the very earliest years of church history."[5]

Going with the Global South

This amazing trend raises the question for some as to whether the West is done sending missionaries. Will it not now be left to the Global South to finish the Great Commission? The clear answer is no. First, don't discount the power of gospel-advancing partnerships between the West and the Global South. But second, these partnerships should mean sending not merely Western money, but Western people. Going is necessary for discipling.

According to www.JoshuaProject.net (which tracks the global progress of the gospel among the world's unreached peoples), there are an estimated 6,650 unreached people groups in the world out of a total of about 16,300 ethnolinguistic peoples. The Joshua Project lists 1,540 of these unreached peoples as *unengaged*, meaning that there is no current missionary work among them. With so much work yet to be done, it will take the gospel partnership of the whole global church—Western, Hispanic, Asian, African, Eastern European, Russian, Middle Eastern, and more—to take the message about Jesus to the world's final missionary frontier, the peoples most hostile to the gospel.

But not only does this new global situation create promise for new ways of partnering both in sending people and in resources; it also gives rise to new possibilities and problems in the West.

The Promise and Potential Danger of Missional

In the last decade, a new term related to *missions* has come into use among evangelicals doing domestic ministry: *missional*. The most insightful of those using the term recognize that the West is quickly becoming post-Christian and that this shift raises important questions about what it means to do domestic ministry. Europe and North America have become more and more like a mission field—but a post-Christian, rather than pre-Christian, field. Since the term *evangelism* carries for many the baggage of Christendom—recalling days when the general biblical worldview was prevalent enough in society that street-corner confrontations and stadium crusades found more traction and produced more genuine converts—the

---

[5]Ibid.

emergence of the term *missional* (in place of *evangelistic* and as a more holistic kind of evangelism) signifies that the times are changing in some significant degree, calling for new missions-like engagement. This new thinking is a good development, but with it comes a danger.

The danger is that with the discussions about "being missional" and "every Christian being a missionary," the pursuit of all the peoples by prioritizing the unreached may be obscured. We need to preserve a place for the biblical category of reaching the unreached. The biblical theme is not merely that God reaches as many *people* as possible, but *all the peoples*. He intends to create worshippers of his Son from every nation. The push for being *missional* captures something very important in the heart of God, but the danger is when it comes at the cost of something else essential in the heart of God: pursuing *all the nations*, not merely those who share our language and culture.

The Priority of the Unreached

We need *both-and*. Our churches should pursue both *mission* among our own people and *missions* among the world's unreached peoples. One way to sum it up is to say that we can't be truly *missional* without preserving a place for, and giving priority to, the pursuit of the unreached. It doesn't matter how much a church may say that it is being *missional*; it is not fully *missional* in the biblical sense if it is not both pursuing mission at home (traditionally called *evangelism*) among native reached people and being an engaged sender in support of missionaries to the unreached.

As the West grows increasingly post-Christian, it is easy to see the intensifying need for the gospel around us to the neglect of the frontiers. Missions is a summons to the frontiers. And more and more those frontiers aren't savages living in the woods that make for the idealized missions stories of the previous generation, like *Bruchko*, *Peace Child*, and *Through the Gates of Splendor*. Today's "frontiers" are home to the globe's most hostile peoples to the gospel. Don't think jungles and loin cloths. Think flat, hot, and crowded in the world's urban megacenters. God is bringing the unreached peoples out of the woods and into the cities for the completion of the Great Commission.

There Will Be Suffering and Martyrdom

This means there will be suffering. Many of the 6,650 unreached peoples (and the 1,540 unengaged peoples) are unreached (and unengaged) for a reason. They are profoundly hostile to the gospel. But the suffering and martyrdom to come—and they will come[6]—will not be a setback for our sovereign Savior.

Suffering is not only the consequence of completing the commission, but it is God's appointed means by which he will show the superior worth of his Son to all the peoples. Just as it was "fitting that he . . . should make the founder of [our] salvation perfect through suffering" (Heb. 2:10), so it is fitting that God save a people from all the peoples from eternal suffering through the redemptive suffering of Jesus displayed in the temporal sufferings of his missionaries.

This is why Paul could rejoice in his sufferings—because he knew that in them he was "filling up what is lacking in Christ's afflictions" (Col. 1:24). What is lacking in Jesus' sufferings is not their redemptive value but their personal presentation to the peoples he died to save. And in the sufferings and martyrdoms of missions, "the sent ones" fill up what is lacking by showing Jesus' superior value and pointing to his sufferings in their own.

So the call to the Great Commission is a call for martyrs. Not a call for kamikazes, but a call for missionaries bent on Jesus' worldwide fame and satisfied so deeply in him that they can say with Paul, "To die is gain" (Phil. 1:21).

Jesus Will Be with Us (Matt. 28:20)
The power for life-reorienting giving for missions and life-risking going in missions, for suffering and for martyrdom, is the enjoyment of the One whom we preach. Missions is not only powered by Jesus' universal authority, founded on his finished work, and modeled in his ministry; missions is sustained by the promise of his presence and the pleasure we have in him. He says "behold" to make sure he has our attention because this is really precious. "*Behold*, I am with you always, to the end of the age."

He will be with you. At the border of the "closed" country, in the learning of an arduous language, and in the disorientation of a new culture, he will be with you. In speaking the gospel when your hearers may turn on you, in persecution, and in jail, he will be with you. And when you're pressed to renounce the faith or die, he will be with you.

---

[6]It is generally accepted that there were more Christian martyrs in the twentieth century than the nineteen previous centuries combined.

He loves to be with his people to give them the grace to say with Martin Luther, from the heart:

> Let goods and kindred go,
> This mortal life also.
> The body they may kill;
> God's truth abideth still.
> His kingdom is forever.

Missions is about the worship of Jesus and the joy of all peoples. And as surely as Jesus is Lord of the universe, the Great Commission will finish. He will build his church. He will be worshipped among every people. And in him will his redeemed people, from all the peoples, forever "rejoice with joy that is inexpressible and filled with glory" (1 Pet. 1:8). To Jesus be the glory. Amen.

FOR FURTHER STUDY

Köstenberger, Andreas J., and Peter T. O'Brien. *Salvation to the Ends of the Earth: A Biblical Theology of Mission.* Downers Grove, IL: InterVarsity, 2001.

Mandryk, Jason. *Operation World.* 7th ed. Colorado Springs: Biblica, 2010.

Piper, John. *Let the Nations Be Glad: The Supremacy of God in Missions.* 3rd ed. Grand Rapids: Baker, 2010.

Contributors

Thabiti Anyabwile, Senior Pastor, First Baptist Church of Grand Cayman, Cayman Islands

Denny Burk, Dean of Boyce College and Associate Professor of New Testament, The Southern Baptist Theological Seminary, Louisville, Kentucky

Tim Challies, author and blogger

Kevin DeYoung, Senior Pastor, University Reformed Church, East Lansing, Michigan

Greg Gilbert, Senior Pastor, Third Avenue Baptist Church, Louisville, Kentucky

Collin Hansen, Editorial Director, The Gospel Coalition

Jay Harvey, Senior Pastor, Evangelical Presbyterian Church of Newark, Delaware

Ted Kluck, author, founder, Gut Check Press, Grand Ledge, Michigan

Jonathan Leeman, Director of Communications, 9Marks, Washington, DC

David Mathis, Elder, Bethlehem Baptist Church in Minneapolis, Minnesota, and Executive Pastoral Assistant to John Piper

Russell Moore, Dean of the School of Theology, Senior Vice President for Academic Administration, and Professor of Christian Theology and Ethics, The Southern Baptist Theological Seminary, Louisville, Kentucky

Andy Naselli, Research Manager for D. A. Carson and Administrator of *Themelios*

Darrin Patrick, Lead Pastor, The Journey Church, St. Louis, Missouri

Ben Peays, Executive Director, The Gospel Coalition

Eric Redmond, Senior Pastor, Reformation Alive Baptist Church, Temple Hills, Maryland, and Assistant Professor of Bible and Theology, Washington Bible College, Lanham, Maryland

Owen Strachan, Instructor of Christian Theology and Church History, Boyce College, Louisville, Kentucky

Justin Taylor, Vice President of Book Publishing, Crossway, Wheaton, Illinois

Tullian Tchividjian, Senior Pastor, Coral Ridge Presbyterian Church, Fort Lauderdale, Florida

General Index

Scripture Index

The Gospel Coalition

The Gospel Coalition is a fellowship of evangelical churches deeply committed to renewing our faith in the gospel of Christ and to reforming our ministry practices to conform fully to the Scriptures. We have become deeply concerned about some movements within traditional evangelicalism that seem to be diminishing the church's life and leading us away from our historic beliefs and practices. On the one hand, we are troubled by the idolatry of personal consumerism and the politicization of faith; on the other hand, we are distressed by the unchallenged acceptance of theological and moral relativism. These movements have led to the easy abandonment of both biblical truth and the transformed living mandated by our historic faith. We not only hear of these influences, we see their effects. We have committed ourselves to invigorating churches with new hope and compelling joy based on the promises received by grace alone through faith alone in Christ alone.

We believe that in many evangelical churches a deep and broad consensus exists regarding the truths of the gospel. Yet we often see the celebration of our union with Christ replaced by the age-old attractions of power and affluence, or by monastic retreats into ritual, liturgy, and sacrament. What replaces the gospel will never promote a mission-hearted faith anchored in enduring truth working itself out in unashamed discipleship eager to stand the tests of kingdom calling and sacrifice. We desire to advance along the King's highway, always aiming to provide gospel advocacy, encouragement, and education so that current- and next-generation church leaders are better equipped to fuel their ministries with principles and practices that glorify the Savior and do good to those for whom he shed his life's blood.

We want to generate a unified effort among all peoples—an effort that is zealous to honor Christ and multiply his disciples, joining in a true coalition for Jesus. Such a biblically grounded and united mission is the only enduring future for the church. This reality compels us to stand with others who are stirred by the conviction that the mercy of God in Jesus Christ is our only hope of eternal salvation. We desire to champion this gospel with clarity, compassion, courage, and joy—gladly linking hearts with fellow believers across denominational, ethnic, and class lines.

Our desire is to serve the church we love by inviting all of our brothers and sisters to join us in an effort to renew the contemporary church in the ancient gospel of Christ so that we truly speak and live for him in a way that clearly communicates to our age. We intend to do this through the ordinary means of his grace: prayer, the ministry of the Word, baptism and the Lord's Supper, and the fellowship of the saints. We yearn to work with all who, in addition to embracing the confession and vision set out here, seek the lordship of Christ over the whole of life with unabashed hope in the power of the Holy Spirit to transform individuals, communities, and cultures.